BLOWS LIKE A HORN

BLOWS LIKE A HORN

Beat Writing, Jazz, Style, and
Markets in the Transformation
of U.S. Culture

PRESTON WHALEY, JR.

Harvard University Press

Cambridge, Massachusetts, and London, England   2004

Library of Congress Cataloging-in-Publication Data

Whaley, Preston.
　　Blows Like a Horn : beat writing, jazz, style, and markets in the transformation
　of U.S. culture / Preston Whaley, Jr.
　　　p.　cm.
　Includes bibliographical references and index.
　ISBN 0-674-01311-5 (alk. paper)
　　　1. American literature—20th century—History and criticism.　2. Beat generation
　3. Music and literature—History—20th century.　4. United States—Civilization—
　1945–　5. Markets—United States.　6. Jazz—United States.　I. Title.

PS228.B6W48　　2004
810.9′0054—dc22　　　2004042426

For my parents, Elizabeth and Preston Whaley

ACKNOWLEDGMENTS

I would like to thank Linda Jordan for her invaluable help at Bancroft Library, Berkeley, California. The advice of the following members of the faculty at Florida State University has been invaluable: William J. Cloonan, David K. Kirby, Jerrilyn M. McGregory, Peter H. Spencer, and especially W. T. Lhamon, Jr.—editor, fellow author, and friend. Thank you to the very special Carrie Price for help reading the proofs. I thank my brother William Whaley and Katherine Evans for sharing the film *The Subterraneans* with me. My family's support and patience, especially on Whiteside Mountain, enabled the completion of this book. I am grateful to ruth weiss for sharing her knowledge and art, and to Robert E. Johnson—artist, scholar, gentleman, and generous soul. My experience as a student, songwriter, and musician of rhythm & blues, rock 'n' roll, and jazz helped make this book possible, as did my mom's helping me to understand, by example, civil rights and social justice.

BLOWS LIKE A HORN

INTRODUCTION
OPENING MEASURES

Critical work on the cultural significance of the Beat Generation writers up to now, if it has been positive, has stressed the artists' rebellion from aesthetic and cultural norms. It has stressed the sense in which Beat literature was intrinsically oppositional and radical and symbolized the struggle of the individual spirit against regimes of governmental-corporate, ideological, and aesthetic power. This oppositional assessment of the Beats clusters around prominent signs in the 1950s such as McCarthyite demagoguery, the FBI black lists, HUAC, the suppression of working class and civil rights, the "Howl" obscenity trial and other censorship incidents, the barriers to publication and academic recognition, and culture industry images that pictured a homogeneous United States whose constituents were white, affluent, heterosexual, suburbanite American families that seemed to know themselves through nonessential shopping.[1]

This assessment constitutes much of the complex material background that helped produce the Beat movement. Analyses of the role of speech in the formation and establishment of Western institutions (punishment, madness, sexuality, and rebellion), however, have shown how it is more accurate to think of power as dispersed rather than concentrated in a singular capitalism or state apparatus, for example, or contained exclusively within a neo-Marxian theoretical model.[2] Power is a relation of resistances. And while it is evident in British and U.S. cultural theory that "culture is grounded in unequal relations and is differentially related to people and groups in different social positions," resistance cannot be found outside of power, even multinational corporate power; as Michel Foucault has said, there is no "single locus of great refusal, no soul of revolt, source of all rebellions, or pure law of the revolutionary." William Burroughs has put it more bluntly: "All agents defect, and all resisters sell out." Hence, to appropriate jazz argot, the Beats were inside and outside; they did resist, and they did conform, variously, in different moments and different circumstances—some more than others.[3]

The Beats were conforming and resisting, but they were also destabilizing the very social and subjective power constituted in the terms. Much the same was occurring in modern jazz (bebop—hot and cool, modal, free jazz, and fusion), which was challenging the musical, linguistic, and institutional structures that produced and defined the music and its makers. To a great extent, the Beats followed the trail jazz blazed. They were participating in power, yes, but also transmuting it by denaturalizing aesthetic and narrative standards and the performance of social, racial, and sexual identities in nuanced and personal ways. The Beats and jazz multiplied the possibilities of agitating performance and creative experience that even today disturb the certain lines framing a dialectic of power and resistance and head off at the pass the critic's attempts to reify. My goal is not to overanalyze, civilize, and effectively kill interest in the Beat Generation and jazz but to explore it, discover it, and I hope groove with it.[4]

Markets

Beat writers used markets to transform U.S. culture. They lured capital to themselves through their actions and antics, their personal
charisma, and their work. They enlarged capitalism's symbolic repertoire. To be sure, the mass media often reduced Beat artists to silly
beatnik caricatures—dulled their critical edge. But it is reasonable to
think that, while mass-mediated folderol persuaded many people to
dismiss the Beats, it likely encouraged others to take a closer look. It
encouraged many to read the Beat writers, to gather and talk, and to
exchange poems and prose and records. In other words, mass media
helped spur the vernacular dissemination of Beat Generation subordinate values and a pluralism of style.

Pluralism of Style

Like artists, audiences engage in creative cultural work. Audiences'
desires, though influenced by the culture industries, are not determined or "manufactured" by them. Consumers use what they want
and dismiss what they do not want, in ways that conform to their
personal socio-political orientations and stylistic preferences. Consumers frequently engage in play and inventively manipulate signs.
Sometimes they overtly affirm intended messages, and at other
times they vigorously oppose them—they may do the former one
day and the latter the next. Whatever they do with media and meanings, they do it from their own seat of knowledge, experience, and
pleasure.[5] Thus, the overlapping activities of artists and audiences,
their interactive participation in the making of meanings, can evolve
into the more cohesive organization of subcultures or widely practiced trends, which can effect social transformation. I think many
people in consumer audiences, indeed, spy a trick when they see

hyperbole, sharply drawn dichotomies, or stereotypes. Some members of audiences interrogate spectacles and investigate their subjects. They learn and act on new knowledge, exchange and spread it, often critically.

The Beats modeled these processes of cultural transmission in their social lives and creative work. They were promiscuous consumers of both high and popular culture and vernacular strains of subordinate groups in the Americas. They were pluralists and also great talkers, and to a large extent they transmitted these diverse sources through their own speech of imitation, parody, and pastiche—sometimes erroneous, sometimes offensive, and at other times incisive. The results of this kind of spontaneous, oral community mirrored the practices of jazz and vitalized writings by Jack Kerouac, Allen Ginsberg, and lesser known writers, such as Bob Kaufman and ruth weiss. But it did not stop there. The vernacular mores that both influenced and characterized the Beats also influenced mainstream culture. Beat Generation interests, values, and style muscled into widely distributed spectacles of popular magazines, television, and feature films. These spectacles contained the Beat movement, but also revealed aspects of its appealing, creative edge. Participants in contemporaneous audiences saw these contradictions and used them.

The most dominant vernacular influence on the Beat writers was African American: not just talk, but gesture, art, and especially jazz—in short, a far-flung African American style. The influence of African American mores on whites was not new. It was happening in antebellum New York City when slave and free blacks were showing working-class whites how to dance for eels at Catherine Market. Today we see it manifested in superficial and deep ways, as white youth from virtually every socioeconomic background affect the dress, gestures, and argot of hip hop. There they are: white suburban high-school youth tooling down the road with a hydraulic car-trunk full of rap and pavement-cracking bass. There he is: 50 Cent. Where is

Eminem? Last seen at the box office with Ice Cube. There are others at the annual Tropical Heat Wave festival in Ybor City in Tampa: May 3, 2003, midnight on stage 4 in the Cuban Club Cantina. It's time for the Florida Hip Hop Showcase of five artists from Tampa, Orlando, and Gainesville. Dark and light skin takes the stage. They rap, spin, bounce, sing to synthetic melodies, beats, and grooves. A light and dark audience spreads out over the dance floor. Some eyes turn toward the stage. Others watch the circle of black and white acrobats taking break dance turns: one slides in on a knee, another on his head, another gradually spirals to the center before unleashing the beautiful, wild dog of his act. All of this is happening at the same time.

In the 1950s African American style was in the nascent stage of its mass commodification. Then, mostly white entrepreneurs and institutions took ownership of the style, its simulacra, and its means of production, promotion, and distribution; they appropriated it. The Beats did something different. Like these contemporary Heat Wave folk, they did not appropriate African American style, they consumed it just as it seized upon their desires. Then they enacted its influence through their art.[6]

Jazz

The Beat use of jazz must be considered apart from African American vernacular style. Jazz both overlaps and sidesteps the idea of the vernacular. It simultaneously retains and dismisses aspects of folk music, pop music, and high art music. As a signifier, jazz is as slippery as a fish. Some dismiss the term altogether because it so intertwines the ideologies and social hierarchies of race. Indeed, past guardians of society and culture have tried to keep the music in its subordinate position by loading it up with derogatory racial meanings. Nevertheless, the term evades attempts to essentialize it because the idiom itself is so multifarious and changeable; for these reasons I believe jazz is both a healthy signifier and a healthy music. In the 1950s African American style and jazz were more than a repertoire of cosmetic gestures for the Beats. "Blow as deep as you want to blow" went the Kerouac bromide.[7] Beat writing blew like a horn because black style and jazz influenced the very structures of its art and social life.

Jazz's impact was aesthetic and social. Its improvisational and pluralistic bent compelled the Beats to open their art to immediate expression and diverse voices in the culture. New voices became salient features of Beat texts, socially marked by the motley community of artists and their audiences in the Bay Area and other cities in the country. These artists and publics converted disaffection and powerlessness into affirmative emotions that shifted the marginal into the center, the disdained into the celebrated, the beat into beatitude. Thus Beat writing was the agent of a protean, desiring American consciousness that sought out cultural multiplicity. It was about creating a new art and a new earth. It derived its ambition from jazz; as Jack Kerouac called it, the "conglomerating music of the world." In *On the Road* it looks like this:

> That grand wild sound of bop floated from beer parlors: it mixed medleys with every kind of cowboy and boogie-woogie in the American night . . . Wild Negroes with bop caps and goatees came laughing by; then long-haired brokendown hipsters straight off Route 66 from New York; then old desert rats, carrying packs and heading for a park bench at the Plaza; then Methodist ministers with raveled sleeves, and an occasional Nature Boy saint in beard and sandals. I wanted to meet them all, talk to everybody.[8]

Jazz's meanings are always being contested. From its beginnings in the musics of the African diaspora, however, jazz has accommodated itself to sophisticated, mercurial desire. It has sought new connections and produced new combinations of sonic and performative meaning and audiences. And while this view may be complicated by jazz's mid-1960s turn toward black power and nationalist politics, it is also true that during the same period, jazz was lassoing ever larger, mixed audiences into the psychedelic corral of fusion. Moreover, although many participants in the influential Black Arts movement—including Anthony Braxton, Ornette Coleman, John Coltrane, Eric Dolphy, Archie Shepp, Abbey Lincoln, and Cecil Taylor—were seeking a means to a pan-African identity, perhaps an ahistorical black or global identity, they did so for the purposes of spiritual goals that were universal in scope and for all humanity. Jazz has simultaneously moved in multiple directions not as a result of diminished desire but as means and strategy for setting desire free. Even today, as Stanley Crouch and Wynton Marsalis pursue a traditionalist project, other jazz artists such as Jane Bunnett, Steve Coleman, David Murray, and Matthew Shipp remain experimental and internationalist in focus. All of these artists and critics in their own ways seek to build bridges to vernacular publics of rock 'n' roll, rhythm and blues, hip-hop, slam poetry, and music and art around the world.[9] Jazz continues as a free-floating and improvisatorially exciting signifier.

In broad terms, *Blows Like a Horn* looks at two sides of the Beat movement and the San Francisco poetry renaissance. One side is on the ground, oral, personal, social, and hence ethnographic and the other side is capital-driven, superficial, spectacular, and mass-mediated. The complex relations between these two sides make up the Beats' world, one of constantly shifting interplay of writing, jazz, and styles of vernacular life and in the popular mediated image.

The rigors of an agile cultural studies have in few instances been brought to bear on the Beat movement. Reasons for this neglect have to do with lingering ambivalence in academies about the Beats' importance. The Beats themselves and their audiences have long cocked a suspect eye toward both the industry of critics and academia for their occasional arrogance and frequent remoteness from what audiences and students experience. Finally, on the one hand, cultural studies itself is still often seen as an upstart, disruptive discipline in the academy, but the language of cultural studies can be arcane and jargon-laden to those who are interested in the Beats. I have tried to strike a balance by bringing an accessible scholarship to the subject.

1

THE HORN OF FAME

Four sentences in a San Francisco newspaper obituary announced Robert Michael Seider's death in 1979. He had been one of the hottest tenor saxophone players on the North Beach scene in the 1950s when jazz and painting and poetry were in renaissance, when everyone was relatively unknown, before the fame of the Beat generation and the subsequent beatnik fad. Seider never cut a record. He never held a stable gig. His performances were often impromptu in nature, for example, at the Coffee Gallery's Sunday sessions or after-hour jams at Jimbo's Bop City. His lifestyle was also impromptu. In and out of San Francisco General Hospital, he epitomized a certain hip grace while he suffered and a certain hip style when he played. Lester Young had been his exemplar of sound and dress—down to the economy of notes, the oversized trench coat, and pork pie hat. He was thin and eccentric looking, a kind of cool Beat era archetype. When Seider entered a club or café with his saxophone, a feeling of expectancy charged the air because when he was on, he was as good as anyone, known and little known.

Along with poetry and painting, San Francisco's jazz scene bristled at that time in North Beach, and, after hours, into the Fillmore and Tenderloin areas. One night in 1957 Seider went with Thomas

Albright and a few other friends to the Jazz Workshop on Broadway in North Beach. According to Albright, Seider engaged in a spur-of-the-moment cutting contest with Sonny Rollins. The tune was "Lover Man." Albright wrote, "by the time Seider had finished his first chorus, it was clear to everyone that Rollins had been carved. He had played all kinds of notes, fast, as was his custom. Seider had played very few, but each note had told a story." Like much jazz and poetry in the 1950s, Seider was telling stories that would not necessarily be told again. In this respect he echoed the lore of Bay Area poets like Bob Kaufman, who was said to have created most of his work live and on the spot. Occasionally, someone wrote down what they heard. Like zephyrs off the Pacific, creativity was blowing through San Francisco. The painter Robert E. Johnson was in the Bay Area in those days. Seider's story exemplifies "how easy things were," he said. "No one was a star then in San Francisco. No, you were on the street, exchanging ideas. Live music was carrying people along during a pretty mixed up, rotten time. In the middle of it, it was dark. We didn't know it was a renaissance." But this would change. The culture was changing. The Beat generation would graft itself into the San Francisco renaissance, launch it and usurp it as a national spectacle by way of jazz and scandal, flamboyant personality, charismatic literature, and through the invention of literary-historical Beat fiction.[1]

With the advent of the *Howl* trial in San Francisco in 1957, Beat generation writers crossed the threshold from being a small contingent of an obscure U.S. avant-garde, to becoming controversial symbols of a new generation. Although the transformation seemed to happen in a day, the Beats had long been building momentum, developing their style, and waiting for an opening. For example, it had been over half a decade since Jack Kerouac had published his stylistic homage to Tom Wolfe, *The Town and the City*, in 1950. He had written at least seven other novels in the early 1950s, which no publisher would touch. The publication of *On the Road* in the late summer of 1957 coincided with the momentum of the trial. The novel was fast, picaresque, and thrummed with the energy of Kerouac's jazz-derived, spontaneous prose. Soaring on Benzedrine, he wrote the book in three weeks using a scroll of taped-together typing paper, over one hundred feet long. It was a remarkable feat and fortuitously aligned with the sensationalized *Howl* trial.

Others were as productive in the early 1950s, if not as prolific. William Burroughs had published *Junky* (1953) and written his then unpublishable *Queer* in 1954. When he moved to Tangier the same year, he began writing the nihilistic, proto-psychedelic *Naked Lunch* (1959). John Clellon Holmes—a Beat-associated writer and friend to the New York group of Kerouac, Neal Cassady, Allen Ginsberg, Joan Vollmer, Burroughs, and others—published his novel *Go* (1952), the jazz novel *Horn* (1953), and for the mainstream public, the *New York Times Magazine* piece "This Is the Beat Generation" (1952). Holmes wrote in a more familiar narrative style and in that sense was on the Beat periphery. But until 1957, he was probably the most successful of New York's Beat-associated writers. It was not until after they arrived in San Francisco between 1954 and 1957 that the Beats broke through the public surface with enduring effect.

San Francisco was open to the Beats. The city had long been fertile ground for writers and artists of all stripes, radical politics, and independent lifestyles. The overlapping groups of writers in the area in the 1950s made a supportive and challenging environment for the Beats to develop and differentiate themselves by means of a uniquely spontaneous and publicly oriented style. Traditionally, most avant-garde movements have been insular, even arcane, and infused with sizable disdain for popular culture. Many Bay Area artists were gregarious, however. They wrote works less to be read than heard in discussion groups, art galleries, cafes, parties, and the streets. Often poems were about popular subjects. Jack Spicer wrote works about baseball, or with titles like "Billy the Kid" (1958) and "Buster Keaton's Ride" (1957). Lawrence Ferlinghetti's poetry had "Coney Island" on the mind. Kenneth Rexroth broadcast verse, prose, and talk over his KPFA radio program, and in response to the death of Dylan Thomas in 1953, he wrote his near-hysterical, public jeremiad, "Thou Shalt Not Kill." He mimeographed it marked "not for publication" and passed it around. Like the news of Thomas's untimely death, the poem went out across the country and nations: England, France, Japan, and others. Here, as John Arthur Maynard wrote, "the whole affair showed that it was possible for a noncommercial writer to create an immense and popular sensation in America in the early 1950s."[2]

Not unmindful of the success of "Thou Shalt Not Kill"—its outrageous language and incantatory-prophetic technique—in 1955 Allen Ginsberg composed a poem with similar features and combined it with Kerouacian jazz spontaneity: "Howl." He whirled up considerable fanfare when he read the poem at the 6 Gallery two years before the obscenity trial. City Lights publisher Lawrence Ferlinghetti, who was at the reading, heard "Howl" as a radical but hot commodity. Later, on the night of the reading, he typed a note to Ginsberg echoing Ralph Waldo Emerson's auspicious response to Walt Whitman after having read *Leaves of Grass*: "I greet you at the beginning of a great career, when do I get the manuscript?"[3] City Lights published the Ginsberg number as *"Howl" and Other Poems* (1956).

Like the jazz performances of Robert Michael Seider and others, poetry readings evoked ritual significance and began to gain popular momentum throughout the Bay Area. Local poet ruth weiss and musicians such as Sonny Nelson, Wil Carlson, and Jack Minger started merging poetry and jazz in 1956 at the Cellar, a North Beach spot that sold beer and wine. Soon Rexroth and Ferlinghetti were recording poetry and jazz at the Cellar for Fantasy Records (1957), which stirred up more publicity and enlarged the audience. At the height of its popularity, jazz-poetry may have seemed as much like a gimmick as it did a well-executed aesthetic mix. At its best, however, as with jazz, it marked an important, creative, and social interplay of black and white. It also revealed jazz to be a source of energy, method, and style for much 1950s poetry and other arts. Meanwhile, Rexroth, Ferlinghetti, and Ginsberg began talking up the Bay Area scene to media heavyweights such as *The New York Times Book Review, Mademoiselle,* and the Grove Press journal *Evergreen Review.* All of these published momentum-building features on the arts in San Francisco before the *Howl* trial arrived to blow the shutters off the public's eyes.

The Beat generation registered the exponential rise in the capacity of postwar media to spread culture. Most Bay Area artists were keen to the emerging youth culture and its symbolic relationship to Hollywood, the popular press, and music industries. Ginsberg, Ferlinghetti, Lawrence Lipton in Venice Beach, and to a lesser extent Rexroth and Kerouac mixed this awareness with an ambition and savvy for fame—all combined with a desire to get poetry into the hands of as many readers as possible. The behind-the-scenes agency of Ginsberg, Ferlinghetti, and others superseded the avant-garde status of the Bay Area. They became honking horns of popular dissent, using poetry, jazz, myth, personality, and scandal to help make a Beat generation sensation of the San Francisco renaissance. They left many local artists in their shadow, but at the same time opened up the avant-garde culture to the masses.

The spectacle of the *Howl* trial blasted the Beats across the country in an explosion of fame and controversy. Its fragmenting effects necessitated clarifying responses that would give coherence to Bay Area art and portray its compelling vitality for present and future use. The 6 Gallery "Howl" readings began a new literary and cultural movement in America. It was one event of many that presented a rarified view of the Bay Area scene, but its genesis and layered symbolic power helped to make it an original image of the Beat movement. But to understand how the beginning happened, we must start with what followed.

The *Howl* trial was officially called the *People vs. Ferlinghetti:* San Francisco, 1957. The case is well known, but here are its important elements. Captain William Hanrahan of the Juvenile Bureau issued warrants to arrest Lawrence Ferlinghetti, the publisher and book-seller, and Shigeyoshi Murao, City Lights manager.[4] The charges were that they "did willfully and lewdly publish and sell obscene and inde-cent writings." The press seized upon these titillating words that pinned *Howl* as a sexual scandal. Revealing pervasive obsessions, the incident was ready-made for a spate of headlines.

LIFE magazine called its story "Big Day for the Bards at Bay: Trial Over '*Howl*' and Other Poems." Norman Podhoretz, writing for the *New Republic*, described the trial as a "Howl of Protest in San Fran-cisco." *The Nation* marked its article as a "New Test for Obscenity." The *San Francisco Chronicle* said the courtroom could not contain the "sell out crowd." It captioned photographs of the trial with lines like "Battle of the Books Is On" and played up the attendance of sus-pect North Beach types and the infamous Henry Miller, who was also photographed. By the time the trial was over, David Perlman of the *Reporter* simplified the results of all the bluster with the caption "How Captain Hanrahan Made 'Howl' a Bestseller." No longer was *Howl* a book of poems; it was spectacle.[5]

To say that *Howl* had become a spectacle is to say that it had be-come a social event with a trajectory that could be watched, talked about, toasted, cursed, speculated upon, and analyzed. It became currency for social exchange and a touchstone where opinions and ideologies converged and dispersed again, leaving behind a kind of intaglio of thought that occluded concerns outside of its design. It made commodities of news and magazine print and television sig-nals. It was not what *Howl* said that was important but what it sym-bolized. To Captain Hanrahan it symbolized "filthy words that are very vulgar"—a threat to the ideal of moral purity. But to concerned San Francisco citizen Evelyn Thorne another ideal was at issue. She wrote to Ferlinghetti: "I have not read 'Howl' but only the reviews in the *Nation*, mainstream and elsewhere. I do not write to champion this . . . book. In fact, I think it might fall short of what I would call poetry . . . But I do want to applaud your decision to fight this legally.

Censorship is a black mark on any state that calls itself democratic
. . . civilized or cultured."[6] Thus, *Howl* became a tool for those with
stakes in an ideological relation. Two ideals—the moral purity of the
community versus individual freedom in the community—rubbed
together like steel and flint and put *Howl* to the fire.

Spectacles are like fruit: consumable, disposable, and displaceable.
Not so with "Howl." The poem's genius was to sustain the guise of
the spectacle while it retained the substance of art. Or as Ferlinghetti
characterized the kind of poetry he was interested in: it must have a
public surface, yet be subversive.[7] "Howl" had the superficial specifications of a commercial prototype; it mirrored postwar relations of
sight and sound; it was an effective bardic vehicle because it was big,
loud, and fast. It had brand name appeal. It could have been a new
brand of TV cartoon, toaster waffle, or cheap wine. An effective
brand name obliterates the competition.

Who remembers *Miscellaneous Man?* Ferlinghetti and Murao were
arrested for selling it, too. Was it bad literature? Not according to
the literary editor of the *San Francisco Chronicle,* William Hogan.
After defending *Howl* in his official statement for the court, he defended the offensive "The Statement of Erica Kieth and Other
Stories," which was reproduced in the literary magazine *Miscellaneous Man,* as "equally the work of a sincere, growing, and dedicated
literary talent, a talent provocative and stimulating enough to interest and excite admiration in serious critics and observers of literary
craftsmanship of our time."[8] But the work was ignored. Gil Orlovitz,
the author of "Erica Kieth," noticed and wrote Ferlinghetti to ask
why he, the *San Francisco Chronicle,* the *New York Times, Publisher's
Weekly,* and the trial itself forgot *Miscellaneous Man.* Orlovitz demanded that Ferlinghetti address the situation "in the press to
which you are so well connected." Obviously not expecting an answer, nor having read Dale Carnegie, Orlovitz threw insults: "I would
be greatly interested to understand the cheap literary cabal—with
apparently no more integrity than its East Coast counterpart—which

attempts to bask one author at the shadow of another . . . I have perhaps forgotten that the behavior of a resurgent group tends to ape
that of the status quo it affects to despise."

Not only does Orlovitz accuse the new West Coast poets of selling
out, he suspects a conspiracy of exclusion against him. There were
others who had conspiratorial suspicions, but it is enough to say,
for now, that Ferlinghetti's responsibility as the publisher of *Howl*
took precedence over his role as a bookseller for *Miscellaneous Man.*
It is also obvious that within the mass media, *Howl* was a better con-
ductor of controversy than a literary magazine called *Miscellaneous
Man.* Moreover, Ferlinghetti and Ginsberg wanted to sell books, distribute messages, and change the culture. They knew fame and in-
famy would come with the mission. It bends Jim Morrison's meaning, but they and a few others were determined to "break on through
to the other side." "Howl" was the hammer for the job. I will return
to the *Howl* trial, Orlovitz, and notions of conspiracy later.[9]

Surprisingly, before the *Howl* trial, there is not much tangible evi-
dence that the 6 Gallery readings took place. There is some, however.
Jack Spicer, a poet, started the 6 Gallery with his students from the
San Francisco College of Art and five painters: Wally Hedrick, David
Simpson, Deborah Remington, Hayward King, and John Allen Ryan;
with Spicer, these became the "6." The gallery was opened in 1955 on
Fillmore Street, in a location that six months earlier had been the
King Ubu Gallery, which was run by poet Robert Duncan; Duncan's
life partner Jess, the artist; and Harry Jacobus. Both galleries sponsored art shows, plays, and poetry readings. Of all of the performances held at the gallery, Ginsberg's became the most famous: "The
birth of the San Francisco Poetry Renaissance," wrote Jack Kerouac
in his novel *Dharma Bums* (1958). *Dharma Bums* contained the first
version of the 6 Gallery story to be published in the United States,
which became the source for virtually every historical/cultural account of the beginnings of the Beat movement and the San Francisco
renaissance.[10]

Even among authoritative, historical accounts of the 6 Gallery readings, however, there are discrepancies about when the event took place, who the participants were, and what poems were read. Multiple versions of the story reflect its oral basis, and while some oral traditions produce folklore and legends, this story slants toward myth in the sense that its facts are variant and its presence ubiquitous, both in oral tradition and later in literary-cultural histories. Moreover, for the Beats, fiction mingled closely with personal history. The tale of the 6 Gallery readings is as much the result of imagination as is *On the Road* (1957) or the poem "West Coast Sounds—1956," by Bob Kaufman. Finally, the story is decidedly antibourgeois in content and tone; to use Roland Barthes's terms, it is mythical in that it undermines bourgeois myth.[11]

Two years before the trial, "Howl" blew like a maelstrom across the poetic waters of the Bay Area. Jack Goodman spread the news and testified to the effect of the poem in a letter to John Allen Ryan one month after he heard it at the 6 Gallery:

> This Carrowac [sic] person sat on the floor downstage right, slugging a gallon of Burgundy and repeating lines after Ginsberg, and singing snatches of scat in between lines; he kept a kind of chanted, revival-meeting rhythm going. Ginsberg's main number was a long descriptive roster of our group, pessimistic dionysian young bohemians and their peculiar and horrible feats, leading up to a thrilling jeremiad at the end, that seemed to pickup the ponderous main body of the poem and float it along stately overhead as if it were a kite. There was a lot of sex, sailors and language of the cocksuckingmotherfucker variety in it; the people gasped and laughed and swayed, they were psychologically had, it was an orgiastic occasion.

Though he had not attended the "orgiastic occasion," William Burroughs indicated he could imagine it, in a letter to Ginsberg dated

March 14, 1956, Tangier. He had just read early drafts of "Howl," parts two and three, and writes, "I don't wonder the poem is causing a stir . . . undoubtedly the best thing you have done."[12]

News of the reading spread. Readings like it popped up like franchises as more and more organizations signed on to sponsor them. Audiences enthusiastically gathered to test the ritualistic strength of each reading. Could they be "psychologically had"? The tumult was basically invisible to the mainstream set, but Rexroth (writer, critic, and mentor), Ferlinghetti, and Ginsberg were notifying mainstream contacts about the excitement of poetry in the Bay Area. Rexroth called Richard Eberhart at the *New York Times Book Review.*

As the first copies of *"Howl" and Other Poems* (1956) came off the press, Eberhart's "West Coast Rhythms" appeared in the *New York Times Book Review* (September 2, 1956). Eberhart called the West Coast "the liveliest spot in the country in poetry today." The article gave a confined overview of the diverse literary personnel and traditions around the Bay Area. It omitted any mention of the Berkeley renaissance and the poets Robin Blaser, Robert Duncan, and Jack Spicer, who spearheaded it. It highlighted the new axis of City Lights, Ferlinghetti, Rexroth, and the young writers who were not content with the traditional obscurity of poets, whom Eberhart said possessed the "young will to kick down the doors of older consciousness." With the exception of Philip Lamantia, Eberhart counted all of the mostly unpublished poets who read at the 6 Gallery, but he did not mention the event itself, which had not yet crystallized as an originating myth. Eberhart went on to say that "the most remarkable poem of the young group, written during the past year, is 'Howl,' by Allen Ginsberg . . . son of Louis Ginsberg, a poet known to newspaper readers in the East."[13]

After Rexroth first contacted Eberhart, Ginsberg helped Eberhart write the article by sending him copies of the soon-to-be published poems in *Howl,* accompanied by a twenty-page explanation of their meaning. In the letter, Ginsberg commended the work of the poets who read at the 6 Gallery and gave special mention to the important influence of Kerouac. Eberhart found Ginsberg's letter convincing. He had previously heard "Howl" at a private reading at Berkeley and surmised then that the poem was little more than a long tirade. After reading the letter, however, he modified his view and noted in the article the poem's "positive force and energy . . . a redemptive quality of love." He admired the poem's social protest and acknowledged its traditional echoes of Walt Whitman and Biblical literature. He also remarked on the humor in the poems "America" and "A Supermarket in California." Eberhart's article pictured a Bay Area literary scene that was taking the shape of a solar system, with Ginsberg at its center.[14]

As local excitement about poetry in San Francisco grew, a mass youth culture was also on the rise. Some youth were swinging to the jazz of David Brubaker, Chet Baker, and Miles Davis. Others were shaking to Elvis, Little Richard, and Chuck Berry. Youth queued up to ogle rebellion. They had watched *Blackboard Jungle* (1955), *The Wild Ones* (1954), and *Rebel Without a Cause* (1955). *Mademoiselle* (February, 1957) circulated the look by publishing Michael Grieg's exposé, "The Lively Arts in San Francisco." The article's first page features a picture of Ginsberg and Kerouac. Ginsberg is described as a "cross between Whitman, Rimbaud and bop pioneer Charlie Parker . . . the enfant terrible of San Francisco letters." Kerouac is the writer to whom "Howl" is dedicated, and "whom Malcolm Cowley called the greatest unknown writer in America . . . one novel published in 1950 . . . another one out soon." Grieg uses two other photographs. One is of contemporary dancers in primitive dress and pose, and the other shows Michael McClure and Jim Harmon with their wives Jo Ann and Beverly. The four describe a circle around a bottle of wine—two on the floor and two on a floor mattress; a cigarette dangles from McClure's lips. Harmon and McClure are noteworthy as editors of the arts journal *Ark II*. Both photos supplement the article's overall tone of dangerous allure.[15] The *New York Times* and *Ma-*

demoiselle reviews represented gold in the marketing establishment. In particular, they set Kerouac and Ginsberg to the specifications of an emergent superficial form—celluloid antiheroes—attractive to those in want of adventure and who would soon be reading *On the Road* (1957). Moreover, both articles gave public shape and content to the San Francisco scene and prepared minds for the idea of a poetry renaissance.

Just below the popular surface, Grove Press was going forward with preparations for its second issue of *Evergreen Review.* Devoted to the "San Francisco Scene," the issue's release (like *On the Road*) was timed to coincide with the beginning of the *Howl* trial in August 1957. The Eberhart article had piqued the interest of Barney Rossett, Grove publisher. The firm's editor Don Allen arranged to interview Ginsberg and Kerouac when they came to New York. This was a serious but controversial literary journal. Positive mention in it would provide national credibility to art, literature, and jazz in the Bay Area. Grove Press used *Evergreen Review* to give unknown and avant-garde writers exposure and to test their appeal for larger, future projects. The San Francisco issue featured all of the 6 Gallery readers except, once again, Philip Lamantia. It used a piece by Ferlinghetti, Kerouac's "October in the Railroad Earth," Ralph Gleason's article on San Francisco jazz, and short works by Bay Area elders Josephine Miles, Kenneth Rexroth, Robert Duncan, and Henry Miller. Circulation for *Evergreen Review,* at its peak, reached an unprecedented (for a literary journal) 250,000. Though it is clear Allen consulted Rexroth and Ferlinghetti, and that he knew poets associated with the Berkeley renaissance (he had been an irregular participant), Ferlinghetti told S. E. Gontarski that Allen "went heavily by what Allen Ginsberg told him to publish . . . I remember there were some omissions. Bob Kaufman wasn't in there . . . Diane Di Prima . . . my poems, 'Dog' and other poems from *A Coney Island of the Mind* . . . I had been using them in the Cellar with jazz."[16]

The response to the legal problems of *Howl* began before

Ferlinghetti and Murao were arrested on May 29. It began when customs agents seized the last shipment of the first edition on March 25. Sales of the book, helped by the early press discussed above, were good but modest; the first edition numbered 1,500 copies. Ferlinghetti responded to the seizure quickly by printing another 3,000 in April.[17] Ginsberg, in Tangier with William Burroughs at the time, responded on April 3 to a letter from Ferlinghetti:

Was surprised by news of Customs seizure . . . Offhand I don't know what to say about MacPhee [Chester MacPhee, Collector of Customs who implemented the seizure]. I don't know what the laws are and what rights I got. I suppose the publicity will be good . . . I'll write to Grove to Don Allen & let him know, and & he'll tell the lady from Time-Life. If you can mimeograph a letter & get some kind of statement from WCWilliams Bogan Eberhart & send it around to magazines might get some publicity that way. Also let Harvey Breit at *NY Times* know for sure definitely—he'd probably run a story . . . My brother is a lawyer & has recently done some research on the subject, I'll write him to get in touch with you & provide any legal aid—if any is useful from him in New York. I guess this puts you up shits creek financially. I didn't think it would really happen. Be sure let the *Life* people in SF know about the situation, they might include it in a story. The woman in NY is Rosaling [Rosalin?] Constable % [care-of] Time-Life, Rockefeller Center. She is very simpatico & would immediately call it to attention of Peter Bunzell who is (I heard) writing up the story for *Life* in NY. Send story too to *Village Voice,* they've been digging the scene. By the way I heard there was a lukewarm review in *Partisan Review,* could you send it to me? Might let them know, too, as they took a poem of mine for later. I guess the best way publicity wise is prepare some sort of outraged & idiotic but dignified statement quoting the Customs man & Eberhart's article & Williams & and *Nation* review, mimeograph it up & send it out as a sort of manifesto publishable by magazines and/or news release. Send one to Lou Carr at United Press[???] Bldg., 42 Street NYC too. If this is worthwhile. Also write, maybe Jarrell at Lib. Of Congress & see if you can get his official intercession. His address is 3916 Jennifer St. NW, Wash. D.C, I imagine these Customs people have to obey orders of their superiors; & that superiors in Wash. D.C. might be informed and requested to intercede by some official in Lib. Of Cong. Maybe I'll write my congressman—is there a friendly congressman in SF? This might be more rapid than a lawsuit . . . if you ever make our money back & make some profit from all your trouble, & we go into a 4th or 17th edition, we divvy the loot.[18]

Though taken by surprise, Ginsberg's response was shrewd. He seemed prepared for legal entanglements. He knew the seizure could be used to stir up publicity for himself, Ferlinghetti, and City Lights, increasing sales of *Howl*. He had an impressive list of influential contacts with addresses at the ready even from Tangier. He wrote that he "didn't think it would really happen," but he obviously thought that it might. Moreover, it is probably more than coincidental that his brother had been "recently researching censorship issues." If Ginsberg learned about media from his work as a market researcher between 1950 and 1955, his savvy shows here.[19] Ferlinghetti immediately contacted the ACLU, whose lawyers felt the book was legitimate and agreed to take the case. The U.S. Attorney in San Francisco backed down.

Ginsberg and Ferlinghetti were acting out another subordinate but increasingly archetypal U.S. role; they resisted the society of organization men by becoming renegade entrepreneurs. Gil Orlovitz did not understand this. He scripted himself as a dependent. He waited for the spectacle to adorn him with its glitter. He took the San Francisco scene for being just another hierarchical organization that should install him in a prominent position. But the San Francisco scene was no organization; it was a volatile scattering of storms. Ferlinghetti and Ginsberg flew through them like improvising acrobats. They selected a society with whom to spiral and spin: Gary Snyder, Michael McClure, and Philip Whalen; Ginsberg always seemed to fly best in the company, or at least the imagined visage, of Kerouac. This society was less real than imaginary, if only genealogically enjoyed in the indelible burn of the 6 Gallery story that Ginsberg helped create.[20] Though they remained friends and collegial, as Ginsberg's notoriety grew, Snyder, McClure, Whalen, and others such as Duncan, Spicer, Rexroth, and even Ferlinghetti, resisted the carpetbagger's Beat generation formation. This is why McClure and Harmon insisted Grieg's "Lively Arts . . ." article include them in a separate photograph with their heterosexual partners and plug *Ark II*. Duncan refused to pose for the *Mademoiselle* article at all. Bay Area writers were mercurial and self-determined. Orlovitz's feeling for San Francisco was anachronistic. He had not participated in the circle of friendship that existed among the others. Moreover, like Lamantia, his writing meandered the surreal periphery rather than the streets. Although caught up in the storm of the *Howl* trial, he was swept away like so much dust and leaves. He, along with Spicer, Blaser, Kaufman, and others, reserved a traditional skepticism and disdain for popular media. Yet with dismay and in some cases outright jealousy, many poets disliked having been left to the obscurity of the Beats' shadow.[21]

Orlovitz was not the only Bay Area writer who felt conspired against. The poet ruth weiss told me she had trouble understanding why Ferlinghetti would not publish her work. Moreover, she said she knew quite a few people who thought Ferlinghetti and Ginsberg orchestrated the *Howl* customs seizure and the trial. In their biography of Spicer and the San Francisco renaissance, Lewis Ellingham and Kevin Killian explain that Spicer believed "Ferlinghetti's notoriety, and Ginsberg's by extension, stemmed from the publisher's mania for publicity. It was part of 'the fix,' Jack snickered, and told George Stanley that, in order to create a scandal, Ferlinghetti had arranged with the printers in England to wrap the boxes in proofs of the poems so that the word 'cocksucker' would appear on the outside of the boxes, making it more likely that the books would be seized for obscenity." Spicer's accusation lacks evidence and is symptomatic of latent resentments, but certainly Ginsberg and Ferlinghetti were ambitious, entrepreneurial, and media wise—altogether extremely successful in promoting their interests and new art into the U.S. mainstream.[22]

In the meantime, police authorities determined the uppity perpetrators of *Howl* were out of control and staged an arrest. They sent two plain-clothes agents to City Lights to buy the Ginsberg number and *Miscellaneous Man*. With this evidence they obtained warrants and arrested Ferlinghetti and Murao. Ferlinghetti sent out news of his arrest with requests for support. People replied with encouragement and some sent money. A variety of academics, critics, and publishers wrote the court defending *Howl;* if not aesthetically, they defended Ginsberg's prerogative to write it and Ferlinghetti's right to publish and sell it. Thus, Ferlinghetti and *Howl* became a flash point of alliance among readers, writers, publishers, lawyers, and academics all over the country who recognized their mutual interest in free speech. Two years to the day after the 6 Gallery readings, on October 7, 1957, the *San Francisco Chronicle* named the "'Howl' Decision" a "Landmark of Law." The editorial called Judge Horn's decision rejecting charges of obscenity against *Howl* "sound and clear, four-square with the Constitution."[23]

The conclusion of the trial prompted more publicity and commentary about the San Francisco scene and especially the Beats. In the midst of the frenzied media spin, Kerouac penned *Dharma Bums* in late 1957. During the same month that Kerouac was speed-typing *Dharma Bums,* the Amsterdam journal *Literair Paspoort 100* published poet Gregory Corso's "The Literary Revolution in America." It includes all of the basic elements of the 6 Gallery story as it has been conveyed throughout its genealogy—the five readers: Philip Lamantia, Michael McClure, Gary Snyder, Philip Whalen, and following the pattern of the Eberhart article, an extended description of "the most brilliant shock of the evening . . . the now-famous rhapsody, 'Howl,'" by Ginsberg who was encouraged by the wine-drenched shouts of Kerouac. Corso took the byline for the article until 1986 when Ginsberg published the fact that he, too, helped write it. Yet he confided in a letter to Ferlinghetti in 1957 that he knew the article would "probably infuriate everybody" (though he does not confess to having written it), because "it's written in English" and once again superimposed Ginsberg's self-interest and vision on the Bay Area scene. Kerouac may have read the article and used it as a source for his account of the 6 readings in *Dharma Bums,* but neither version contains anything outside of what circulated orally.[24]

Interestingly, Kerouac moderated Ginsberg's and Corso's claim to revolution by crystallizing the San Francisco scene down to a rhetoric of renaissance. Having been vindicated by the court decision, it is easy to understand Ginsberg's revolutionary feelings. But Kerouac realized the vindication's basis was intrinsic to the law of the land, not its overthrow. The court decision made *Howl* a legitimate commodity; its pages could be bought and sold or read on any street corner. The invocation of renaissance usurped longstanding renaissance prerogatives assumed by local writers, however, such as Robin Blaser, Robert Duncan, William Everson, Kenneth Rexroth, Jack Spicer, and others. The notion of renaissance was effective because it alluded to the six-hundred-year-old European specter of artistic greatness. In addition, Beat generation renaissance prestige compounded more plausibly by its association with the centennial decade of the United States' own literary moment in the sun. Still more significant, though less apparent, the reading of *Howl* amplified vibrations sounding back to the jazz of renaissance Harlem, an era in which blues and jazz poets found themselves when much of the high culture's generation was "lost." The notion of renaissance served as a talisman against the opposition, if only for the time it took to dismiss the claim as a red herring. A conventional, yet still brilliant stroke, the appropriation of the term protected artists who were signifying change—those who were being recognized and those who were not. It opened a space for artists to work in and protected the moment for posterity and for those backward-glancing critics.[25]

Kerouac's ostensibly fictional narrative crystallized the story of the 6 Gallery readings—the beginning of historical treatments of the Beat movement. He changed the names but described the mien and poetry of the several readers in a way that showed some of the diversity of poetry at the 6 and in the Bay Area. The narrator of *Dharma Bums*, Ray Smith (Kerouac), is fascinated with the way Japhy Ryder's poetry (Ryder, the book's hero, is based on Gary Snyder) combined a mix of cultural strands including Oriental philosophy, Northwest American Indian ritual, and the brave individualism of frontier heroes. Smith shows his preference for plain speech: "Fuck you!" quoting Ryder, "sang Coyote, and ran away!" He notes but is not impressed with politically strident speech (Michael McClure's "For the Death of 100 Whales") or the wrongly described "incomprehensible" academic abstraction of Coughlin's (Philip Whalen's) "unclarified processes." Alluding to the Renaissance, he remarks that the Cervantes's hero would have wept at the "delicate Englishy voice" of Francis DaPavia (Philip Lamantia) while he, himself, laughed and was charmed the same. In the audience, Smith singles out the presence of Rosie Buchanan (Natalie Jackson), "a real gone chick and friend of everybody . . . a writer . . . in love with my old buddy Cody (Neal Cassady). Kerouac liked Jackson and seems to have respected her. Her literary promise, however, as Kerouac thinly fictionalizes later in the novel, was smashed on a San Francisco sidewalk along with her suicidal body—a dissonant turn that linked her to Ginsberg's poem as another of the best minds destroyed.[26]

And it is dissonance—the blue and asymmetrical notes of dissent—that counterpoints the agreeable assertion of a renaissance and signals that the San Francisco poetry scene was a subordinate movement, opposed to dominant features of the culture. Kerouac writes that as the effects of ample wine loosened up the "stiff-audience," Alvah Goldbook (Ginsberg) began to read: "wailing his poem 'Wail' ["Howl"] drunk with arms outspread everybody was yelling 'Go! Go! Go! (like a jam session)." The poem threw people into a remarkable collective enthusiasm that left them "wondering what had happened and what would come next in American poetry." Thus Kerouac provided the jam session as the irrefutable sign of determined and energetic social agreement that an opening of expressive possibility had occurred, that a poetry renaissance was underway.[27]

For Kerouac (and other Beats) the sign of jazz is complex. On the one hand, it often recapitulates and conforms to a charismatic but primitivist-racist view of jazz that has circulated with talk and writing about the music since its inception and which is rooted not only in the colonial beginnings of the United States but in the constructions of the West's intellectual and theological history. More precisely, the inventions of primitivism and racism have all along been symptoms and determinants of socioeconomic and class relations, and it follows in the most simplistic sense that any artist that deploys such conventions becomes an agent of the same, including Kerouac. On the other hand, in later chapters I will explore the idea that Kerouac loosened the soil around the roots of primitivist interpretations of jazz. In *Dharma Bums* he reinvents assumptions about the practices and methods of jazz by encoding them with his own take on Eastern philosophy and art. Yet another layer of meaning of jazz for the Beats embedded in the 6 Gallery readings recollects the sociopolitical energies associated with the birth of bebop in Harlem in the early 1940s. It is well known that bebop was an artistic counter-punch to commercial pressures in the music industry that seemed to privilege white jazz players and stifle improvisation and innovation. Bebop also coincided with and mirrored disruptive social responses of African Americans being asked to support a war in behalf of a country that did not reciprocate that support. The 6 Gallery readings reveal how Beat and associated artists and audiences also tapped into this residual, insubordinate, and positive sense of jazz and expressed it through their art and lives.

Hammer-horn pounding soul marks on unswinging gates.

—Bob Kaufman, "Walking Parker Home"

The Beats certainly trafficked in primitivisms, however ambiguously, often undermining them within the same narrative. Critics seem to miss this latter point, especially with respect to Kerouac. For example, Leo, the narrator of *The Subterraneans* (1958), fantasized at home for days on the serpentine primality of his new African American love Mardou—on her feet, sandals, dark eyes, "little soft brown Rita-Savage-like cheeks and lips, little secretive intimacy and . . . snake-like charm as befits a little thin brown woman." By the end of the novel, however, Leo's ideologically charged fantasy has no enduring hold on its object. Leo cannot master Mardou or love her, blocked as he is by the curtain of his fantasy and a not unrelated infantile attachment to his mother. In *On the Road* (1957) Kerouac treads a fine line between outright indulgence of his fascination with the primitive and brilliant parody of the same right out of *Tom Sawyer*. Here Dean, Sal, and Marylou drive nervously through the swamps of Louisiana and in dialect conjure mysteries: "Man, do you imagine what it would be like if we found a jazzjoint in these swamps, with great big black fellas moanin guitar blues and drinkin snakejuice and makin signs at us?" Of course, it never happens. They find no jazz or juke joints. Kerouac, beneficially I think, airs provincial class and racist discursive symptoms with—as Kerouac's method would have it—as much unadulterated spontaneity as possible. The ideological cul-desacs that Kerouac's method exposed in *The Subterraneans* and *On the Road* are transformed in *Dharma Bums*.[28]

First, a short review of modern primitivism. In the 1920s when jazz began to percolate into the mainstream, a mostly urban white and Harlem-centered black intelligentsia began to take notice. These artists and intellectuals looked for an ideological reason to leave Victorian principles behind and return to the alienated personality what machine-age modernity had taken away—nature. They found their answer in the primitive: one who lives by the senses and instinct—a couple of decades later, Norman Mailer's definition of the hipster. Ideological uses of the *natural* man crossed a vast terrain of categories from the aesthetic, to the educational, to the mass cultural need to create consumers. Black and white writers and musicians—Hart Crane, Countee Cullen, Duke Ellington, George Gershwin, Ernest Hemingway, Langston Hughes, James Weldon Johnson, Marianne Moore, Gertrude Stein, Jean Toomer, William Carlos Williams, Antonin Dvorak—all participated in what David Levering Lewis called the "vogue of the Negro" and often, with the caveat of avoiding complex investigation, they can be said to have indulged in primitivist stereotypes, from Carl Van Vechten's *Nigger Heaven* to Claude Mckay's *Home to Harlem*, to Toomer's *Cane*, to Duke Ellington's jungle performances at the Cotton Club. Combined with the arrival of Sigmund Freud's theories of the psyche, primitivism made the quest for the repressed essence irresistible and paradoxically useful in separating from the past. Primitivism also introduced artists and their audiences to vernacular idioms of music and speech that seemed uniquely American and free of tiresome European sources; it began the process of opening the country to its own diversity, however skewed by racism. Finally, drawing on the work of Ann Douglas in *Terrible Honesty* (1995), Chip Rhodes remarks that "artists' fascination with blacks" helped them fulfill a "desire . . . to embrace a modern, masculinized culture of speed and excitement"—certainly, an important precondition to the exuberance of the 1950s.[29]

But modern primitivism had a more pejorative and destructive side. It was rooted in the peculiar seventeenth-century North American version of race, which was invented from the agrarian-capitalist imperative to have a "social control buffer" that would appease a dissatisfied, unpropertied working class. The result was that blacks became the objects of a new racial speech of inferiority that provided the ideological basis and justification for slave labor. Post–Civil War versions of this racism, whether combined with Victorian religiosity or Darwinian and Freudian social theories, made African Americans and their art a social and cultural threat. Since its inception, reactionaries have scripted much African American music and jazz, in particular, as irrational, undisciplined, vulgar, a threat to or travesty of refined musical tradition, a flaunter of taboos, a clear danger to individual and social morality and character: primitive. Late nineteenth- and early twentieth-century Western society had amassed its wealth through a political economy historically dependent on notions of colonization, slavery, capitalism, and Christian ideology and recoiled at the sight of corrosion on its cage. The academy, high culture, and popular media had ideologized its acquisitive barbarism into a pure discourse of bourgeois freedom, democracy, and piety. Despite the popular rhetoric, some artists and intellectuals, working-class and adventurous middle-class audiences sought after jazz for the very reasons polite minds called it dirty names; they, too, sought to break from the Victorian past—some as a life choice and others only on Saturday night. In addition to its personal and social meanings, audiences liked jazz because it sounded good. They liked how it slipped the on-beat, ducked perfect pitch, and saturated timbres of instruments with the tones of the human voice. They liked it not because it mouthed some composer's ideal, but because it emoted what musicians feel, what audiences feel—what human beings can share. Thus, like the so-called primitive, whereas jazz had been alarming and repulsive to many with refined, sphinctered tastes, it was vitally compelling to fans.[30]

In the 1940s and 1950s, the idea of the primitive seemed to be accumulating oppositional uses. For example, in the poem "America," Ginsberg played the primitivist card against corporate power, which used racism in the 1950s to fan red paranoia about working-class disruptions. Ginsberg puts so-called primitive dialect into the paranoid corporate mouth in order to redefine what primitive is. "Them Russians and them Chinamen . . . make Indians learn read. Him need big black niggers. Hah. Her make us all work sixteen ours a day." In the poem "Walking Parker Home," Charlie Parker shows Bob Kaufman, an African American poet, that his weapon, indeed, is a "hammer horn pounding soul marks on unswinging gates" of Western "Culture gods" of money and nostalgia, who could not hear their souls for their guilty fear of "mob sounds." As now, so then primitivisms were embedded constituents of thought, and the Beats made them versatile.

Reading Kerouac's account of the beginning of the San Francisco renaissance, we might, as many critics have, halt at the inescapable fact that the renaissance was born of a drunken revel. These reviewers, like many in the 1920s, scarcely conceal their wish for prohibition. They captioned their influential articles with titles like Norman Podhoretz's "The Know-Nothing Bohemians," and John Ciardi's "Epitaph for the Dead-Beats." Other critics, such as Sascha Feinstein, Jon Pannish, and Rexroth rightly find fault with Beat primitivisms, but betray their superficial readings when they dismiss whole texts as romantic anachronisms and perpetrators of ignorance. With respect to Kerouac, who catches it the worst, they miss his openness. They overlook the extent to which the then vogue for "new criticism" framed culture as a tradition, made by high minds, to be preserved and transmitted inside scholarly walls and between the covers of academic books and journals. They seem to forget that at a time when individual expression was stifled and vernacular voices were rarely heard, when the United States preferred to conceal its diversity with homogeneous scripts and celluloids, Kerouac prac-

ticed the conviction that "everybody is important and interesting."
This idea was not new or a revolution; it was subordinate and implicit to radical ideas of U.S. democracy. Without a doubt Kerouac
superimposed his own needs on others and trivialized others. Yet
his prose took in vast, teeming surfaces. He saw the capacity for joy
and individuality in diverse peoples despite, or, perhaps, because
they were excluded from U.S. economic and political systems. For
Kerouac, exclusion from the machines of conformity saved the vernacular present, which gave him a very personal "safety of the mind"
and provided subjects, forms, and vitality for his art. Self serving? Yes
(it is also true today that many cultural preservationists argue for the
isolation of indigenous groups). Oblivious to the oppressive aspects
of socioeconomic exclusion? Often, but not always. Still, the main
point is that despite (mis)representational excesses, Kerouac's artistic
stance incisively critiqued the status quo, even if you hesitate to call it
an accomplishment.[31]

Before leaving the subject, however, I want to relate how Kerouac
(by no means alone among the Beat and associated writers) helped
disable the grinding pinions of primitivism through his own vernacular take on oriental mysticism, which strange as it may seem, informed his views on jazz and writing. In *Dharma Bums,* Goldbook's
(Ginsberg's) reading of "Wail" ("Howl") assumed the gestures and
conveyed the communal feeling of a jam session. But later in the
novel, the feeling reoccurs in Ray Smith (Kerouac), who finds himself frozen with fear near the peak of California's Matterhorn Mountain. "Then suddenly everything was like jazz," he says as he watches
Japhy Ryder descend "in huge twenty foot leaps, running, leaping,
landing with a great drive of his booted heels, bouncing five feet or
so, running, then taking another long crazy yelling yodelaying sail
down the sides of the world and in that flash I realized it's impossible
to fall off mountains you fool and with a yodel of my own began
running down the mountain."[32]

On one level, Ryder's descent may be said to resemble jazz (especially Bop) in the way a solo may take unusual "leaps" from one note to the next and give no account to the available, more conventionally used, notes in between. At another moment the solo may seem to be "running" in orderly fashion through diatonic arpeggios or scales, or chromatic runs. Jazz solos seem to "bounce" as they syncopate or swing the beat in a particular way. Finally, the "yodelaying" voice resembles the jazz solo insofar as the latter is heard as an extension of the voice.

There is another level at which Kerouac's prose exhibits Baudelaire-like correspondences to the best and most original jazz solos. Kerouac's passage extends itself, its theme of spectacular descent, not through variation but in uninterrupted release of momentum—conveyed through a line of conspicuously immediate, active present participles—to the end. Compare it, for instance, with Dizzy Gillespie's "A Night in Tunisia." Recorded in 1946, the composition features one of Charlie Parker's famous solos. The piece begins with an Afro-Latinesque introduction, followed by an interlude. A four-measure solo follows the interlude in which Parker releases a time-and-space merging stream of sixteenth-notes—twelve notes per second for five seconds straight—that forms what Thomas Owen called no virtuosic run through a scale or chord, but "a perfectly structured melodic statement." The correspondence of momentum and instantaneous creation between Parker's solo and Kerouac's prose derives from their basis in open psychic conditions. Both Parker's sequence of melodic ideas and Kerouac's sequence of word pictures seem to be conceived and simultaneously expressed, whole and intact, not in accord with convention, but with their own implicit logic of structure and timing. After playing the "A Night in Tunisia" solo, Parker reportedly said, "I'll never make that break again." It is a fair bet that Kerouac thought the same about his own literary jump down the mountain.[33]

Kerouac cultivated mental states that allowed him to write in conformity with the flow of thought. He believed the best jazz musicians at their best moments performed similarly. His influential "Essentials of Spontaneous Prose" is based on the assumption that there is a parallel texture of experience across improvising disciplines—namely between improvised writing and improvised music. The experience supersedes craft. Put another way, Kerouac thinks form takes care of itself as it spontaneously flows through the mind and then through the musical or writing instrument. Norman Podhoretz believed this was indicative of distaste for knowledge—primitive. Irving Howe remarked that the Beats' "contempt for mind" was "at one with the middle class suburbia they think they scorn." Howe's and Podhoretz's views seem to be based, in part, on the media spectacle of beatnik public foolishness, in some cases Kerouac's. As a result I think they superimpose a caricature of primitivism—the occasional, seemingly mindless behavior of crowds—onto a Beat aesthetic that does not jettison knowledge, but conforms itself to Eastern-derived notions of mental concentration and esteem for creativity in the moment.[34]

With all due respect to their many critical contributions, I think Howe and Podhoretz misunderstood the Beats. The Beat writers they criticize revered learning and admired scholars such as Mark Van Doran and Lionel Trilling. The Beats were keen to influences from Euro-American and international traditions. For example, in his 1956 letter about "Howl" to Richard Eberhart, Ginsberg associates influential colleagues with literary forebears or scholarship: Robert Duncan "dug [William Carlos] Williams, Stein . . . Charles Olsen; Gary Snyder, a Zen Buddhist poet and Chinese scholar; Jack Kerouac . . . is the Colossus . . . taught me to write . . . *the* unmistakable . . . prolific Shakespearean *genius*." In "Essentials to Spontaneous Prose," Kerouac likens the act of writing to Elizabethan drama and its requirements of perfect timing: "Nothing is muddy that runs in time and to the laws of time—Shakespeare stress of dramatic need to speak now in own unalterable way or forever hold tongue." Dennis McNally relates the story of Kerouac reading *Henry IV* with his friend Gerard Alvin, when Alvin suddenly realized that Kerouac was not reading his part of Hal but dramatically reciting it from memory. In his letter to Eberhart, Ginsberg specifically explains how past writers—Apollinaire, Baudelaire, Blake, Hart Crane, Dostoyevsky, T. S. Eliot, Lorca, Pound, Whitman, Williams, Wordsworth, Yeats—literary forms such as Haiku, and religious and philosophical ideas—Freud, the "Trilling-esque sense of 'civilization'"—all influenced the form and content of *Howl*, what it was and what it wasn't.[35]

Knowledge of and interaction with aesthetic, intellectual, and religious traditions informed Kaufman, ruth weiss, Corso, Burroughs, Ginsberg, and others who paid attention to Kerouac's "Essentials of Spontaneous Prose." Kerouac's document considered that the best music and writing resulted from diamond-clear awareness: a kind of heightened psychological moment that immediately grasped or set up the object and wrote it, for example, "sketching language . . . undisturbed flow of mind . . . 'blowing' (as per jazz musician) on subject of image." Likewise, improvising musicians set up the object—the arc of a tune's harmonic movement, the lyric of a tune, or the image of a melody, the musical color of a phrase: any one or all of these necessarily combined with a felt sense of rhythm. The setup opened the door to the solo. Once over the threshold of the first note, word, or brush stroke, concentration in the solo must be total. Distinctions break down between thought and action. Imagination and action blend as a singular movement from note to note, word to word, phrase to phrase. The solo blows over like a wind. The motion assumes the effortless intelligence of breathing. Art happens. On paper, canvas, film, or tape, it leaves not itself but its trace. In this idealized sense improvisation is in part meditation, and as such, it facilitates an appreciation for both the crude and finest subtleties of perception. It encourages the pursuit of intuitions that in their implications dissolve rationalist dualities of bad note and good note, bad thought and good thought, to the larger parameters of sinner and saint, mind and body, enemy and friend, civilization and ecology, and notions of discrete difference in sex, race, and ethnicity; it does not deny com-

plexity and difference, rather, it views the whole mountain of interconnected, teeming, ephemeral multiplicity. When Ray Smith said,
"everything was like jazz," he voiced the realization of an attentive
consciousness that knows creative growth occurs through the making of uncharacteristic relations among elements of a given medium
or mediums. He speaks of the safety of apparent risk—the ultimate
security of leaping into an improvisation or into the motley traffic of
steep slopes or, for that matter, like Galileo, from the edge of the flat
earth itself. The cultivation and experience of these moments is a discipline quite remote to a stereotyped primitivism; it speaks to the
years of difficult training (formal or not) and practice most artists
undergo before they can even think about making art in the moment.[36]

The 6 Gallery readings signified commonplace but charismatic
notions of renaissance and, through its association with jazz, socially galvanizing "primitive" energy. Moreover, Kerouac and others
critiqued the latter by infusing it with Eastern concepts of reality,
mind, and creativity. The sign of jazz—especially in its bebop formulation as deployed in the 6 Gallery readings—also indicated an artistic response of independent and creative social dissent on the part
of Beat writers and audiences. These heard the sound of dissent and
liberation in bebop, which exploded out of the context of a commercial music industry that unfairly exploited black musicians and
stifled artistic ambition. Moreover, the socioeconomic inequalities
of the music industry were but symptoms of an overall political
economy systematically arrayed against the interests of African
Americans particularly, and working classes more generally. As a result, Americans of every hue—both disenfranchised and white youth
questioning the benefits of middle-class security—found liberating
(and therefore subversive) meanings in bebop that showed through
Beat art.

Black jazz musicians were well aware of racial inequities in the
music industry and in society as a whole, but their primary motiva-

tions for being involved in bebop had to do with a passion for innovation in music and professional choice. They pursued their art with discipline and pride and usually ducked aesthetic and political labels that could restrict their creative goals. The new Bop style was politicized, less by musicians than by critics and audiences commenting on its meanings. Nevertheless, images of self-possessed black masculinity embodied in such figures as Kenny Clarke, Dizzy Gillespie, Thelonious Monk, or Charlie Parker created a new controversial sound that attracted white musicians and mixed audiences and unsettled the anxieties of those vested in the homogeneity of white stability. Bebop exploded out of the context of a war being fought against fascism abroad while widespread discrimination was entrenched at home. Black activism and urban upheaval rattled U.S. cities. Bebop was contiguous with jazz traditions, but it sounded like an alien country. It was a conspicuous, free-floating sign that lent itself it to transformational shifts in the performance of personal, cultural, and political identities. It seemed to announce the emerging disruptions of late modernity itself.[37]

Holy the Bop Apocalypse!

—Allen Ginsberg

Kerouac and others had their ears to the ground when bebop, developed by a small group of black musicians, sprang loose of its confines to after hours at Minton's and Monroe's Playhouse, two jazz clubs in Harlem. At first, Kerouac said he did not like Bop, but he soon changed his mind. Gerald Nicosia reports that by 1944 Kerouac was an avid student of Bop. He followed Jerry Newman, who recorded the new sounds, around Harlem. By 1944 Burroughs, Lucian Carr, Hal Chase, Ginsberg, Kerouac, and Edie Parker had all met. Cultivating a vital nightlife, they haunted jazz clubs, played records, tuned into Symphony Sid's late-night bebop program, and spent many a Benzedrine night in their cold-water flats contemplating jazz. They were fascinated by all of the displaced creatures who seemed most visible at night: homeless people, petty thieves, hustlers, prostitutes, charity workers, pimps, nuns, junkies, street preachers, artists, the insane, workers on the A.M. shift, and musicians. They imagined a profound wisdom suffused through all ostensibly perverse life, in part, by virtue of its alienation and seeming autonomy from official concerns of winning the war. Displaced by the social and economic structures most Americans were fighting for, many African Americans were also ambivalent about the war. The Beats identified with their displacement. For many, bebop was a musical formulation of social displacement turned active and positive, enfranchising itself in the face of historical and present systematic denial. The obtrusive audacity of bebop hit the Beats like an apocalypse of the possible; it tripped the light of their new cultural vision and gave it an aesthetic—a tangible African American style and performance. Thus, it was a radical moment when the reading of "Howl"—poetry, of all things—invoked a level of audience participation and response similar to that of a Charlie Parker performance or Bud Powell or Dexter Gordon & Wardell Gray or Little Richard or a fired-up preacher in a storefront church or Adam Clayton Powell, Martin Luther King, Jr., or Malcolm X.[38]

Art is not an autonomous entity. Anthropology, ethnomusicology, and to some extent cultural studies have shown the intimate ways in which art bears the marks of social and material conditions of life. Whereas structural features of society may not always be aesthetically marked, the ethnomusicologist Steven Feld has written, "for all societies, everything that is musically salient will undoubtedly be socially marked." Long before Feld, Norman Mailer, in however rarified a manner, provocatively understood jazz was salient. The existentialized Negro hipster and the white version of the same socially marked jazz—a music that "gave voice to the character and quality of his existence, to his rage and the infinite variations of joy, lust, languor, growl, cramp, pinch, scream and despair." LeRoi Jones (Amira Baraka) in his landmark *Blues People* (1963), Charles Keil in *Urban Blues* (1966), and Frank Kofsky in *Black Nationalism and the Revolution in Music* (1970) all express the social contours of black music. Even James Lincoln Collier, shy of materialist interpretations, insinuates that Bop is an extreme case in which jazz mirrors social upheaval: "Rarely has their been a movement in art that showed so clearly as bop the lineaments of the social forces behind it. Not merely was the philosophy of the players a product of currents in the culture, but the shape of the music itself—the actual length and pitches of the notes—to a large degree was determined by shifts in the structure of society, shifts that are in fact still going on." Collier links the oppositional aspects of Bop to post–World War I developments such as the rise of the black arts and jazz in the 1920s and recognition of the implications of segregation on the part of intellectuals. Left-wing political groups were agitating for black rights and a number of African American entertainers had established themselves in the popular and high arts. All of this caused blacks and whites to question assumptions about black inferiority. In addition, the explosion in the popularity of swing in the 1930s and 1940s disproportionately rewarded white practitioners of the music. A clearer vision of these factors, says Collier, caused African Americans to grow "bitter, resentful, and scornful of white society."[39]

Collier's analysis is a good one, but it does not go far enough. U.S. blacks were being asked to support a war on behalf of a country that refused to extend the same social and economic freedoms white citizens were guaranteed. African Americans that fought in the war fought for the "Double V" as the *Pittsburgh Courier* called it: "victory abroad and victory at home." Inequities in employment and education and indignities and dangers faced by African Americans around the country—especially those who were in the military—made Harlem's race relations exceeding tense. Correlating with the development of bebop, in 1943 Harlem exploded. "Word was that a white cop had shot and killed a black soldier in a scuffle involving a black woman. This was mostly true (the soldier lived) . . . The inequity of a black military man gunned down by the white Uncle he had protected overseas hit hard, and Harlem hit back, looting businesses and trashing cars to the tune of several millions. James Baldwin later said that Harlem had needed something to smash."[40]

Social instability, war itself, appeared to register sonically in bebop; with its disjunctive melodies, polyrhythmic accents—*bombs* and *rim shots*—and relentless speed, it seemed to smash the conventions of jazz. Early on, many white critics expressed shock, calling the music "crazy," "heresy," "anti-humanistic," and "on a lower level of musical significance"—in short, riotous, a kind of musical anomie and terror. Critics coined the term "bebop" and publicized it as a "fighting" word for a "fighting" music. Dizzy Gillespie and Kenny Clarke deny these connotations, saying that for them, it was "just music," but they agreed that like the riots themselves, the music was a "wake up" call with a special message to black people summed up by Clarke as "get the fuck outta the way." Clarke is perhaps referring to African Americans who he felt disdained their own culture in order to assimilate into the white mainstream. He was probably also referring to the older generation of jazz audience and to jazz musicians such as Louis Armstrong, who seemed befuddled by the music and criticized it as "weird chords that don't mean nothin'"[41]

Bebop sympathizers adopted nonmusical elements to accent and heighten the divisive effect of the music and to link it symbolically to the spirit of insurrection in the streets. The argot, the zoot suits, the smack, the goatees, the berets, the green-tinted, horn-rimmed glasses spelled out a new style that was serious and relaxed, intellectual and street savvy—in short, hip. Against this backdrop, Mailer's notion of hip in "The White Negro: Superficial Reflections on the Hipster" (1957) seems narrow. The title not withstanding, Mailer's article thinks provocatively about a neo-romanticized macho-primitive, a caricature that does not exist called the hipster, albeit not the zoot-suited hot hipster but the shadowy cool version: white. This existentialist, sensual figure of the present and future derives force and mystique via miscegenation with the myth of black sexual potency and marks nothing less than a total repudiation of the humanist tradition. Mailer's hipster refuses revolution, ideology, even history. Indifferent to all but the libido, his psyche draws nigh to the psychopath's. The hipster in "The White Negro" discloses less street-life or anthropology than Mailer's own role in the semiotic undermining of high modernism—its all-at-once supercession by a late modern return to the body. Mailer is reading signs and in the manner that he does it, whites' absorption and use of black style, he is a progenitor of cultural studies. Moreover, he reads contemporaneous signs against a structure of feeling that comprehended the historical burden of the Holocaust and nuclear annihilation and, for many, the nausea of the U.S. mainstream escape through consumption and suburban life. Mailer also tapped feelings that encompassed the threat of indignity and the peril of African American life: "Any Negro who wishes to live must live with danger from his first day, and no experience can ever be casual . . . no Negro can saunter down a street with any real certainty that violence will not visit him on his walk. The cameos of the security for the average white: mother and the home, job and the family, are not even a mockery to millions of Negroes; they are impossible." Thus, though Mailer is interested in a rarified idea of the hipster, he nevertheless indicates an emotional and psychic fabric that underlies not only a cool version of hip but a hot one too, as well as the street riot.[42]

Hip attitudes, like jazz, also drew from European romanticism to the extent that they valorized art for its own sake, even if it was produced at the nexus of alienation, and with respect to junk, self-destruction. Such attitudes did not stop at nostalgia; they could be unequivocally and presently defiant. Zoot suits were a visible sign of antipatriotism in that they openly defied the War Production Board's rationing of clothing. Psychologists Kenneth Clark and George

Breitman said zoot suits were evidence of a new militancy, and in Los Angeles, after the riots, the city council debated declaring the suits illegal.[43]

Embedded in Kerouac's account of the 6 Gallery readings is Ginsberg's "holy the Bop apocalypse," in part, the "angry fix" from "negro streets," the voice of the oppressed, shooting through and pushing forward the lines of Ginsberg's poem "Howl," as well as the art and thinking of others. For example, Robert Alexander and Wally Berman, white, gay Los Angeles artists who have been associated with the Beats, wrapped themselves around jazz. "Wally and I probably both had our lives saved by jazz music. We identified with the world of jazz and blacks, the pain, the roots. We shared persecution . . . I like the word 'soul' if it's understood . . . as a feeling of the heart that can be shared—smoking a little weed, going to jazz clubs, meeting jazz musicians, getting into the idiom."[44]

ruth weiss, a Holocaust survivor and Bay Area, Beat-associated poet, has been reading poetry with jazz since 1949. "When I heard Bop I said that's my sound." Although weiss's comment does not explicitly mention the social upheaval associated with bebop, she was certainly familiar with persecution. weiss's living partner Paul Blake, Bay Area painter and jazz aficionado, associated jazz and persecution with the comment, "jazz is anarchic and chaotic because it is personal; it's dangerous. Bebop players were underground and persecuted by the police state," as was, as Mailer said, "any Negro who wishes to live." For many people, jazz was the sound of living dangerously if you were black or Beat, though the latter, if white, obviously had a choice. In the Bay Area, police were offended by the exposure of their violence. At the Co-Existence Bagel Shop, they ripped from the wall Bill Margolis's line (placed there by Bob Kaufman) which read that Hitler

> moved to San Francisco, became an ordinary
> policeman, devoted himself to stamping out Beatniks.

Margolis echoed Mary Bethune's words to the Daughters of the American Revolution fifteen years earlier when Bop was taking shape in Harlem. Though many African Americans recognized they would be worse off under Hitler's rule, she said, "we're not blind to the fact that the doors of democratic opportunity are not opened very wide to us." Therefore, she added, America "has the dual task of defeating Hitler abroad and Hitlerism at home."[45]

In the poem "Walking Parker Home," Bob Kaufman writes that Charlie Parker's "realization bronze fingers" sought "ghetto thoughts"; they danced double-time from his horn and Ginsberg's, Kaufman's, Kerouac's, weiss's, and John Clellon Holmes's pens. For example, in the novel Go (1952), Holmes describes the "Go Hole," a New York jazz club populated with conspicuous Negroes, Irish, and Italians, styled out in zoots, long-lapelled shirts, horn rims, and suede shoes—youthful crowds belonging nowhere in wartime America, affecting a walk and talk, hearing in "modern jazz . . . something rebel and nameless that spoke for them." Thus bebop sonically encoded the rebellious act of social mixing and style exchange. Indeed, Holmes writes of a compelling social pluralism that took place in New York City in the 1940s and 1950s. In particular, as bebop began to move downtown to 52nd Street, clubs such as the Village Vanguard and Kelly's Stable became magnets for black and white musicians and audiences. Both hosts and the guests were marked as rebels by the police who watched, harassed, dispersed, and closed down their gathering places. Scott DeVeaux writes: "The sessions at Kelly's ended abruptly in mid-1943, when the police put a padlock on the door. 'Naturally, it had to do with the black-white thing,' according to Monte Kay [the music promoter]. 'We drew an integrated crowd.'" Kay adds, however, "the police action did little to stem the cultural tide."[46]

Holmes's second novel The Horn (1953) shows how jazz auralized explicit feelings of rage toward the U.S. social order. Edgar Pool, or "Horn," a great tenor sax player in decline, had used his musical skill to escape the strictures of an imposed identity. In a flashback to the beginning of his career, on his way to New York for the first time, he refused the interior of a Jim Crow train and told his companion: "I'd rather ride cold and nothing back here, than warm and nigger up there." Holmes writes outrage as the central emotion of Pool's art and self-destructive bent—outrage that there was no social precedent for a free black self. Pool raged because the compromises a black man had to make for economic necessity brooked no pride.[47]

Bebop was not about rage, however. It was generous enough to permit rage and every other emotion, too. Nor did Beat writing and the 6 Gallery readings simply reduce the music's emotions to social spleen. Musicians often felt empowered, free, and full of happiness. It is true that just as the Beats and San Francisco poets felt the academic establishment had put a stranglehold on poetry, jazz musicians felt commercialized swing jazz discouraged collective and individual innovation and improvisation. Yet poets and musicians were no longer "waiting" like the voice in Ferlinghetti's poem but experiencing a "rebirth of wonder." Jazz players and audiences stood in awe as they heard the various conventional blues and 32-bar song forms opened up by oddly configured, complex chords and more of them, a field of sound where improvisers, out of the corral, could romp and dance or run down new melodic moves as fast as cheetahs chasing gazelles across savannas. Bop players restored the African American roots-music practice of striking melodic and percussive notes in polyrhythmic relation to the beat—ahead of it, behind it, or on it depending on the exigency of the moment. Dexter Gordon has said he felt very lucky to have come up at such an exciting time when the music was changing so dramatically. Kerouac felt the excitement, too. In passage after passage of *On the Road*, Bop tracks the wild automobile rides of Sal Paradise and Dean Moriarty across the vast U.S. geography. Like Bop musicians, Kerouac made a new, obtrusively compelling aesthetic of vernacular and sometimes conventional materials: his own speeding *jouissance* of the text. And bebop was its underlying musical counterpart.[48]

The "angry-fix" was palpable in "Howl," yes, but so was its flip side—the poem's invitation to participate in a community sheltered under "the gold-horn shadow of the band." Ginsberg conceived this community as bound together by "America's naked mind for love." He heard this feeling of vulnerable openness in jazz. He imagined jazz as an art of human relevance. He did not limit its span or contain its strength because he perceived African American struggle as one of its sources. Through its music, this community enveloped him: white, American, and Jewish. Why not believe jazz could help transform the postwar machinery of capitalism into an "intelligent kindness of the soul!"?[49]

While such language may seem naïve, it is both ambitious and practical. Jazz has always been at the vanguard of transforming recalcitrant cultural boundaries into art and art communities. Born of European and African traditions, it has throughout its history freely absorbed Spanish, Caribbean, Middle Eastern, near and far Asian, and North and South American Indian traditions. The jazz community—players, audience, and personnel of its commerce—has been a global community. Paul Berliner has found that jazz players are often knowledgeable about the music's history. Informed by symbolic links to the past, many performers "can assume a spiritual quality" and may have a sense of "participating in a global discourse among music thinkers, negotiating musical ideas that transcend cultural and historical boundaries." I prefer the word transform to transcend, however. The cultural openness of jazz and bebop—in particular, its seemingly innate ability to realize communal and individual expression along with its technical feats—not only made John Coltrane's *A Love Supreme* (1964) possible but the cultural vision and style of "Howl" and the story of the 6 Gallery readings before it. The story of the 6 Gallery readings and the story of Bop function as insurgent cousin myths. The latter was the benefactor of the former, but in the ensuing decade of the 1960s, both stories conveyed energies that turned increasingly reciprocal and pluralistic via the counter culture, rock 'n' roll, civil rights, and Vietnam protests.

The cultural energy and meanings flowing through the pipeline connecting New York and San Francisco also flowed to other cities. Chicago, Seattle, Boston, and Los Angeles all had constituencies that identified with similar jazz rituals and feelings that had gathered and dispersed from the 6 Gallery. Even Ginsberg spread the ritualized form of the reading; he used it like a jazz musician uses a chord chart, covering the content but improvising the delivery according to the needs of the moment at various parties, the San Francisco Poetry Center, Berkeley, and with great controversy in Los Angeles in the summer of 1956. In response to jeers in the audience, he stripped off his clothes and dared the troublemakers to come on the stage and do likewise. "Come and stand here, stand naked before the world," he shouted. "The poet always stands naked before the world!"[50]

If it is true that many people saw the 6 Gallery reading as a watershed event for San Francisco poetry and beyond, it is also true that Lawrence Lipton—the master of ceremonies for the L.A. reading, elder spokesman, and inventive promoter of the Beat generation in Southern California—thought that Ginsberg's later reading signaled a new opportunity. "L.A. will never be the same," he victoriously wrote his San Francisco competitor Kenneth Rexroth. The L.A. reading showed that much of the mythical aura of the 6 Gallery reading preceded it. Ginsberg invited Anais Nin to the L.A. reading, introducing himself and asking her to invite Christopher Isherwood, Aldous Huxley, Marlon Brando, and James Dean (who was dead). The charisma of these readings was closely bound to Ginsberg's personality. The poem also had huge charisma, but Lipton was not referring as much to qualities in Ginsberg's art or art in Venice Beach, as to the quantity of mass media attention he could help generate through the spectacle of conspicuous beatniks. Indeed, after the

Howl trial and an article by Herb Caen in the *San Francisco Chronicle* (April 2, 1958) that coined the pejorative term, beatniks suddenly sprang from obscure beaches and dark urban corners to the pop culture surface. Lipton was quick to promote his views on the new scene. In his hot-selling popular sociological study, *The Holy Barbarians* (1959), Lipton championed Venice Beats as purveyors of a spiritual-material revolution of voluntary poverty, sex, kicks, jazz, and poetry. Lipton's text was simultaneously learned and hyperbolic, and it helped draw a large migration of beatniks and tourists to Venice Beach. Everyone from Metro-Goldwyn-Mayer to Caroline Freud in London to UCLA consulted with Lipton about the scene. Subsequently, he hosted a nationwide CBS radio special called "Beatniks" (1959), and he helped *LIFE* magazine engineer the article "Squaresville U.S.A. vs. Beatsville U.S.A." (1959). The latter was an especially cynical and distorted portrayal of American life that invented a story in order to reinforce a false dichotomy. It sold lots of ad copy and promoted Lipton. Though the article made it easy for some to dismiss Beat-types, I believe others saw beyond the spectacle and the expensive ads it attracted. These were the ones who read the poetry and discovered jazz. They read books, listened to records, and talked about them with their friends. Perhaps they hit the road. They opened up, performed new identities, and engaged the substance of cultural change.[51]

Writing retrospectively in 1980, Michael McClure confirmed the genealogical strength of the 6 Gallery reading of "Howl"—a strength it absorbed from the liberational meanings surrounding bebop: "Ginsberg read . . . left us standing in wonder, or cheering and wondering, but knowing at the deepest level that a barrier had been broken, that a human voice and body had been hurled against the harsh wall of America and its supporting armies and navies and academies and institutions and ownership systems and power-support bases." Time has only served to amplify the 6 Gallery's subversive mythical edge. As we have seen, Kenneth Rexroth became loath to champion the Beats as their popularity eclipsed established San Francisco writers. Yet by 1970, in his book *American Poetry in the Twentieth Century* (1971), he had recovered his earlier enthusiasm. Writing in the context of American postwar poetry, Rexroth wrote: "The climacteric was not the publication of a book, it was the famous Six Gallery reading, the culmination of twenty years of the oral presentation of poetry in San Francisco." The Beat media spectacle and the 6 Gallery story had short-term exclusionary effects on the breadth of writing in the Bay Area in the 1950s. Part of the 6 Gallery's enduring meaning lies in how it opened up a space for new voices to be heard, identities performed, and bodies seen, whether they were recognized by fame and money or not.[52]

In summary, then, the spectacle of the *Howl* trial projected the Beat and associated writers on to the surface of popular consciousness. Although the spectacle excluded many of the issues that the Beats were concerned about, Corso, Ferlinghetti, Ginsberg, Kerouac, and others were able to act, to align themselves with subordinate but vested interests and win a modicum of legitimacy under the law. Mass-mediated caricatures, parodies, and outright distortions ensued. Nevertheless, the Beats fashioned narratives that have defined and preserved the movement and have empowered artists, audiences, and critics, then and since. The 6 Gallery story has been a starting place for virtually every account of the literary and cultural history of the Beats and the San Francisco poetry renaissance. It is a piquant story, malleable and tough. Like gum it has stuck in the memory and resisted the distractions of hyped images and rhetoric.

On the other hand, it is necessary to scrutinize the overdetermined and exclusionary features of a lineage that has helped obscure other important Bay Area artists. The next chapter discusses two of them: ruth weiss and Bob Kaufman, who both confirm and challenge assumptions about the Beat generation and indeed, richly expand its breadth. The 6 Gallery story and much of Beat generation society and art derived its vitality and style from jazz. Writing and attitudes

about jazz had long ensnared the music in a pejorative, or less frequently, a romantic charismatic primitivism. While the Beats drew
upon the latter, Kerouac and others began to disentangle jazz from
its associations with the irrational. Kerouac wrote of the music's de-
mand for mental acuity of the highest order. More significant, a
closer examination of the 6 Gallery readings reveals how the Beat
generation, participants in the San Francisco poetry renaissance, and
other artists in other cities identified with the radical socio-political
energies stemming from bebop's formative years in wartime Harlem.
Bebop was a sophisticated and intellectual art, but it also demonstrated how social and cultural marginalization and inequality could
be made into new forms of expression, identity, and community.
This African American music and the style of its players supported
disaffected artists across the country searching for a means to trans-
figure their own experience into an art that cut to the quick of U.S.
hypocrisy and unrealized potential. Moreover, the symbolic and social mixing of the Beat generation undermined U.S. chauvinism and
led to more cultural pluralism and exchange in the next decade. Thus
the Beats were effective agents for social change through their art and
through their media savvy. At the same time they shaped stories that
packed the necessary mythical force to fend off mainstream distortions and preserve the memory of their work.

2

ON THE BRINK

go to the round house
he can't corner you there
mirror where?
table and table and mirror
and he said why talk
we'll only confuse

—ruth weiss, *The Brink*

No, I am not anything that is anything I am not.

—Bob Kaufman, "I, Too, Know What I Am Not"

Beat writers' populism, their consumption of vernacular voices and mores in the making of art, foreshadows cultural studies itself. Ideally, cultural studies attempts to listen to voices from the fringes in order to learn more about the complex, shifting relationships that comprise centers and edges—middles and margins. Through its study of aesthetics, style, and life, cultural studies tilts its ambition toward ethnography.[1]

In this chapter, too, I lean toward ethnography by focusing on two Bay Area writers who, as best as I can put it, wrote from the margin of the margin in the 1950s—in some cases, off the edge of it: ruth weiss and Bob Kaufman. Kaufman is the best known of the two writers. He is an international legend to outcast poets and radical Beat audiences. But unlike the story of the 6 Gallery, neither the story of Kaufman or his works are widely known; they make scattered, brief appearances in the cultural histories of the Beats as well as in African American literature, but relative to the celebrity status of Kerouac and Ginsberg, he is obscure, and weiss, even more so. Kaufman was black and distantly Jewish. weiss is a white, bisexual woman and part of the Jewish Diaspora. She and her parents immigrated to the United States, narrowly escaping the Nazis in World War II. Although I reject strict claims of cause and effect, knowledge of Kaufman's and weiss's social positions—difficult as it is to ascertain facts of their biographies—brightens the light on how their work interacts with the work of other Beat writers.[2] These interactions are significant in the way they dance around both poets' vagabond approach to the confessional voice—the *narrative I*—the very brink of self.

Lawrence Ferlinghetti wrote, "the only thing that will stand will be the 'narrative I'—whether in prose or poetry—the voice of him sounding thru [sic] the American experience."[3] Yet weiss's and Kaufman's poetry illustrates that the category of the *narrative I* did not stand as firmly as Ferlinghetti's statement seems to indicate. Beginning with weiss, the I is an i. It is a contingent entity and not a controlling one—a sign among signs. She uses it in her autobiographical work. Much of her poetry and film, however, cuts off the structural logic of the *narrative I* and its content of restricted desire which stutters,

> and i   i have no more to say
> may i have another blade of grass?[4]

By way of contrast, many of Kaufman's poems drop the subjective voice altogether in favor of an often politically charged, gleefully absurd, descriptive sketching. Still others of Kaufman's poems use the *narrative I*, not to reveal an internal condition but to evade or disguise it:

My body is a torn mattress,
Disheveled throbbing place
For the comings and goings
of loveless transients.
The whole of me
is an unfurnished room
Filled with dank breath
Escaping in gasps to nowhere.

The voice of Kaufman's poem makes a full antidisclosure: "The whole of me is an unfurnished room." The voice evaporates into a cipher, which is unusual but not unprecedented. For example, the beginning of Ginsberg's poem "America" evokes a similar feeling: "America I've given you all now I am nothing." This is the poem's ruse or negative capability, however, because the ensuing lines are a blast of substance from the vacuum. Kerouac also threw selves into contingency. They splinter off into multiple voices in *Visions of Cody* (ms.1952, 1972). And in *On the Road* (1957), Sal Paradise tells us one red morning by the railroad tracks in Des Moines, Iowa, "I didn't know who I was."[5] Ginsberg's and Kerouac's turbulent flights through uncertain identity and multiplicity return to the safety of a unified, though greatly expanded, narrator's vision, however. weiss and Kaufman avoid the narrator's grand vision.

In the following pages I examine how both Kaufman and weiss undermine the controlling authority of the narrating self and selves. weiss deconstructs selves into fragments and leaves them there, a text permitting neither self or other, especially in her film *The Brink* (1961) and in her poems in *Gallery of Women* (1959). But Kaufman uses the structure of the narrative form in order to exploit its superficial qualities as an occasion for absurd entertainment—parody and pastiche. In Kaufman's poetry that is all there is, a spectacular surface, a virtuosic series of masks signifying an absence of self, not an invisible man but no-man.

It is useful here to note that the observed phenomenon of fragmented subjectivities characterizing postmodernism is not a new condition but a proliferating one. Beat writers such as Kerouac and Ginsberg registered this pervasive feature among their middle- and working-class generation stemming, in part, from the aftermath of World War II and the rapid growth of the consumer economy. At the same time they tended to romanticize disenfranchised minorities—African Americans, Native Americans, and Mexicans. Many of the Beats imagined that these *fellaheen* retained something of the utopia long since lost to Anglo-Americans. This was often a misperception. Disorientation and fragmented identity often suffuse disenfranchised and oppressed peoples. Widespread cracking of the psyche preceded the superimposed periodization of postmodernism.[6] Thus we should frame Kaufman's and weiss's life and work in terms of their bearing the compounded pressures of both disenfranchised minority status and the effects of late capitalism and the Cold War. And this leads us to ethnography.

Kaufman's and weiss's treatment of subjectivity instructs us about social experiences in the Bay Area and the United States in the late 1950s. Relatively speaking, the Beat movement and the Bay Area were open to exceptional voices, especially politically charged, dissenting voices against censorship, the Cold War, and materialism, and this attracted weiss and Kaufman. Kaufman's and weiss's work also helps us gauge the status and development of nascent voices in the Bay Area: queer voices, feminist voices, environmentally conscious voices, and voices about black identity—all of which spoke at a low volume, sometimes not at all, or shrewdly, in a diversionary way for protection from a hostile public. Kaufman's and weiss's treatment of the subjective and the narrative I takes shape in this plurality of voices with which they interact; they alternately observe them, assume them, and occlude them. They help us to see better the complex social and artistic interaction that comprised the Bay Area scene and the Beat movement.

In contrast to weiss, Kaufman exploited the pleasure of the text. He mastered the art of the witty, political, satirical surface, and he was popular for it. Ferlinghetti appreciated Kaufman's accessible hilarity and so did Bay Area audiences. Ferlinghetti's City Lights published three of Kaufman's works as broadsides: "Abomunist Manifesto" (1959), "Second April" (1959), and "Does the Secret Mind Whisper?" (1960)—all of which sold more than *Howl*.[7] I will look at the "Abomunist Manifesto" because it appealed to Bay Area libertarian sentiment. It highlights what the bohemians wanted to hear and ignores other important but less overtly public, subordinate issues.

The "Abomunist Manifesto" was not a contradiction in terms but a paradoxical smile.[8] It was popular because it reflected the long-standing western frontier love of anarchy and because it was timely in its reference to current issues. It threw outrageous wit in the face of all things presumed serious. Authority wishes to be taken seriously, but "ABOMUNISTS REJECT EVERYTHING EXCEPT SNOWMEN." Here are a few more of the documents' principles:

> ABOMUNISTS JOIN NOTHING BUT THEIR HANDS OR LEGS OR OTHER SAME.

> ABOMUNISTS DO NOT FEEL PAIN NO MATTER HOW MUCH IT HURTS.

> ABOMUNISTS NEVER CARRY MORE THAN FIFTY DOLLARS IN DEBT ON THEM.

> ABOMUNISTS DO NOT WRITE FOR MONEY; THEY WRITE THE MONEY ITSELF.

These are five of fourteen principles that occur in the manifesto. The manifesto also includes ten other subsidiary documents, for example: "NOTES DIS- AND RE-GARDING ABOMUNISM"; "$$ ABOMUNUS CRAXIOMS $$"; "EXCERPTS FROM THE LEXICON ABOMUNON";

"Abomunist election manifesto"; "Boms"; "Abomunist documents (*discovered at the tomb of the unknown draft dodger*)." Enjoy the free wheeling satire of the Abomnewscast . . . on the hour . . ."

America collides with iceberg piloted by Lindbergh baby . . . Civilian Defense Headquarters unveils new bomb shelter with two-car garage, complete with indoor patio and barbecue unit that operates on radioactivity, comes in decorator colors, no down payment for vets, to be sold only to those willing to sign loyalty oath . . . Forest Lawn Cemetery opens new subdivision of split-level tombs for middle-income group . . . President inaugurates new policy of aggressive leadership, declares December 25th Christmas Day . . . Pope may allow priests to marry, said to be aiming at one big holy family . . . Norman Rockwell cover, "The Lynching Bee" from "Post" Americana series, wins D.A.R. Americanism award . . . Cubans seize Cuba, outraged U.S. acts quickly, cuts off tourist quota, administration introduces measure to confine all rhumba bands to detention camps during emergency . . . Both sides in Cold War stockpiling atomic missiles to preserve peace, end of mankind seen if peace is declared, End of news . . . Remember your national emergency signal, when you see one small mushroom cloud and three large ones, it is not a drill, turn the TV off and get under it . . . Foregoing sponsored by your friendly neighborhood Abomunist . . . Tune in next world.

The pleasures of satire supersede the fears of a generation witnessing the consumer explosion, the booming war economy, threat of nuclear fallout, Cold War imperialism, and systematic racism. "Abomunist Manifesto" was more than a joke. It was a message to a generation: confront official authority with critical absurdities of every conceivable kind.

Kaufman saw all authority as a manifestation of war against hu-

man beings. ruth weiss—with the exception of her autobiographical
writing in which she says that she and her family caught the last train
out of Vienna in 1938 to escape the Nazis—exiles war to the oblivion of silence. Kaufman attacks it on three fronts. He attacks the
technologicalization of actual war (its apotheosis being the bomb).
He attacks U.S. politics as war on freedom in times of peace—that is,
war on minorities and dissent at home and abroad via the rule of
law, the HUAC, the police, the FBI, the CIA, the State Department,
and the Pentagon.[9] And he attacks commercialization as war on art.
Abomunism used crazy wit to expose diffuse institutional surveil-
lance and power. On occasion, such as in the poem "War Memoir,"
Kaufman went for authority's jugular by displacing humor with the
shock of the image of atrocity, for example, "the burning/ Of Japanese in atomic colorcinemascope . . . stereophonic screaming." Here
Kaufman deplores not only the act of war itself, but also the
aestheticization of war through Hollywood film and sound technologies (in the poem "Hollywood," which I will discuss below, he sa-
lutes Hollywood as an "artistic cancer"). And he attacks the various
national security agencies that approve images of "flagwrapped cre-
mations" for propaganda purposes.[10]

These kinds of poems gave Kaufman a reputation for being politically radical and funny in North Beach, a scene that he documented
in one of his well-known poems, "Bagel Shop Jazz." The poem is interesting for what it includes and what it omits. "Bagel Shop Jazz"
framed a classic picture of North Beach pluralism. Here he studied
the strange sight of motley "nightfall creatures, eating each other
over a noisy cup of coffee": "Mulberry-eyed girls . . . love tinted, beat
angels . . . lost in the beat . . . angel guys . . . black-haired dungaree
guys, Caesar-jawed with synagogue eyes . . . lost [too] . . . where time
is told with a beat," and "coffee faced Ivy Leaguers . . . hoping the beat
is really the truth." Kaufman threads all of this unlikely sociality—
men and women who were variously Italian or Jewish or black—together via the beat of jazz. This is not a romanticized pluralism. The

bagel shop crowd harbors fierce social tensions. It sublimates "secret terrible hurts." The air is hazed, too, by the nervous anxiety of the imminent "guilty police," who did not appreciate such gatherings.[11] "Bagel Shop Jazz" shows a crowd enacting its outlaw desire for a transformed social life. But not all desires were spoken for here.

Specifically, Maria Damon has written about how a poem such as "Bagel Shop Jazz" excludes the then conspicuous presence of queer desire and queer/straight interaction in the Bay Area. Damon believes this exclusion is remarkable given what she knows about Kaufman. She writes,

> It is not the case that queers were simply part of a vague backdrop of undifferentiated Bohemia. Kaufman was actively enmeshed in a triangle involving queer men; he was their friend, he engaged them *as queers* in public if playful verbal sparring. The queer scene to which he lived in such close and even overlapping proximity (in light of his protracted flirtation with Russell Fitzgerald [a writer and Jack Spicer's lover who was obsessed with Kaufman]), with its far more believable and regular bar busts and its coded communications, its shadow existence . . . forms the world that this Bagel Shop world protects the Beats against as much as it does against the police.[12]

Kaufman and other Beat associated writers were committed to free, spontaneous expression, but their words and images often obscured the social presence of *queers*.

The San Francisco poetry renaissance included a number of important gay writers such as Robin Blaser, Robert Duncan, Stan Persky, Jack Spicer, George Stanley, John Wieners, and of course Allen Ginsberg, one of few to publish his sexual preference: "I'm putting my queer shoulder to the wheel." A letter that Ginsberg sent to Ferlinghetti in December 1956 supplements Damon's research that the queer presence was substantial and overt: "Regards to . . .

Spicer if he's there. Did he give big queer reading at 6 gallery [sic] thanksgiving as promised??" Ginsberg was pushing queerness out of the Bay Area shade and into the media lights, and he made people nervous. Recall that in 1956 Michael McClure and Jim Harmon, the editors of the small literary magazine *Ark II*, agreed to participate in Michael Grieg's exposé on the San Francisco scene in *Mademoiselle* as long as the article did not associate them with Ginsberg. Grieg complied and had William Eichel photograph Harmon and McClure separately with their wives. Robert Duncan refused to participate at all. Kerouac posed with Ginsberg. All of this may seem like petty gossip, but it gives us a sense of the kinds of social pressures Bay Area writing negotiated—how the conflicts influenced what the writing said and what it did not say.[13]

weiss's *Gallery of Women* (1959) and her film *The Brink* (1961) negotiated similar tensions. She has said that there were many gay people frequenting the clubs and cafes in North Beach. In fact, the leading man in *The Brink,* Sutter Marin, was homosexual, but in the film he enacts a heterosexual affair. The film breaks down the schematic of patriarchy that usually informs heterosexual relationships, but the image does not broach homoerotic love, as *Gallery of Women* does. weiss said the book "was an homage to women with whom i felt a sisterhood. Poets Laura Ulewicz and Idell Tarlow were included in those poem-portraits." Boo Pleasant, who played piano when weiss read at the Cellar, and fifty-five other women were also honored in the work by first name only. There is a subtle eroticism in some of the poems. For example, the poem "Tale about Dori or a Lioness with a Mane" symbolically evokes strange identity and desire for personal freedom. Dori is androgynous because she is a "lioness with mane." She is also radiantly childlike and therefore doubly innocent of gendered distinctions: "(still partly cub) / leapt laughing in / one sunny afternoon." The poem's speaking voice offers Dori her impassioned organ of "rich sluicing meat." Then she describes Dori's reaction

refusing smiling still
she only nibbled grass
and smiled and nibbled
and stroked the dog
and shaking her golden mane
laughed about alaska.

Dori refuses. But the propositioner does not act out the disappointment of rejection. Instead, she embraces Dori's autonomy (contained
in her response of refusal); the lioness wants grass not meat. Then
she blithely changes the subject to Alaska. The narrator expresses
erotic desire subtly. She obliquely codes it because it was unspeakable. And Dori's androgynous qualities make it even more ambiguous. weiss sets out to free desire from gendered determinants. This
sisterhood is hip to desire liberated from ego-bound needs to control
selfishly and possess the other.[14]

Although Kaufman occludes queer desire in "Bagel Shop Jazz," in
the poem "Hollywood" he uses it as a weapon. He smears Hollywood
with the charge of profligate homosexuality: "Two dozen homos,
to every sapiens . . . Fastest guns in video West slinging lisps with
the slowest fairies in ivy East." For Kaufman Hollywood was a huge
symptom of commercialism gone riot. He reacted to it like it was
a disease; at the mention of Hollywood, he would pillory them mer-
cilessly. More than any of the Beat writers I have come across,
Kaufman took the principle of improvisation to heart. He was ambivalent about publishing, too. Most of his poems were lost speech,
composed on the fly for a particular moment and never written
down. We have some of his work because his wife Eileen steadfastly
encouraged him to write out poems, and she saved many of them. To
Kaufman, Hollywood seemed like the crass antithesis of genuine
feeling and spontaneity in art. Thus, the poem fights caricature with
caricature.

"Hollywood" depicts the movie industry as a kind of machine in which technology and enormous but desperately insecure wealth and talent produce cultural poverty. Its multidisciplinary operatives are a group of pimps and whores, hustlers, pushers, junkies, and homosexuals (all of them caricatures of Beats), selling art for the buck and donning guises of business executives, directors, producers, screenplay writers, actors, agents, musicians, critics, cosmetologists, painters, and stage designers. As I discuss in the chapter on the film *The Subterraneans* (1960), by the late 1950s, Kaufman, Kerouac, and others of the Beats were disturbed by the explosion in consumable simulacra as if they were so much fast food—"hamburger . . . served in laminated fortune cookies." Kerouac's and Kaufman's feelings were strongly negative because Hollywood and the media had appropriated the Beats and transformed them into merchandise—consumable images: "Ranch Market [a popular L.A. night club for tourists] hipsters who lost their cool in grade school . . . plastic beatniks . . . with artistically dirtied feet . . . recreated Jimmy Deans, pompadours looking for sports-car mothers." Hollywood exploited "broadway actors with . . . talent trying to look stupid." It neglected its "yesterday idols" like Cecil B. De Mille and overlooked "small chested actresses bosomed out by the big breast scene." There is more: "carping critics refuse to see what's good, just because it isn't present." Hollywood's "five square miles" is full of "no coast jazz musicians, uncommitted"—extracted from the street-sources of their musical vitality—"waiting to be committed." They wait to be told what to play on vinyl and celluloid and what divisive constituency they belong to: East/West; hot/cool; black/white. These marketing ploys hindered jazz freedom and openness. Indeed, Hollywood was making the "San Francisco poets looking for an out place," look "way out of place."

As to Kaufman's sex charges against Hollywood, I do not superimpose contemporary political standards on writers active in the 1950s. Instead of suing, he slandered the movie industry for slander in order to protect his own community. His actions conformed to the wishes of many gay artists in the Bay Area who wanted to divert the public gaze from their private lives. Ginsberg threw insulting language as a kind of game in order to test egos and ease social tension. Nevertheless, the queer community absorbed the Beats and especially Ginsberg before it began to come out in the next decade. It was not ready then, but soon it showed that its own bold, public style had learned much from Beat style.[15]

Kaufman had no protective instinct for commercialism. As he saw it, the forces of commodification were as coercive as they were ridiculous. He and many other Bay Area poets such as Robert Duncan, Philip Lamantia, Jack Spicer, ruth weiss, and Philip Whalen tried to orbit clear of commodification's decadent, magnetic pull. Kerouac felt the same way, though he circled closer to commercial interests. He despised the editorial compromises he had made in order to publish *On the Road*. And after he saw the movie *The Subterraneans*, he expressed open shame for having sold the film rights to MGM. Ginsberg, however, felt he could use the commercial media to his benefit. He would tickle it here and needle it there. He would stir up a spectacle around his personality in order to sell his uncompromised but accessible work and promote others' work, too. He would attract lecture and reading invitations from around the world. Ginsberg believed the Beats were about art, yes, and social change, too. He felt that there was no way to avoid using markets and communications technologies to mediate his ambitious agenda. Ginsberg accepted what Kaufman, Kerouac, weiss, and others did not accept—that their culture of spontaneous intelligence, openness, and pluralism was cresting and would break in the 1960s in part because of opportunistic and manipulative media.

The media acted in its own interests to stir controversies and attract audiences. At the same time it aided and abetted the influential force of a creative community of dissent. If it stifled artists, it is because they allowed it. If it misled audiences, it is because they chose their leader. These are important points for cultural studies because by the time the media had exhausted its clichés and stereotypes, the work of the movement had already been accomplished. The books and the poems had been written and many of them published and sold. Readers were already in the process of transforming the disparate energies of Beat art and social movement into the new styles of the coming decades.

These multiple, volatile energies uniquely registered in ruth weiss's work *Gallery of Women* and the film *The Brink*. It may not have been new ground for a woman to write books and direct a film in the late 1950s, but it was not often trodden ground, either. What is more, weiss' works show women pushing doors open into unfamiliar identities and experiences. Women summoned extraordinary confidence to push open the doors that the Beat generation men more easily walked through. I have already shown how in "Tale about Dori" one woman preferred a nonpossessive, same-sex love to heterosexual love. Three additional poems in *Gallery of Women* also mark the social presence of women's bold desire, though they are not necessarily flamboyant or charged with Kaufman-like wit.[16] The poems' surfaces resemble the simple language of a child or a neophyte to the language. weiss uses language as if to return desire to innocence. "Pattie" wants to surrender domesticity to the jazz dance:

> Pattie cake pattie cake
> home momma home
>
> don't wanna be a momma
> no more
>
> don't wanna sew
> all the lost buttons
> no more
>
> the dance
> calling me
> calling

This is a jazz poem. Like many jazz solos it begins with a familiar colloquialism, in this case a nursery rhyme. Moreover, the poem utilizes motifs of call and response. The response feeds back into the call through vocal-rhythmic repetition: call, "home momma home"; response, "don't wanna be a momma/no more/don't wanna sew . . . no more." Not dissimilar to a jazz solo, weiss ends the poem with a new phrase and repetition: "The dance calling me/calling." It is an open ending—just as easily a new beginning—but an ending because weiss does not develop it further for a logical reason. The poem leaves Pattie in want. She hears the call of the dance, but there is no indication that she acts. The potential exists for a new experience. Similarly, a jazz soloist can transform a finish line into a new start. Pattie wants a new start. She may have the accoutrements of domestic comfort, but her selfhood is as lost as the unattached buttons. The self seems disembodied, floating without a rudder and blocked off from the sky. It calls its vessel back to itself in the dance. Pattie was not the first to recover a sense of her body in the rhythms of jazz. She, too, is one among a generation with jazz fever and as the next poem suggests, it is a freer generation.

> This poem is named for "Any," presumably anybody,
> > Ah'll stick a rose
> > in mah hair
> > fare forth in a hansom
> > and go
> > rick-a-rocking
> > through town

The poem shouts out to any woman who will hear: do what you want! It echoes Emily Dickinson's carriage rides. Emily, do what you want, with aplomb! The poem makes desire a spectacle, a thing of rhythmic style. Feel the joy of your existential freedom.

The poem "To Dee or Robin's Nest" says the city is the congenial nest, the place in which to seize freedom; there are no limits on it in the city:

> is a world so full of things to do to be
> is a world so going that being is
> where?
> in a WHAM of lights is the city

The first two lines speak fast jazz talk in rhythmic repetition and subtle variation: "is a world so full . . . is a world so going"; and here, again, syllabic variation with a familiar tonal ring, "things . . . going . . . being." The voice of the poem is charged with surplus desire, surplus joy, the kind of desire that burned in Kerouac's lines, "the only people for me are the mad ones . . . desirous of everything at the same time."[17] Similarly, women in the gallery want it all now—"the wailing wailing wonder of the now." They desire perfectly like a child: "head first and seeking," always asking "when will the milk come?" The city is mother; her modern machinery has become like nature itself. The poem's romanticism invokes women's "blood/the sacred tie" as the purchase of union with the city's kinetic forces. Through the cultivation of an emphatic urban mysticism the woman becomes skillfully present, "now belonging is for now/then will tell of itself." weiss's poem is as enthralled with the city as any Beat poem ever was.

The striking thing about all of these poems is the way they show women's and men's desire of a piece and touching each other: a shared structure of feeling. What did they want? Everything, now and with style—a jazz flight *through* the domestic trap, not *from* it. Desire transforms 1950s domestic relations in the United States, freeing them from the cultural and ideological mire. The subject of jazz points to weiss's biography and the role of the music in her life and work.

"The first time I heard Bop, I knew it was my sound."

—ruth weiss

weiss's love of jazz burst upon her in an instant. But its seeds were planted early. Immediately after her family's escape from the Nazi occupation of Austria and their arrival in the United States in 1939, weiss lived in Harlem. She was placed in a Jewish home for children nine and younger until they discovered that she was eleven. She remembers Harlem's rhythms and its

> streets oh so wide. smiling. and everybody is out there at one time or another. or from the window. and there's skipping & jumping & clapping. and stopping. and sitting & talking. and always the dance.

And she remembers school and formative bonds with Americans,

> the only white girl in the class. and i don't speak yet too much english. and this one & that one takes me home to show mama & sister & brother.
>   don't you have a mama. yes i have a mama & a papa too. but where are they. i see them on sunday. and where are your sisters. and where are your brothers. i don't have a sister. i don't have a brother. you do now. yes i do.

More than most of the Beat writers, weiss's art marks the collision of white biography on the fringe with African American culture.[18]

In 1948 weiss took a room at the Art Circle on the near north side of Chicago. She began listening to Bop and reading her poetry to audiences there. In 1949 an African American painter named Ernest Alexander asked her to read with the Art Circle jazz ensemble. She accepted the invitation, and she has been reading to jazz ever since. In late 1949 she moved to Greenwich Village, New York, where she soaked up the same music, art, and bohemian society that Kerouac, Ginsberg, Kaufman, Burroughs, John Clellon Holmes, and others were enjoying.

weiss took more road trips, but to this day she does not drive.

From New York she hitched to New Orleans and from there back to Chicago and from there to San Francisco in 1952, where she remained and grew roots for the first time in her life. She married twice: first, to Mel Weitsman, a painter and musician, in 1957 and second, to Roy Isbell, a sculptor, in 1966. In 1963 Weitsman and weiss parted as friends when he left to become a Zen Buddhist priest. Her second marriage ended when Isbell was jailed on a drug charge and subsequently killed by prison guards. She now lives with painter Paul Blake, seventeen years younger, in Albion, California. They have been together for over thirty years.

The experience of reading poetry to jazz at the Art Circle in 1949 stayed with weiss, and according to Herb Caen, "she launched the readings at the Cellar" in North Beach when it opened in 1956. Sonny Nelson, the drummer for the Cellar Jazz Quintet, said of weiss's role, "she was a big part of it, believe me." The experiment took off. "We had huge crowds," said Nelson. Locals came to hear the sessions and soon, so did celebrities such as Lenny Bruce, Dizzy Gillespie, widely read local critic Ralph Gleason, Charles Mingus, and William Carlos Williams.[19]

Kenneth Rexroth and Lawrence Ferlinghetti contributed to the fame of the Cellar when they held six jazz-poetry sessions there in the spring of 1957 for Fantasy Records: *Poetry Readings in the Cellar* (1958). Contemporary jazz critic Ted Gioia calls these readings "a seminal event in San Francisco's cultural history."[20] The sessions delivered on their hype as bold experiments with popular appeal. The conflicts among participants at the Cellar are revealing, however. They expose contemporaneous tensions between critical authority and women artists and between critical authority and whites' and blacks' practice of jazz and poetry in the 1950s.

Ralph Gleason's album-cover notes for *Poetry Readings in the Cellar* liberally quote from an interview he conducted with Rexroth and Ferlinghetti, who say that jazz is useful because it can help bring poetry to a wider audience.[21] Gleason writes about and quotes Rexroth, who "was motivated in his activity with jazz by an attempt to broaden the audience for modern poetry. 'It is very important to get poetry out of the hands of the professors and out of the hands of the squares,' he says. 'If we can get poetry out into the life of the country it can be creative,' he adds. 'Homer, or the guy who recited Beowulf, was show business. We simply want to make poetry a part of show business.'"

Gleason quotes Ferlinghetti: "The big thing is the oral message. My whole kick has been oral poetry. The poets today are talking to themselves . . . no audience. The competition from the mass media is too much. We're trying to capture an audience. Gutenberg had a good idea with printing but it . . . ruined it for the poets! The jazz comes in as part of the attempt to get the audience back."

Both Ferlinghetti's and Rexroth's comments couch the emerging oral style of poetry in Western terms, that is, it was something the European tradition lost with the advent of the printing press, the En-lightenment, and the mass media. They understand jazz as a popular music that can bring poetry back to the people on the streets. More-over, North Beach, relatively speaking, was a multicultural bastion of creative energy, and it is frequently remembered for its racial pro-gressiveness and nascent feminism during the 1950s. Rexroth's com-ments, however, expose pervasive chauvinistic assumptions that trip-ped up the progress of race and gender politics even where they were most congenial in the Beat generation / jazz milieu. Rexroth told Gleason, "You know almost all the poetry written for jazz is strictly corn. That's true of the negro poets, too." Apparently, Rexroth thought it true for the women poets. According to Sonny Nelson, Kaufman also read at the Cellar. Rexroth continues, "Now the real problem in putting jazz and poetry together is in finding people who are flexible enough. You have to find people who can play different kinds of jazz . . . lots of musicians are anti-verbal, you know. The group at the Cellar is young and flexible. This is a tremendous ad-vantage. Where bands understand poetry and poets understand jazz, it will catch on."

Rexroth's remarks suggest his wont to delegitimize critical authority by replacing it with his own. Indeed, Rexroth did exactly that. He was a controversial and popular intellectual and artist. And certainly through his home poetry circles, his regular radio broadcasts on KPFA public radio, and his critical writings in publications such as the *Nation* and the *New York Times Book Review,* he was an established critic of the establishment—an authoritative gatekeeper of aesthetic taste. His comments not only rendered weiss invisible but reflected stereotypical assumptions about the literacy and flexible intelligence of black jazz players, if not poets. On the one hand, Rexroth was a gifted, productive, and complex man, but like the more famous jazz players and beat writers, he benefited from and, in part, constituted the institutional and social preference that avant-garde artists, rebels, and gadflies be white men. On the other hand, weiss—her view perhaps aided by its outside-the-loop vantage point—recalled that in 1958 the Cellar was not an archeological ruin; it was not the site for the recovery of lost, European oral roots. Rather it was an exemplary location for an emerging modern culture of "white skin. black and blue sounds." For example, weiss regarded her brief collaboration at the Cellar with Boo Pleasant—"lean, tall, and black. hovering over the keys that talked before she touched them. how she unlocked those sounds"—as among her most satisfying artistic experiences.[22]

Certainly, there were institutional biases in the United States that overlooked or looked condescendingly upon women and African American writers. The smaller, more adventurous publishers and critics in the Bay Area were not necessarily exempt from such biases. weiss believes Auerhahn Press and City Lights turned down *Gallery of Women* because they "were not interested in women poets. And my work was not considered political." She said poet Philip Lamantia presented her work to Auerhahn Press, and they declined to read it; as a matter of policy, they did not publish women. City Lights did publish two women poets in the pocket poet series in the 1950s: Marie Ponsot and Denise Levertov. In fact, Rexroth enthusiastically rec-

ommended Levertov to Ferlinghetti's City Lights.[23] It is more likely
that City Lights turned down weiss because her work frustrates readers. We will see that she inflicts havoc on the authority of the narrative I, avoids sustained subjectivity, overt politics, and the pleasures
of easily accessible wit. These were Ferlinghetti's publishing criteria.
Kaufman's broadsides met them but weiss's poetry did not. For example, after Dori turns to grazing grass in the poem "Tale about
Dori," subjectivity and narrative voice break like glass:

> The dark
> she waits
> the profile
> is explode
> my mouth
> to fill
> the question
> I am to about
> to loose the   if I were the
> light   rooster to
> am dark   wash my hand free
>   I would
>   to feather off
>   night
> DAWN
>   the open mouth
> the rooster is shrieking
> to
> let
> go
> grain[24]

Beat and other Bay Area writers shared weiss's feeling that the ego-
bound self was an exhausted category that had come to naught.

Yet writers such as Kerouac, Ginsberg, and Ferlinghetti did not jettison the self. Instead, they took the leash off the dog. They let the narrative I run wild with the techniques of spontaneity and improvisation. weiss instead uses the poem to enter language from every portal. Every syntactical unit is a window into alternative arrangements of poetic line. She looses syntactical units from their functionary straightjackets.

Thus to readers seeking meaning, weiss delivers disappointment. To readers seeking essentialist abstraction, she delivers bewilderment. Viewers and critics found abstract essentials in the pure color and line of Kandinsky and Mondrian, but weiss is no platonist. Nor does she drip the expressive sweat of Jackson Pollock or Jack Kerouac. Other negations obtain. weiss has no yen for a golden mean between the subjective and objective; her work provides no fulcrum that balances these categories. She cracks the opaque glass of sense and arranges the pieces not so much for a reader as for a body seeking a look, a tone, a rhythm, and a feeling.

weiss's art throws a party for the senses. It invites the multimedia of jazz and other sounds—composed, improvised, found, and aleatory—painting, and film. It works the crowd and dances with all of the guests. weiss's forty-minute experimental film *The Brink* (1961), particularly, demonstrates these aims.[25] The film's use of multimedia blurs categorical distinctions among the visual image, music, speech, noise, and the ways they signify. weiss was not the only radical experimentalist of the Beat generation. Kerouac, too, exposes the contingent basis of meanings, regardless of medium, in *Visions of Cody* (unpublishable until 1972) and in his narration for Robert Frank's film *Pull My Daisy* (1959). weiss, with Kerouac, Frank, and Kaufman, is marking and effecting cultural change in the United States. They play with the signs, images, and sounds to unhinge Cartesian exactitude and bend open thought's vise to an aesthetic of multiple desires.

In the opening scene of *The Brink* a couple discuss their relationship in a bustling Bay Area cafe. weiss's voice narration affects the dialogue. The woman asks the man, "am i to walk with you . . . talk with you?" Are we complements, "cup and saucer"? We have choices, "coffee or tea"? The woman says to herself, "go to the round house . . . he can't corner you there." He cannot corner her because she keeps moving—dodging and slipping her way around the circle replete with signs and roles. Surely, the man is her complement. Aware of the coercive medium of speech, he echoes Kaufman's attitude of silence in the 1960s, when he asks "why talk" at all?

This introduction to the couple sets up a discussion of how weiss conveys her poems not as meaning but sound after the manner of the rule-breaking sequences of notes, tones, and rhythms of free jazz. As she puts it, *The Brink* features "a voice bouncing against images . . . ear language." The voice bounces against urban, domestic, and natural images along the seacoast and in the woods—night and day. For example, a man in a small sailboat approaches a dock. The bright sunlight shimmers on the rippling water. The music of a swinging jazz trio, led by a loping bass line, brushes on a trap set, and brass instrument, accompanies the image. weiss's narration floats along impressionistically signifying generalized decay and creation:

> and he built his house of wood with one plank
> plunk plunk plunk by the sea
> paddle broken waterline
> wind splintering the beached boat
>
> And the dark caves were rocks . . .
> sun sun sun warm salt to sink in
> i'm the begin said water
> i was before you said sand
> and the shells rubbed screaming against each other

Sensitivity to sound trumps the particularities of meanings and continuities of syntax. The priority of the aesthetics of tone color subordinates the mechanics of signifying chains. weiss says that she makes this happen through "instantaneous response" to and with "no fore-knowledge" of her subject: free improvisation. Certainly *The Brink* is improvisational and verité in style: 16mm, black and white, natural lighting, no-prop location sets. weiss carefully choreographed the film's eighteen scenes with her narration and Bill Spencer's soundtrack, however. Like Frank's *Pull My Daisy* and Ornette Coleman's *Free Jazz* (1960), *The Brink* utilizes improvisation but within a framework and according to specific protocols—loose ones.[26] weiss rarely seeks literally to emulate jazz with her poetry. They are different media. Instead, she applies the music's principles. She associates her work with jazz and reads it with jazz. She frequently sabotages textual meaning so that audiences hear the tones and rhythms of words just as they hear tone color and time in jazz. She cuts through knowledge to the core of sensual awareness and other intuitive kinds of knowing.

By opening up the thought-performance structures of identity, *The Brink* is able to probe the effects of divided consciousness—the contemporaneous linguistic, social, and material scene, which circles round to reinforce habits of divided thought again, and around again it goes. For example, such· habits underlie the physical reality of suburbanization and its cultural and environmental consequences. weiss's film precociously formulates the issue when the camera pans rows and rows of identical houses. Bill Spencer's soundtrack accompanies the immaculate image with sullied noise, the simulacra of industrial pain—the clash of development and the preindustrial order. It is the sound of cosmic assault, and it bears mimetic relationship to the appalled tone of weiss's lyric and what the characters feel:

> arrest the trees
> chop'em all down
> STOP!
> they've cut the trees
> the flood! the flood!

all around the town
blow the men and women down
make 'em into sticks
stop all their tricks
put 'em into rows and rows of boxes
where the trees once were
they'll be of some use then
do you love me she said.

The rationalized replacement of nature with homogenized habitations of utility does not bode well for love. For weiss, love is manifest when varieties congenially share space. When uniformities displace particulars love becomes vacuous and ineffective. Thus, weiss takes us to the brink between nature and rationalized environments, love and complacency, and life and death. *The Brink* does not linger on this critical intervention, however. The couple knows a few tricks. They know they transform their world by committing their feelings, not to angst but to a joyful image of life.

Gallery of Women and *The Brink* register the social limits of gendered desire in the United States in the late 1950s. Then they wreck the vehicle of those limits—the narrative I and its content of restricted desire. Her work unhinges the curve along the vicious hermeneutic circle of language and its solipsistic patterns of self-awareness and individuality, conformity and deviance, and the fiction of objectivity, itself. For weiss, the patterns are preset and already written. Where do the patterns lead? Perhaps to those unspeakable events weiss rarely speaks about, such as Leopold's Congo, Germany's Dachau, the U.S.S.R.'s Babi Yar, the United States' Hiroshima, and many other such events. weiss is not the only one who could find little to say after Auschwitz. Her work swings free of the destructive circle. It drops the master plot and features the concrete sound and the decentered image.[27] Her works radically question and destabilize the iconic order of things: authority, race, gender, and nature. Their strategy stems from a biography that has witnessed nightmare and has sought a means to transform it.

Attack: The sound of jazz.
The city falls.

—Bob Kaufman, "Battle Report"

Before turning to poetry Kaufman sought to transform the world through politics. He left home in New Orleans at age eighteen in 1943 to become a merchant seaman until the middle of the 1950s. His travels gave him international exposure. As it had been with many black seaman and black military personnel who went abroad, his years at sea were what Maria Damon called "a redemptive response to the Middle Passage" and, I would add, to personal experience. Kaufman's body had learned violence early when at age thirteen a lynch mob strung him up from the thumbs to hang all night in an icehouse. International travel taught him, as it had taught many jazz expatriates, that the U.S. brand of racism was not universal. New York City was his home base. During this period Kaufman worked hard for the left-leaning National Maritime Union. He educated sailors about workers' rights mostly in New York and probably at ports along the West Coast from Spokane to San Diego. After the war he joined the Progressive Party and became an area director for the Henry Wallace presidential campaign in 1948. He carried his socialist vision to unemployed farmers and miners in Tennessee, West Virginia, and Kentucky where authorities violently opposed him. Police beat him up several times, and he spent significant periods in jails. Kaufman's conflicts with police never let up. According to poet Raymond Foye, police records show Kaufman went to jail thirty-six times in 1959. He seemed to know no fear. The more dangerous the circumstances, the louder he spoke his mind. Until his vow of silence in 1963—perhaps precipitated less by the Kennedy assassination than 50–100 involuntary electroshock treatments—he was not just a voice but the very animal force of free speech. He invoked the awe (consternation and admiration) of many witnesses. Kaufman made his reputation on two North American coasts. Mass media did not talk about him; the streets did. More accurately, communities with outcast politics and communities of poets that romanticized the streets spun tales about Kaufman, which comprise his legend and symbolize both an anticonformist ideal and a bygone era that nevertheless still reverberates.[28]

In the 1940s and 1950s Kaufman plunged into New York's jazz and avant-garde scenes. Billie Holiday and Charlie Parker were reputed to be casual friends and with certainty, so was Jack Kerouac. Kaufman absorbed the influences of action painting and abstract expressionism, the Beats, and André Breton's surrealist aficionados. He wore sharp clothes and drove a flashy car. He began writing in 1954 and moved to San Francisco because he felt powerful artistic energies there; he wanted to eat them and feed them, too.

Earlier I noted that Kaufman kept relatively silent about the sensitive issue of queerness. Or he volleyed it like a hot potato into the hands of the enemy, Hollywood. There was a second hot potato issue, Kaufman's own black self. Norman Mailer was right when he said the aura of hip black men fascinated white males. Myths of black men's nearness to life and sexual prowess with white women lured white copycatting.[29] Black musical talent seemed to verify that myths were truths. On the page and in life, Kaufman played a shadow game with white men's projections of race and sex. His poetry and biography consistently show that whites, particularly men, failed to relate to Kaufman as a person. For example, Jack Spicer's young lover and understudy Russell Fitzgerald committed most of his unpublished diary to his obsession with Kaufman. At one point Fitzgerald renounces his indulgent fantasies of Kaufman, "Dark brother, I free you from my legend, I love you real. No more masturbation, no more black magic . . . forgive me." Still, Damon observes that Fitzgerald never called on Kaufman to "reveal himself, to put his cards on the table as it were, since he was presumed to have no interiority." In 1960 Jack Kerouac was enjoying his greatest success professionally, but emotionally he was at a nadir. He and Kaufman spent an evening together drinking on a day just before Kerouac was to leave San Francisco and return to his mother in Lowell. He slept over at Kaufman's apartment. In the morning Kaufman entered the kitchen and fixed him breakfast. But when he returned to serve it, Kerouac was gone. He left a poem scribbled on the wall:

> To Bob Kaufman—
> Though I have known you
> And slept with you
> And loved you,
> Yet I don't even know your name.

Whether or not sex was involved is immaterial. These examples are symptoms showing that even Kaufman's friends could not see beyond their dark adumbrations. Black jazz musicians contended with a similar problem with their white fans and detractors.[30]

Perhaps Kaufman thought Kerouac, Fitzgerald, and others were seeking the light because they felt their blindness. There is no doubt that he admired many of the white poets that came to exemplify the poetry renaissance:

> Jazz sounds, wig sounds,
> Earthquake sounds, others,
> Allen on Chestnut Street,
> Giving poetry to squares,
> Corso on knees, pleading,
> God eyes.
> Rexroth, Ferlinghetti,
> Swinging, in cellars,

Kerouac . . .
writing Neil [sic]
On high typewriter
Neil, booting a choo-choo,
On zigzag tracks.[31]

But crowded as Kaufman's world was with fans, friends, artists, even family, he was quite lonely.

Kaufman's solitude was trying, but it was also liberating. His invisibility assumed guises. In the poem "Cincophrenicpoet," Kaufman writes of one of them, "coughing poetry for revenge, beseeching all horizontal reserves to cross, spiral, and whirl"—like oral speech and like jazz.[32] Jazz is about swinging cross-rhythms and arpeggios and chromatic runs that whirl and spiral with hungry surprise. Kaufman, too, is voracious for new associations and connections made on the rhythmic fly. His poems move in unexpected flows of images just as jazz styles can move in unexpected flows of chords that rewrite familiar tunes and progressions. For Kaufman, jazz had revolutionary potential to reorient peoples' feelings toward one another. He thought jazz's sounds and its practices enacted a model whose implications could transfer into large-scale social relationships. Jazz could cause the old city walls to fall and inform the building of new, open cities via "windy saxophone revolutions." This potential hinged on the idea that selves were malleable; they could demolish barriers, adapt, and participate together.

Like weiss, Kaufman is reluctant to assert a familiar self or interiority. Moreover, he did not assert his own because there was not social space for it. Few of Kaufman's poems unfold the perspective of a confessional I, except obliquely by way of what he calls "the strange landscapes of my head"—inevitably fatal terrain for even stalwart selves.[33] Kaufman does not disrupt the syntactical properties of language as radically as weiss. His poetry's alien content inhabits formal language patterns. It sketches out recognizable forms of speech and then infuses them with absurd wit. Kaufman intoxicates customary methods of organizing reality—spoken or written. He sends them on their way like staggering nihilisms:

> I have heard the song of the broken giraffe and sung it . . .
> The frozen sun has browned me to a rumor and slanted my
>   navel.
> I have consorted with vulgar crocodiles on banks
>   of lewd rivers.
> Yes, it is true, God has become mad, from centuries
>   of frustration
> When I think of all the girls I never made love to,
>   I am shocked.
> Every time they elect me president, I hide in the bathroom.
> When you come, bring me a tourniquet for our wounded
>   moon.
> In an emergency, I can rearrange your beautiful wreckage
> With broken giraffe demolitions and lovely colorless
>   explosions.
> Come, you sexy Ferris wheel, ignore my illustrated
>   bathing suit.
> Don't laugh at my ignorance, I may be a great
>   bullfighter, olé!
> I wanted to compose a great mass, but I couldn't kneel
>   properly.
> Yes, they did tempt me with airplanes, but I wouldn't bite,
>   no sir-ee.
> Unable to avoid hospitals, I still refused to become a doctor.
> They continued to throw reason, but I failed
>   in the clutch again.
> It's true, I no longer use my family as a frame of reference.
> The clothing they gave me was smart but no good
>   for train wrecks.

I continued to love despite all the traffic-light difficulties.
In most cases, a sane hermit will beat a good big man.
We waited in vain for the forest fire, but the bus was late.
All night we baked the government into a big mud pie.
Not one century passed without Shakespeare calling us
    dirty names.
With all those syllables, we couldn't write a cheerful
    death notice.[34]

The "Song of the Broken Giraffe" is Bop parody of a confessional poem. The singer affects poses of selves and rejects them all for a textual masochism of wit. The singer is as vacant as the Sex Pistols but prettier.[35] He does not write the death notice but sings—as I and as we—a New Orleans wake for selves and authors: a late-modern jazz wake.

At various historical moments jazz itself has conducted wakes for exhausted jazz styles. In a sense, bebop was a wake for swing, and free jazz was a wake for bebop. Various critics have claimed these ceremonies were antijazz voodoo. But antijazz is an implicit truth of jazz. Jazz has always protected the need to splinter the wood of its habits in order to open itself up to new influences and combinations of ways of playing. Kaufman skidded across the far edge. He went out of the analogical plane of antijazz into antiliterature that heralded the death of authors. The singer joined a society of dead authors: truth tellers and Beat writers. They cheered the death of the pretensions of authorship much as aficionados of free jazz cheered the death of the pretensions of playership. Most of the Beats used the confessional self to pave a road over the field of narrative authority and its tricks. Writers such as Ginsberg and Ferlinghetti followed the self as idealized by Whitman to utopia. But where they saw utopia, Kaufman saw dystopia. He utilized the form of the narrative self only to write its entropic path to self-sabotage. The singer ends his song at the vanguard of a transgressing community: the oblivion of "Rumpelstiltskin", the violent dismembering of the male textual self: black and white. What is left? Multifaceted style, the destroyed self's abstract, Bop jive: its tone colors, rhythms, and speed remain.

"Song of the Broken Giraffe" does to confessional sentence structure what bop does to standard song structure. The basic frame remains the same. Bop retains the standard's introduction, chorus, and bridge format (32 bars, AABA, ABAC, and so on). It keeps to the blues and standard general harmonic outlines (I–IV–V; II–V–I with variations and modulations). Then it infuses these forms with the rhythmic disruption of highly syncopated accents and doubled tempos. Triads and seventh chords suddenly acquire a taste for ninths, elevenths, thirteenths—flat and sharp—and the trademark flatted fifth. What is more, III and IV chords bully out tonic chords, and chromatically embellished V chords displace II chords. The result is that strange progressions substitute for familiar ones. These substitutions effect agitated movements from one chord to the next and jagged resolutions back to the tonic. The result is that Gershwin's "I've Got Rhythm" becomes the abstracted, popular nonsense of "Salt Peanuts," and a Kansas City blues injects the vernacular fix of "Oop Bop Sh' Bam." Similarly, the foolishness of the "Song of the Broken Giraffe" explodes the sincere logic of the confessional form.[36]

Therefore, for weiss and Kaufman the narrative I would not stand. The final image of *The Brink* showed a caterpillar crossing the white surface of an unaddressed envelope. It continued over the edge and out of view of the camera into oblivion. Indeed, the film opened with this image. The caterpillar lived on the edge of the simultaneity of destruction and creation: death and new life—the brink. In the late 1950s and early 1960s, U.S. culture tottered along a similar edge. It was a permeable, slippery threshold of openings and closings, emergings and residuals. Homogeneities and heterodoxies diffused their ways through it. It comprised immanent vectors of peril and safety. The Beats took part in the form of this threshold and helped the culture see itself. Kaufman and weiss, for reasons of their social marginality and philosophical and creative sensibilities, also wrote from the boundary, the very brink of selfhood. They displaced and deconstructed the self in order to cross the boundary. The next generation would cross back with a counterculture of new spirituality, environmental consciousness, civil rights, black power, and feminism. The markets did not follow Kaufman and weiss. They were shy of promoting minorities and art that did not master and signify. Nevertheless, Kaufman and weiss drew upon vernacular style and jazz and quite radically opened up performance spaces for new identities and community. They helped transform U.S. culture.

3

CELLULOID BEATNIKS

Metro Goldwyn Mayer (MGM)'s film version of Jack Kerouac's novel *The Subterraneans* (1958) has been too hastily dismissed. The film measures the influence of subordinate Beat generation interests on a mainstream movie.[1] These influences seep into the film and undermine its otherwise conservative intentions that trivialize features of cultural change that the Beat writers and their audiences were helping to effect. This seepage occurs not only through some of the film's dialogue, but primarily in the artistic scenes of jazz and painting and in the film's confessional games in which participants affect a kind of authentic speech of the heart. Portions of dialogue and especially the artistic tableaus help to make the film a complex and volatile surface of dominant and subordinate interests that fiercely compete with each other. Conventional domestic arrangements, patriarchy, the war economy, consumer mania, race ideology, and traditional aesthetics—the film throws all of these themes into contradiction in ways audiences can use critically and creatively. These audiences include readers of Beat literature and jazz aficionados, bohemian types in various cities, and an emerging predominantly white middle-class youth culture.

Plastic beatniks in pubic beards

—Bob Kaufman

With Benzedrine rushing through his bloodstream, Jack Kerouac wrote *The Subterraneans* on Long Island in three dusk-to-dawn typing sessions in his mother's kitchen in the summer of 1953. When he circulated the manuscript among friends, they were impressed. Philip Whalen wrote to Ginsberg that *The Subterraneans* showed Kerouac was a "true individual and a break-through artist." Amazed at the force of the prose and the speed in which it was written, William Burroughs and Allen Ginsberg asked Kerouac to explain his technique. In the fall of 1953 Kerouac wrote "The Essentials of Spontaneous Prose," his attempt to encapsulate a way of accessing a "prose of the future," a prose that reflected the merging of time with mind: "uninterrupted and unrevised full confessions." By 1954 Burroughs was in Tangiers, kicking his habit and writing his phantasmagoric divulgence *Naked Lunch* (1959). In a 1955 letter to Kerouac, he wrote, "I have been attempting something similar to your sketch method. That is I write what I see and feel right now trying to arrive at some absolute, direct transmission of fact on all levels." Ginsberg tacked the informal treatise on the wall of his room in the Marconi Hotel in San Francisco. Here, such visitors as Robert Duncan, Jack Spicer, Al Sublette, Sheila Williams Boucher, and other literary acquaintances could read it. By 1955—prodded by Rexroth, who told him to drop the Columbia University formalities—Ginsberg was writing the spontaneous lines of *Howl* (1956). But however much Kerouac influenced the Beats and other Bay Area writers, he could not fend off the way MGM would exploit the beatnik fad and travesty his novel seven years later.[2]

Kerouac's books had become a hot-selling commodity by the time Grove Press, building on the sales momentum of *On the Road* (1957) and *Dharma Bums* (1958), published *The Subterraneans* in 1958.

Kerouac sold the movie rights the same year and MGM released its celluloid version in 1960. Most biographies, Beat histories, and museum exhibitions remember MGM's *The Subterraneans* as a notable burlesque of Kerouac's book, just one more trivialization of the Beat generation and not worth the trouble of a closer look.[3] In addition, the film has been inaccessible in MGM's archive, where it has been stored for over forty years. Turner Classic Films bought the MGM archive in the 1990s, but the company does not sell video rights. To my knowledge, the company has never broadcast the film for a television audience, but I have managed to see the film, and I do not dismiss it. The film's relationship to the novel and U.S. culture in the late 1950s is instructive; it provides a specific example of how the strength of subordinate, performative identities, art, and values can compellingly insinuate themselves in popular media.

As with the *Howl* spectacle, the economic productivity of the film *The Subterraneans* derived from its internalization of the structural conflict between square and not-square—cool, hip, or beat. These simplistic oppositions define the film and censor Kerouac's book. The film superimposes a European-derived, comedic model of dramatic action, an old form dating back to the Restoration period with plays like Shakespeare's *Taming of the Shrew* and *As You Like It*. This model shrinks the scope of the novel's treatment of subterranean lifestyle, alienation, art, patriarchy, and race. It is important to note this appropriation of Renaissance form because it illustrates the utility and adaptability of conventional forms across periodic interventions from the Enlightenment to postmodernity. The film's appropriation of the comedic model was part of a larger strategy of containment of the Beat generation.

By the time MGM bought rights to the film, the derisive and laughable beatnik spectacle had already eclipsed the Beat generation and its art. Beatnik fortune cookies were for sale and beatniks themselves for rent. In July 1960 *Mad Magazine* published its spoof, "Beatnik: The Magazine for Hipsters." Also, by 1960 90 percent of U.S.

households owned a television, and from 1959 to 1962 the work-phobic, jazz-loving, cuddly beatnik Maynard Krebs entertained viewers of the popular show *The Many Loves of Dobie Gillis*. Although some audiences laughed at beatniks, others feared the term's encoded sociopathology, which Mailer augured in the "White Negro" (1957), and which lent itself to facile cinematic fodder. The B-movie *The Beat Generation* (1959), for example, exploited prejudices that the Beats were by nature thieves, dope fiends, and rapists. Beat artists and their friends were appalled; the attention accorded them seemed opportunistic and out of balance. Rexroth admitted the Beats were no longer human beings but "comical bogies conjured up by [among others] the Luce publications." In his poem "Hollywood," Bob Kaufman satirized the entertainment industry's profiteering on "plastic beatniks . . . pubic beards, with artistically dirtied feet." Kerouac, wounded and angry, invoked the righteousness of the Sermon on the Mount in his article "Beatific: the Origins of the Beat Generation." He condemned those who believed in atomic bombs, who hated sex and love, who thrived on conflict and violence, and added, "woe unto those who spit on the Beat Generation, the wind'll blow it back." The film *The Subterraneans* did not assuage Kerouac's pain. Its mise-en-scene and use of dramatic form occluded serious cultural issues in the book and ran roughshod over its method.[4]

More criticism is in order. Robert Thom, the screenwriter, and Ranald MacDougall, the director, sought to reenact the Procrustean myth. They fit the body of Kerouac's spontaneous, confessional, and indeterminate prose to an ill-shaped bed. The Renaissance comedic form is conservative and corrective. Its plot moves in three-part succession from beginning to middle to end. Its action proceeds from chaos to order, from distress to peace, or from foolishness to wisdom. Renaissance comedy exaggerates, caricatures, and makes ridiculous on its way to achieving its happy equilibrium. In a similar way mass media, too, made comedy of the Beats through its silly caricatures.

MacDougall and Thom follow suit. Moreover, the film compounded the clash with Kerouac's prose because it assumed classical notions of mimetic art, whose "purpose" Shakespeare has stated "was and is to hold . . . the mirror up to nature." Kerouac admired Shakespeare, learned from him, committed large portions of his works to memory, and referred to him as a model of dramatic timing in the "Essentials of Spontaneous Prose." After *The Town and the City* (1950), however, his prose attacked the limiting notion that art imitated life.[5] A brief review of *The Town and the City* helps to illustrate the point.

Popular critics faulted *The Town and the City* (1950) for its exuberance, but in general, they felt the novel was auspicious.[6] The novel tracks an American family that moves from prewar cohesiveness in the town to postwar disintegration in the city. It depicts the postwar implosion of distinctions between the small town and the metropolis. *The Town and the City* seeks to mirror the speed of technological change. It shows how the alienated and disenfranchised fended off psychic fragmentation and buttressed their minds with art and intimacy. It also shows how they experimented with incoherence and fragmentation through madness, drugs, and mysticism. The text boldly takes up the life of the new generation, as do Kerouac's later books, but its style is fraught with symptoms of canonical anxiety, such as omniscient narration, careful plotting, syntactical orderliness, and a contrived use of symbols. This mimetic staging of the novel deeply troubled Kerouac. It proscribed the artistic expression of the multiple flows of his mind and experience.

Kerouac and other Beats refused to perpetuate illusory structures of consciousness by recapitulating traditional literary craft. *The Subterraneans* was a spontaneous confession. It did not imitate life. Writing *The Subterraneans* occasioned the enactment of imaginary life, which melted the difference between reality and perception of reality. In *The Subterraneans* Kerouac writes of "the light rack of my brain" where Mardou is "seen," and where "visions of great words in rhyth-

mic order go roaring . . . so I lie in the dark also seeing, also hearing
. . . the flow of river sounds, words, dark, leading to the future and at-
testing to the madness, hollowness, ring and roar of my mind . . .
where trees sing—in a funny wind . . . 'Smart went Crazy,' wrote Allen Ginsberg" (41–42).

In this passage Kerouac affirms his investment in the semiotic order of sound-images and concepts. Life presents itself as a river of
light and sound flowing through the senses and processed in the
mind where concepts (words) constantly chase the flow of images.
Smart goes crazy in the disavowal of certain temporal and spatial categories, however. For example, the moment of sensory input is irrelevant. The procession of signs is primary, whether or not it occurs at
the moment of sensation, through memory, or dreams. Kerouac ap-
propriates temporal and spatial indicators, but they do not contra-
dict his method so long as they are true to the original flow of words
that name and position the sounds and images. Kerouac's method
undermines the central assumption of mimetic artistic models. It vaporizes the duality of the external and internal world. It discards
contrived schemes of mastery and understanding much as the abstract expressionist painters discarded the practice of transforming a
two-dimensional canvas into a three-dimensional illusion. Mimetic
theory presupposes otherness. Ultimately, for Kerouac, there is no
other. Where mimetic art presents discrete pictures of the world,
Kerouac's prose presents open pictures of consciousness.

In contrast to Kerouac's aesthetic assumptions, MacDougall and
Thom's film opens with an almost documentarian claim that it will
show the audience a new world: "This is the story of a new Bohemia
. . . where the young gather to create and to destroy. In all times, in all
cities, for good or for evil, the young bohemians have been the makers of the future. They are foolish and they have genius. You will find
them on the Left Bank in Paris, in London's Soho, in Greenwich Village and here in San Francisco, in the area known as the North
Beach." The camera then proceeds to tell a story in which writer Leo

Percepied (George Peppard) and Mardou Fox (Leslie Caron) fall in love. They have some kicks. They hear good jazz, attend "Blabber Mouth Night," and loiter at the Poet and Painters Mission. Conflict then ensues as Leo blames Mardou for standing between him and the progress of his book. In order to break the monotony of the blank page, Leo has an affair with the shrew Roxanne, a painter and dancer, who professes a hatred of men and male writers, in particular. By the end, the chaotic whirl of these relationships slows to the ordered prospect of domestic convention. The film's plot sidesteps Kerouac's subjective, mercurial, and nontotalizing prose, which leaves the reader with Leo's irresolute confession and an independent Mardou. The film instead deploys the device of Mardou's pregnancy in order to snap the wayward Leo into observing the proper rites of man-hood. Roxanne, too, having learned from Leo that she can love de-cides to leave the North Beach scene, a decision that permits her to wear a skirt for the first time since she left home. She will give up art, marry a businessman or a plumber, and have a couple of kids—in short, rejoin civilization. Thus the film's action conforms to the ex-pectations of romantic comedies stemming back to *The Taming of the Shrew*. It restores domestic order and affirms its privileged posi-tion over and above the film's bohemianism. This domestic tranquil-ity exacts a price, however: the novel's African American and Native American Mardou is displaced by a blonde, white, French immigrant version.

It is easy to critique the film's avoidance of interracial love. Yet the omission is perhaps the film's most authentic mimetic maneuver; it imitates xenophobic habits of U.S. culture, which in the main would not permit domestic tranquility between blacks and whites. Kerouac's novel imagined the unthinkable. It imagined the anxieties that caused the film to censor the book. The novel's Mardou and Leo feel these anxieties profoundly, and they are worth considering now.

The novel's Mardou is a contemporary renaissance woman: well-educated, spontaneous, intellectually independent, artistic, adept at social charms, and physically attractive to Leo. She has turned away from the light of her African American and Native American heritage, which, nevertheless, casts itself in her shadow. Indeed, Kerouac's profile of Mardou is not far removed from Castiglione's courtly ideal, only for Kerouac, she is dark.[7] Mardou's cultural heritage has much to do with Leo's attraction to her. But it terrifies Mardou. She assumes untethered relations to her peoples' past. Leo knows she is at least as tethered to African American culture as he is. Leo reflects on the rapport between him and Mardou as having its basis in "the amazing fact she is the only girl I've ever known who could really understand bop and sing it" (67). While Mardou can freely and with great pleasure vocally improvise on the music, in a more frightened mood, she states, "I don't like bop . . . I hear the junk in it" (99). Leo is dismayed. He disagrees with her resistance and tells her: "You never like what you come from" (99). Kerouac has the narrator spin out pictures of Mardou's origins in precolonial African and Native American cultures, combined with contemporary images of their fallen dominion—the desolation of minorities in the Americas (16, 19–26). These passages insist on the importance of marginalized peoples in the United States. For example, of Mardou's father Kerouac writes: "I kept imagining that Cherokee-halfbreed hobo father of her[s] lying bellydown on a flatcar with the wind furling back his rags and black hat, his brown sad face facing all that land and desolation.—At other moments I imagined him instead working as a picker around Indio and on a hot night he's sitting on a chair on the sidewalk among the joking shirtsleeved men, and he spits and they say, 'Hey Hawk Taw, tell us that story agin about the time you stole a taxicab and drove it clear to Manitoba, Canada—d'jever hear him tell that one, Cy?'—I saw the vision of her father, he's standing straight up, proudly, handsome, in the bleak dim red light of America on a corner, nobody knows his name, nobody cares" (19).

If the red light is emblematic of the official, modern United States, the significance of the specter of Mardou's unknown father far outshines it. The obscure Cherokee's hobo face seems as vast, desolate, and romantic as the myth-couched plains it observes—plains where ancestors lived their original way of life. Moreover, Kerouac imagines the stories her father tells. He can imagine them because he paid attention to oral traditions, certainly his own as well as the scraps and toss-offs he had observed from others and B-movie depictions of others.[8] However imperfectly, he attends to the telling—the style, the gestures, and the idiosyncrasies of speech. He valorizes the small act of defiant necessity. Like *The Subterraneans,* the stories common to groups such as American Indians and African Americans combine memory and imagination spontaneously expressed. For Kerouac vernacular traditions were true. They were not the truth of theory, statistics, science, or theology; they were the truth of basic human experience in an unofficial, less notable America. But for Mardou, her cultural lore is too painful to enjoy. She sees no advantage in seeking it out. Her modern liberal arts education disdains the vernacular arts and culture that Leo idealizes. Moreover, being Native American and black precludes Mardou from enjoying an outside vantage point. Her race implicates her in a history she has learned to repress. Kerouac's prose, on the other hand, in the midst of segregation, House Un-American Activities Committee, McCarthy, and New Criticism, marked and facilitated the culture's opening to its vernacular traditions. Future decades would show these traditions less and less spoken for but speaking for themselves.

Mardou's resistance to African and Native American cultures is concomitant with her fear of the majority American culture. She seems to fear the hostile acts of individuals because the power structure often allows them to occur with impunity; in effect, it encourages them. Leo remarks that she was always speaking of this. Her talk becomes palpable when she refuses to hold his hand in public streets or accompany him to unfamiliar bars. Leo does not berate her for paranoia, but "tried to console her, show her she could do anything with me, 'In fact baby I'll be a famous man and you'll be the digni-

fied wife of a famous man so don't worry'" (68). To this Mardou
could only reply, "You don't understand" (68). Nevertheless, rolled
in the skein of Leo's positive emotions for his relationship with
Mardou—the calm, the affection, the hope for a life together—there
are threads of doubt candidly enumerated, some of them emotionally loaded racial myths. Leo dispels some by talking to Mardou
about them, or by being observant: imagined sloppiness or klepto-
maniacal tendencies, for example. If too painful for her, he dispels
them through writing, a transmutation of instilled Catholic rite:
"ably assisted by a driving paranoia . . . my confession—doubts, then,
all gone" (50). Ultimately he fears marrying Mardou will make him
as rootless as she is; that it will irreparably separate him from his
mother, sister, and southern brother-in-law, and proscribe his dream
of actually living in the South. Despite this, in another moment, Leo
claims readiness to realize "the dumb phantasy [sic] of the two of us
. . . a shack in the middle of the Mississippi woods, Mardou with me,
damn the lynchers" (60). What comes through in the novel is not just
the anxiety and danger of Leo's and Mardou's position but also the
loneliness of it. The film avoids explicit treatment of the social and
personal anxieties surrounding interracial relationships and the his-
torical-cultural past that informs them.

As the film's opening statement indicates, MacDougall and Thom
avoided the new literary practices of the Beat generation in order to
use a dramatic form that would take the viewer into a discrete image
of the bohemian world. The film presents an essentialized bohemia
in order to contain it and subordinate it. Bohemia is the domain of
the young who do not yet bear the burdens and strictures of middle-
class life. Yet the film suggests it is youth, sometimes frivolous, sometimes creative, that revitalize the larger culture. Responsible adults
(squares) cannot be found in bohemia. Responsible adults do not oc-
cupy themselves with art. They are not psychologically intimate with
their friends. They do not critique society. But if you are Beat but not
young, like the forty-six-year-old Burroughs, the forty-five-year-old

Huncke, or even Kerouac, who was thirty-eight in 1960; then by the film's values, you are a pathetic anachronism—in street slang, you're nowhere man. Bohemia, then, is a rite of passage. Mardou, Roxanne, and Leo pass through it on their way to domestic conformity.

But the film undermines its own conservative strategy. *The Subterraneans* presents the viewer with contrasting but unstable pictures of youthful resistance and adult conformity. There are challenging points of dialogue in the film. Despite the avoidance of interracial love, the film is open in its use of visual and musical art to symbolize the social convergence of European and African cultures. Painting, dance, and music, especially jazz, disturb the film's superimposed form and the safety of its conventions of resolution that favor conservative U.S. values. The film's use of visual and musical art does not constitute an accessible subtext any viewer could translate. One could make a case, perhaps, for the presence of the film's subversive, occult code for the hip, but such arguments are tedious and probably irrelevant. My argument is that a number of points in the dialogue and several of the performance tableaus are compelling. These tableaus' scripting, choreography, and execution undermine the overall terms of the comedic form that couches them. Moreover, I do not view audience consumption as a simple act of receiving the product. Consumption is a symbolic act that can be creative. When viewers consume a cultural product such as a film they receive meanings, yes, and they make them. Thus viewers can see the contradictions embedded in cultural productions. Seeing them, they become unnerved or curious. They may test the products' messages against their knowledge and experience. They wonder and perhaps discover new avenues of expression and community. In short, this film provides an example of how marginal art and its interests seeped into popular culture in the late 1950s. Moreover, the film contains raw material that members of a contemporaneous audience could use to produce challenging meanings.[9]

The instability of the film's denouement can be seen in the last scene, which presents Leo's and Mardou's happy prospects for the future. Soon to be parents, Leo and Mardou are beaming. Mardou's pregnancy has intervened to resolve the earlier problems of Leo's unfaithfulness and writer's block. The subterranean clan, descending the street outside the window of Mardou's apartment like a reveling, theatrical chorus, sounds a warp on this record of romantic bliss. The chorus betrays the superficiality of the film's ending. Nothing has changed. There is no indication that Leo will be anything but a determined and struggling writer and a half-committed husband. Although his first book received favorable comment in the *Saturday Review*, it sold poorly. Through Roxanne, the film suggests that there is no other life for Leo: "For your sake I hope you are . . . good." The act of writing constitutes the protagonist's identity. Leo's writerly disposition conflicts with Mardou's stereotyped need to be loved, a guise, a recapitulation of conventional desire, for the film's need for domestic resolution. In his final dialogue in the film, Leo tells Mardou: "Nothing really terrible can happen to anyone that's young. You'll be the mother, and I'll be the kid brother, okay?" This line implicitly critiques a determinative subtext in Kerouac's novel—Leo's attachment to his mother—and it also destabilizes the film's superficial happiness, which now has a double function. Ostensibly, the happy ending meets the film's formal requirements, but it also undermines them by refusing to resolve the complex tensions between creative life and domestic norms. Though Leo insists on the safety of his youth, some viewers may question the safety of a young man on the cusp of thirty. Audiences might hear Leo voicing a compelling artistic stance sympathetic to many Beat generation writers, and ask why his stance is so perilous. Does the larger society bear the burden of neglecting the gifts and talents of its youth? Why are youth the only group from whom official authority will (up to a point) tolerate resistance? Such are the film's ending tensions. Some viewers ignore or dismiss them. Others consider them.

For all of the compromises MacDougall and Thom make to accommodate the commercial requirements of a feature movie, the force of the Beat generation since the *Howl* trial—many of its values and concerns—infiltrate the popular media of the film. For example, the film shows concern about hydrogen bombs and the narrow range of identities available to people living in a society bent on rampant commercial development; the latter notion occurs throughout the film. In the opening scene Leo's mother wants him to marry a nice girl, and voices concern that his writing career brings in less money than her career as a registered nurse. Leo responds with a fatly loaded comment, "I hate nice girls," meaning men who marry nice girls do not challenge the culture. "Nobody likes a trouble maker," his mother tells him. And Leo makes trouble. He is acutely aware of the incompatibility between hanging out to dry the security blanket of the military economy and maintaining the appearance of a pristine household. Leo recoils at the idea of living his life according to the norms of popular images of U.S. families whose members bond through rituals of consumption. To his mother's complaint about his deficient earning power, he, nevertheless, testifies to the coercive force of such rituals when he reminds her, as if to justify himself as a responsible human being, that he bought her a television set with his pay from the railroad. Thus the film attends to Beat writers' views that conformity to pervasive U.S. domestic ideals smothers artistic expression and precludes sincere portrayals of the world and its characters.

Poet and Painters Mission

The role of the Poet and Painters Mission in the film is instructive because it shows that MacDougall and Thom tried to ratchet up a modicum of authenticity from the North Beach scene. The filmmakers based the film's mission on the Bread and Wine Mission, a popular center for artists, musicians, and poets, located at 510

Greenwich Street in North Beach. MacDougall, Thom, and the film's producer, Hollywood mogul Arthur Freed, consulted with Pierre Delattre, who was a graduate of divinity and comparative religion from the University of Chicago and a writer, who with his wife Lois opened the Bread and Wine Mission to serve an alternative "very powerful spiritual movement in America." The movement, Delattre added, was "not in the churches" but "in the streets where a whole group of prophets and singers were energizing and coming together: singers, poets, jazz musicians." Monday spaghetti and wine and Sunday *agape* dinners were favorites at the mission. Spiritual and social ecumenicalism seemed to flourish there along with an impressive roster of poetry readings: Robert Duncan, Allen Ginsberg, Bob Kaufman, Joanne Kyger, Gary Snyder, Philip Whalen, and many others, even Jack Spicer. In addition, the important street poetry magazine *Beatitude* began at the mission where it printed a number of issues under the various editors such as Bob Kaufman, Allen Ginsberg, and Delattre himself. The Bread and Wine Mission recalled better times for artists, the days of the Federal Arts Projects and Works Projects Administration (1934–1943), when influential constituencies rejected the spectacle of starving artists and considered them makers of a usable past. The film's Poet and Painters Mission emulates service to these themes.[10]

In the film, the mission's spiritual overseer is Reverend Joshua Hoskins (Gerry Mulligan), a composite figure of Gerry Mulligan himself, Delattre, and Brother Antoninus (William Everson), who was also a poet and, as *Time* magazine called him, "The Beat Friar." Born in 1912, Everson was a contemporary of Kenneth Rexroth. They had known each other since the early 1940s. By the 1950s, Everson had won a Guggenheim Fellowship (1948) and had published twelve books of poetry. He had edited for the Untide Press (1944) and founded Equinox Press (1947). Years before, in the mid-1930s, he converted while reading Robinson Jeffers: "Jeffers showed me God. In Jeffers I found my voice." He was a practicing Catholic and became a lay brother in a Dominican monastery in 1948, which gave him his name. In 1956 he began reading his poetry to an enthusiastic public. Dressed in a white tunic and black scapular, he invented a charismatic persona and reading style that vibrated to Bay Area energies—a priestly street bard who came to realize "people will not read my poems, but when I read them I can spellbind."[11]

Like Brother Antoninus and Pierre Delattre, the film's Reverend Hoskins commands respect among the subterraneans for his wisdom and counsel and also for his art—not poetry but well-crafted, soulful baritone saxophone solos. Hoskins parallels Kerouac's saintly figure, Charlie Parker, whose eyes are "separate and interested and humane, the kindest jazz musician there could be . . . and therefore naturally the greatest" (14). Thus the film's Poet and Painters Mission correlates with the way Kerouac and other Beats envisioned artistic and spiritual life. They saw it as an expression of connections among individuals and spheres of community, work, and nature in the modern world. The Poet and Painters Mission is a prototypical holistic ministry. In addition to clothing, food, and shelter, it projects art as a central human need loaded with potential for bringing people together. The larger culture, particularly youth, felt this need. The film uses the mission to reflect emerging responses of youth eager to express themselves in a diversified, modern world.

The Poet and Painters Mission is the site of most of the art and performance in the film. The film's creative action coheres around André Previn's soundtrack, which delineates a pluralistic jazz practice that extends its influence into an eclectic range of social and artistic life. The idea that jazz realized the cultural convergence of African and European culture and that it expressed a democratic vision of creative social relations between blacks and whites was not new; a brief review of it is in order.

Arthur Knight points out that early jazz histories such as Doug

Ramsey's and Charles Edward Smith's *Jazzmen* (1939) pictorially and textually show the mixed origins of jazz. In 1937 *Reader's Digest* reprinted an essay from the *Delineator* called "It's Swing!" that stressed the crossing of color lines in the origins of jazz in New Orleans, but avoided the more sensitive relevance of then-current mixing. John Hammond, an impresario from the early 1930s, sought to realize a pluralistic version of jazz when he convinced Benny Goodman to record with Billie Holiday, Ethel Waters, Teddy Wilson, and Coleman Hawkins. Moreover, beginning in 1934, Goodman hired African American arrangers such as Fletcher Henderson, Edgar Sampson, and Jimmy Mundy, who helped make Goodman's band famous. The record product and associated sales packaging effectively deracinated the recording sessions, so that only the well informed knew about the race of the contributors.[12]

By the late 1930s, Benny Goodman had black players on the stage with him. In 1937 he formed his trio with Teddy Wilson and in the same year added Lionel Hampton to make it a quartet. The trio and quartet played during special interludes at concerts when the big band left the stage. In 1937 Goodman's organization performed at Carnegie Hall, a watershed event that featured the trio, the quartet, and the big band. At two points during the show larger mixed bands took the stage. According to Knight,

the first instance of this came in a section called "Twenty Years of Jazz," which pastiched white (ODJB [Original Dixieland Jazz Band], Beiderbecke, Ted Lewis) and black (Louis Armstrong, Ellington) jazz and employed three key members of the Ellington orchestra. The second was a "jam session" using six members from Basie's band (including Basie and Lester Young) and one of the Ellington men; here, significantly, the black players outnumbered the white players on stage, shifting the established ratios of racial mixture in the Goodman band's mixed jazz . . .

The Goodman concert ensured that its audience literally saw jazz's own "artistic" terms not just as "popular" but as racially mixed.[13]

A pluralistic version of jazz registered in Hollywood (institutionally frightened of racial controversy) when Goodman's quartet appeared in the Warner Brothers' film *Hollywood Hotel* (1937). Warner Brothers arranged two distributions of the film, one for the North and the other for the South; Goodman's quartet was not in the latter.

In the 1940s and 1950s Norman Granz built on the work of Hammond and Goodman with his Jazz at the Philharmonic concerts. These concerts were popular and remunerative (for Granz and the musicians) featuring mixed bands playing for crossover audiences. They formalized in respectable concert packaging the informal and sometimes perilous mixing of jazz audiences and musicians in Los Angeles's clubs and bars. Sonny Criss commented, "Blacks and whites were mixing then, and the police didn't like that. A mixed group—it didn't even have to be a man and a woman—was likely to be stopped." Granz took the Jazz at the Philharmonic concerts across the country. Whether the venue was in the North or South, he insisted on the same standards. In cities like Houston and Charleston, South Carolina, costly altercations ensued, but Granz paid the price. For example, he insisted that audiences be integrated. Tickets would be sold first come first served. The musicians would make good money, and they would travel, sleep, and dine well; no back door treatment would be allowed. Aside from Granz's peculiar fixation that the musicians compete with each other on stage and off, he helped open doors. Dizzy Gillespie relates how Granz would arrange each performance to include an extended cutting contest and suggest the participants travel and sleep separately afterward so as to avoid offstage confrontation. It was a strange, racially tinged fetish. Nevertheless, Gillespie wrote, "the importance of Jazz at the Philharmonic is that it was the original 'first class' treatment for jazz musicians."[14]

With the exception of Norman Granz's and Warner Brothers' production of *Jammin' the Blues,* directed by *Life* photographer Gjon Mili in 1944, Hollywood film has avoided representing jazz's artistic terms and racial diversity. I will return to *Jammin' the Blues,* but films such as *A Day at the Races* (1937), *Radio City Revels* (1938), *Hellzapoppin'* (1938), *The Hot Mikado* (1938), and *Swinging the Dream* (1939) exemplify the way Hollywood frequently connected African Americans to jazz by using the music as background for black lindy hop dancers. Though the dancers were artists in their own right, Hollywood paraded them as entertainers, which displaced visual presentation of the bands and obscured the evolving terms of jazz as an art form. In addition, with respect to the popularity of danceable swing, many musicians felt the craze for dancing marginalized their talents as players. Goodman's concert was important, in part, because Carnegie Hall was no dance hall. Also, a central point about African American dance scenes in Hollywood films is that while they presented talented African Americans to the public, they nevertheless conformed to segregationist politics. As with *The Cabin in the Sky* (1943), an all-black film produced by whites for a crossover audience, Hollywood typically linked jazz not to heavenly homes in the sky but to folly on Earth, that is, the negative polarity of immorality and blackness. Thus Hollywood representations of jazz tended to avoid meaningful negotiation of the tensions between segregationist ideology and pluralistic realizations of the music.[15]

If Hollywood denied jazz's artistic interests and its social implications, I will discuss an instance in which television more effectively charted a course through the tensions of ideology and musical practice. This is an important instance because it shifted the relationship of these tensions in favor of jazz. It illustrates the persuasive cultural force of a then relatively obscure art. In 1952 Charlie Parker and Dizzy Gillespie appeared on the variety show *Stage Entrance* to receive their *Down Beat* award and to play.[16] Newspaper columnist Earl Wilson hosted the show. He was blatantly condescending. Before cuing Gillespie and Parker to come out he joked with his sidekick, "What do I do say, gimme five or gimme some skin?" He referred repeatedly to Gillespie (whom he obviously did not know) as "Diz." After presenting the awards he asked, "You boys got any more to say?" To this point they had not said anything because they had not been asked any questions. Parker, motionless, face fixed in "a look that could kill," according to Parker's wife, Chan Richardson, replied, "Well, Earl, they say music speaks louder than words, so we'd really rather express our opinion that way." Wilson responded, "Well, I think that would be alright little buddy, if you really want to do it." Neither Parker nor Gillespie played into Wilson's attempt to be hip, nor did they cooperate with his alternative Jim Crow rhetorical approach. Next to the two musicians, who were dignified and formally dressed (no beret on Gillespie), Wilson's comments and manner, in our day, seem pathetically out of place. But for the average viewer in 1952, they probably were not. To hip or open-minded viewers, it was as if in a span of sixty seconds Parker and Gillespie transformed media industries, the makers of commercial images of hipsters and Negro musicians, into caricatures of themselves—idiot industries that promoted uncritical, babbling stereotypes out of habit. Parker and Gillespie had participated in a mass medium. As guests, they proved the medium's potential for intelligence and verity, particularly if the show was filmed live and thus uncensored. Whoever controlled the camera made the image real.

After the award presentation the camera trained in on the excellent performance, which further destabilized the solidity of Wilson's prejudice, the segregationist assumptions implicit to it, and its social effects. The quartet was mixed. A white piano player and a white bass player backed up Gillespie and Parker in an astonishingly clear and virtuosic performance of "Hot House." Parker's demeanor was cool as a statue of pharaoh as he blew eighth and sixteenth notes fast enough to melt his horn. Gillespie was loose. As was his wont, he blew through the scalic range of his trumpet. He mixed the highs, the middles, and the lows. Peeling sequences of notes gave way to sustained tones of sonic emotion. Despite the theme of the song and the speed of the choruses, Parker's solo was relaxed, a gentle torrent fluttering from his horn like hummingbird wings flashing colors.

The show withheld the names of the other two players, but the camera disclosed their mien and musicianship. Both were smiling and their playing was sharp. The camera telescoped the pianist's hands: the left hand, in the comp mode, suggested the proceeding chordal pattern; the right hand assuredly spelled out a complex bop melody. The drummer did not take a solo but kept the time in vintage bop style on the ride cymbal. The high hat clapped the beat. He delivered an occasional bomb to the kick drum and tastefully added snare and tom tom to the mix. During a chorus Gillespie dropped his horn to his side. Head down, he listened to the others. As the song rounded the last verse, he raised his head. He was smiling and laughing: seemingly pleased with the performance; perhaps, pleased that the ten-year-old jazz style was reaching at that moment a new popular audience; and pleased at the symbolic disruption of institutionalized media stereotypes.[17] The camera had portrayed the interview and the performance on their own terms within the unusual context of a nationally broadcast variety show. The performance did not serve as background for a conversation, or a dance, or a singer, or some other spectacle. No props symbolically intruded on the performance. Instrumental music was the featured presentation in a generic performance space. Seen through the black and white lens of the camera, the space was almost abstract. A curtain was drawn across the rear of the stage. Gillespie and Parker arranged themselves just in front of the other musicians, while the studio audience remained invisible and silent until the end of the tune. The space was deep and wide enough for camera gymnastics: wide-angle shots of the whole ensemble; focus shots of individual players soloing, with cuts to close-ups of hands and embouchure. The cuts were asymmetrical in their effect and thus agreeable complements for the disjunctions of Bop. Quite frankly, the camera produced images that were inaccessible to even the most ardent concert and club audiences. *Stage Entrance*, to some extent unwittingly, delivered an unprecedented jazz performance to an unsuspecting audience.

The *Stage Entrance* performance defied pervasive racial stereotypes and segregationist ideology with convincing force. It presented an image of modern jazz that thrived on masculinist democratic participation of musicians regardless of ethnicity and race. It showed Parker and Gillespie as professional musicians and artists, not simply entertainers.[18] Most Hollywood images of jazz conformed to the confining norms of caricature and unequal power relations among races. With few exceptions Hollywood presented blacks as entertainment for whites, not as artists. I have set up this contrast between Hollywood films and the televised *Stage Entrance* because it suggests how established structures of prejudice and resistance to them helped shape images of jazz. Moreover, the contrast is an appropriate backdrop for discussing performance vignettes in MGM's *The Subterraneans*, which I argue sought to mirror jazz's artistic values and its preference for democratic participation.

The opening credits of *The Subterraneans* identify all of the film's musicians in bold type, not just the big names. This unusual happenstance is the first sign that the film took its musicians and performances seriously. In addition, unlike most Hollywood portrayals of jazz, the film syncs the music with the gestures of the performers. The jazz scenes have the look of live performance; the editor carefully dubbed (with one exception) the sound to match the visual image.[19]

Cool Bop at Coffee Time

The film's first jazz scene takes place in a rather generic space that looks more like a hotel banquet room for business luncheons than a jazz venue in North Beach—with a bar, booths, murals, night club lighting. The room is full of people sitting around tables with drinks. A smoky haze and diffuse light add atmosphere. The light distributes equal emphasis on the audience and the performers. Mardou, Leo, and Adam Moorad (the figure based on Allen Ginsberg in the book) sit at a table. The jazz combo's sound is clear, fast, and tight: white boys—Shelly Manne, Red Mitchell, and André Previn. The camera picks up the trio finishing a cool Bop tune with four stop-time chorus breaks. The breaks feature Manne with brushes soloing on drums. Previn, stoically virtuosic, mixes up the melody between chorus breaks and on the verses. The camera pans from Manne to Mardou's table, and back to Previn. The lens pulls back to take in the combo before it cuts back to the table, at which Leo, cigarette caught in his teeth, beats with his hands while Mardou watches him and seems to absorb the groove through him. The camera performs this cycle four times—uninterrupted by dialogue—for sixty seconds, making the point that the film values musical authenticity. The camera supplements a compelling authenticity; its movements portray the synergy between Leo (audience) and the combo and simulate the dizzy disjunctions of the bebop style, which the best cool musicians kept intact.

After the first number the lights dim. The combo recedes to the background as the spotlight shines on Carmen McRae, the African American singer. Other than a jerky cut, the action seems routine, like any night at a jazz club. Dialogue remains suspended. The din of peoples' conversations and movement pervades while McRae and the combo set up for the next tune. McRae sometimes played piano, but not here. Clothed in an ideologically meaningful gold leopard-spotted satin dress, she continues the film's displacement of dialogue with the song "Coffee Time":

Coffee time.
My dreamy friend its coffee time.

Let's listen to some jazz and rhyme
and have a cup of coffee.

Let me show,
a little coffee house I know,
where all the new bohemians go,
to have a cup of coffee.

Chorus:

Greetin' time.
The music box is beatin' time.
It's good old fashion meetin' time.
So grab a chair and dig me . . .

Moorad's monologue breaks off the chorus, but the tune and its presentation touch salient contemporary issues. The film spotlights McRae singing intimately to a white audience about simple rituals in bohemian settings. Middle-class practices of the nuclear family, its divisions of labor and consumption patterns have displaced "old fashioned" pleasures of conversation, friendship, play, and art—pleasures not controlled by a clock but in accord with a beat. McRae sings both to the Beat generation's realizations and youth's nostalgia for a community that values imaginative expression. Moorad's ruminations about the geometry Cézanne perceived in nature and his conclusion that "yea . . . Cézanne was a beat man," exemplify McRae's gentle imperative. McRae's song and presence suggest generally what Kaufman made specific in his poem "Bagel Shop Jazz," referring to coffee haunts in North Beach where a motley assortment of "nightfall creatures eat each other over a noisy cup of coffee. Mulberry eyed girls . . . angels" gather with "dungaree guys . . . synagogue eyes" and "coffee-faced Ivy Leaguers." Together they speak "jazz and paint talk, high rent, Bartok, classical murders, the pot shortage, and last night's bust . . . Bird and Diz and Miles" blow the group's "secret terrible hurts" concealed by "cool hipster smiles." McRae relaxes the uneasy tensions of these gatherings wrought taut by the cultural patterns they confront and by the always impending threat of Kaufman's "guilty police."[20] The social values of jazz disarm these anxieties.

Moreover, in the film's world, jazz is a present force for reconciliation of the most personal relationships. In one of the film's final scenes—set in a club whose interior redwoods and mortared stone walls give it the character and warmth of a mountain lodge—a mixed quintet performs a soulful blues. Light again disperses throughout the space. Despite the mythic preference for nocturnal jazz, here the film delivers jazz in afternoon light. Conversations are in progress. Bar service is open. Because there are few patrons, the presence of one African American woman listening to the music, perhaps, qualifies the audience as mixed. The Reverend Hoskins (Gerry Mulligan) takes the first solo. The black skin of the quintet's drummer and trumpet player Art Farmer is considerably less ambiguous and difficult to discern than Barney Kessel's white skin in Norman Granz's and Gjon Mili's important film short *Jammin' the Blues* (1944).

Jammin' the Blues was the first Hollywood film to show the artistry of black jazz players. Moreover, Warner Brothers distributed the film to theaters around the country. In addition to Barney Kessel, the film featured Marie Bryant, Red Callender, Sid Catlett, Harry Edison, Illinois Jacquet, Jo Jones, Marlowe Morris, John Simmons, and Lester Young. Using techniques of "art" photography the film couched African American jazz in the terms of modern art: abstract, asymmetrical, stylized, and fast. Barney Kessel's skin color is erased until the last of three tunes, when in a cautious gesture of inverted tokenism *Jammin' the Blues* broached the integrative character of jazz by showing Kessel's image in an ambiguous, doubly exposed close-up. Another shot shows Kessel's hands, the right straight, and the left strobed, picking out a guitar solo in the context of an otherwise black ensemble. The studio objected to Kessel's inclusion in the film and asked Norman Granz, if he insisted on having Kessel's guitar-playing on the soundtrack, to at least "get a Negro guitarist to 'fake' his playing in the picture." Granz refused to accommodate Hollywood's segregationist conventions, yet only attentive eyes will notice Kessel's whiteness.[21]

The Subterraneans' quintet pushes the reverse tokenism of *Jammin' the Blues* toward equality of representation, although it does so conservatively. Mulligan is clearly the front man. His image occupies the center of the performance shot. Art Farmer stands to Mulligan's left toward the top of the screen. The drummer sits behind Mulligan on the left side of the screen. Viewers must glance at the screen's periphery to see them. If it were not for the sound of piano chords, one would probably miss the presence of the black piano player, Russ Freeman; with his back to the camera, he sits behind and to the left of Farmer. Viewers watch the quintet perform the introductory bars of the blues "Things Are Looking Down" (composed by André Previn) and two bars of Mulligan's solo before the camera cuts to Leo having a telephone conversation with his mother, primarily about the whereabouts of Mardou. The camera then follows Roxanne's entrance into the bar. She joins Leo at a table and the two have their parting conversation. At this point Farmer's trumpet solo ensues in legato, blues-inflected notes that are much more prominent in the sound mix than Mulligan's soft, low-frequency tones. The solo builds up compelling intensity and interweaves meaningfully with the dialogue; it gathers the actors' voices into itself and transmutes them into a multivocal talking-blues of loneliness, regret, unrequited love, and the perplexed difficulty of communication between the sexes. The conversation ends generously. Roxanne offers her best wishes for Leo as a writer and an apartment—rent paid until the end of the month. Roxanne is leaving bohemia for a more certain conventionality. Here Farmer's trumpet solo gives way to two bars of piano before the camera cuts to show the quintet ending the blues with a recapitulation of its opening lines. Farmer and Mulligan take the bars in unison. Their agreement matches the sad concord of the conversation. Thus, this scene emulates jazz's crossover ethic and extends its salubrious implications to the most personal relationships between the sexes.[22]

Blabber Mouth Night

John Gibbons introduced the speak-your-mind free-for-all "Blabber Mouth Night" at The Place in San Francisco, where he tended bar in the late 1950s. Borrowed from bohemian watering holes in Chicago, the weekly event became a popular competition. A magnum of champagne went to the best wit of the night as judged by an audience of writers, painters, and musicians who were quite free with their cheers, boos, and catcalls. The event was similar to the 6 Gallery readings in the way it organized interaction between a type of speech and the audience. "Howl" was so effective, in part, because it drew the audience into a groove traversing a range of emotions. Similarly, on Blabber Mouth Night, good talk was as much about rhythm as it was about compelling speech, which in the film—mirroring the way the Beats often spoke with each other—became quite intimate.

The design of the film's Blabber Mouth Night shows the provocative link between sharing confessions and useful revelation; it also critiques it. In this scene a motley crowd gathers in a dark gallery with a mezzanine balcony. An elder emcee (a Rexroth type) in sunglasses opens the event and announces its purpose: "We are the subterraneans. We live underground, but we are looking for the light!" A spotlight shines in consecutive order on the film's central characters that, along with the crowd's chant of encouragement, "Go, Go Go!" obliges them to speak. Julienne Alexander (Art Pepper) speaks first and briefly: "I'm a thinker. I have but one thought tonight: that women are cannibals." Julienne's thought follows the breakup of his relationship with Mardou earlier the same night. Ostensibly, the decision to separate was mutual, although Julienne initiated it. Mardou's icy words of termination to Julienne seem to stem from her desire to hurt him in return. By this point in the film Mardou is responsive to Leo, which gives the lie to Julienne's claim to be a thinker. Like Mardou, he uses cool affect to regulate boiling emotions.

When the spotlight shines on Roxanne, she responds to Julienne.

She explains that the black paint around her eyes imitates an Eastern medieval practice to keep evil spirits from entering the soul—"like you, Julienne. I think you're an evil spirit." Roxanne's comment speaks to Julienne's duplicity. His misogyny bleeds from a wounded ego, denied its desire to control Mardou and women in general. Power is his unrequited need. Roxanne's and Julienne's exchange suggests the attitude of contemporaneous relationships between men and women in Beat circles.

If after the war a generation of men chose alternatives to middle-class routines and images of success, many women did too. Women drew exhilaration from the risks inherent in acts of rebellion and creativity. For the most part men were the notable artists, but as Maria Damon and Lisa Phillips point out, many women who encouraged their male companions, cooked for them and typed their manuscripts, also wrote and painted their experience and their visions. Roxanne forgoes servile activities in order to embrace artistic ones exclusively. She is independent. She rents apartment space to subterranean boarders, which frees her to dance and paint. Before the arrival of Leo, art had replaced intimate relationships with men. Her stance critiques Beat artists who opened up new forms of identity but failed to transform their chauvinistic behavior. Roxanne sees more clearly what perplexes Julienne Alexander, and for that matter, Kerouac, who acknowledged in *On the Road* (1957): "we don't understand our women; we blame them and it's all our fault." *The Subterraneans* narrator Leo arrived at a similar befuddled conclusion after he deserted Mardou in a cab so that he could get to the liquor store before closing time and take another cab to join a party. Mardou was exhausted, hungry, and wanted to go home. They had been partying all night. But Leo wanted more night, and he took her sandwich money to help get him through it. This was one of many of Leo's erratic acts when he was with Mardou. The next day he was remorseful: "women all mean well—this I knew—women love, bend over you—you'd as soon betray a woman's love as spit on your own feet, clay" (104). Though Roxanne comes round to serve the conventional ends of the film's plot, her character implies resources of critique and offers life options that viewers can use. She critiques the whole structure of desire informing Hollywood film then and in many ways since. To borrow from Laura Mulvey's take on Hollywood, Roxanne is no "silent image of woman still tied to her place as bearer, not maker, of meaning."[23]

"Go, Go, Go!" chants the crowd to Yuri Gligoric (the Gregory Corso character in the novel, played here by Roddy McDowall). Yuri explains he is not a thinker. He has no great thoughts about life, "I don't care. It doesn't make any difference." He admits his intention to write an epic that tells everyone not to suffer. "Life is a party," he exclaims. It is a celebration of pleasures as simple as talking to a pigeon on a park bench in the morning. For Yuri, poverty makes such pleasures more accessible. His revelation is that of the monastic. It is the security, he insists, of knowing that when you do not have anything, you have the world. As clichéd as Yuri's speech may seem, it nevertheless spoke to what remains a compelling simplicity. It recognizes that the fulfillment of desires suggested by advertisers do not, in the end, satisfy. The postwar economy promised to fulfill desires while it strategized to exacerbate and multiply them. Though the Beats, and Kerouac in particular, imaginatively appropriated commodified images, they would have happily exchanged window-shopping at Macy's for conversations with street folk on the Bowery.

More interesting than Yuri's speech, however, is the purpose of the black man dressed in a brown leather jacket sitting next to him and sharing the spotlight. The camera shows the man listening to Yuri and smiling slightly as if amused. He could just as easily have been the one uttering Yuri's speech, but he has no lines. His placement and silence is unsettling and suggestive. It is symptomatic of Hollywood's limited vocabulary for portraying African American personalities, but to the film's credit it does not indulge here in invidious cliché.

The man sitting next to Yuri is not a mere ambient extra such as the lone black man standing in the extreme background against a wall at the dance in *West Side Story* (1961), where the two rival gangs, one Italian, the other Puerto Rican, declare war on each other. Nor does the subterranean character play the genteel crossover figure Sidney Poitier had made popular in such films as *The Blackboard Jungle* (1955) and *The Defiant Ones* (1958). The man is a token to be sure. But the camera studies his silence—a dignified refusal to comply with caricatures or sympathetic Uncle Toms. Like the students in Greensboro the same year, he was sitting in.[24]

The film's Blabber Mouth Night also exhibits interest in the fluidities of gender performance and identity. Arial Lavalina (a character supposedly based on Gore Vidal in the book) is the film's successful writer who prefers the society of subterraneans to the more enfranchised communities of established artists and academics. He is not overtly homosexual as he is in the book; rather, the film accents his highly affected effeminate glamour. Arial dons ruffled sleeves and collars, a dark vest, and a gold watch chain. He smokes his cigarettes from a svelte holder and exudes giddy self-delight. He confesses that, since his mother died when he was eleven, no woman has ever taken him seriously. He tells the audience that his books are his dreams, and that "everywhere I go I'm slumming," and that "I love spotlights." Arial's persona is a double critique. With smooth nonchalance he exploits mainstream society's reliance on surface appearances while he violates their circumscribed and inflexible parameters. On the other hand, he mocks the tendency of some Beats to over-indulge interiority. Unlike the film's Leo, Arial lightens the burden of artistic inspiration and the Beat's emphasis on plumbing the depths of sincere emotion. For Arial, emotion is no more a reliable reservoir for creative work than the bottle. Speech, like costume, gesture, and posing, is an element in a game of style. He plays the game with a jaunty delight that can only infuriate or disarm the self-certain. Arial reveals the unreliability of fixed ideas—including the fixed idea that fluid emotion spurs imagination—through the guise of silliness. His role suggests that frivolity does not so much uncap the repressed unconscious where emotions are trapped as dissolve superimposed notions of a compartmentalized psyche. His glamorous mien follows the colorful trail blazed by such figures as Oscar Wilde and Salvador Dalí and widens it for future celebrities such as David Bowie and Boy George.

Finally, Mardou speaks of oppressions. She confides she is from a small French village that changed hands several times during the war, as did her mother, she adds. Her mother loved life and men—vices that were intolerable to the occupying authorities. At war's end, officials ordered Mardou's mother's head shaved in the streets and her body whisked off by train. The "committee" then sent Mardou to live with an American family. Her despair is embedded in the complaint, "No one has been able to tell me who to love." Mardou's experience parallels and obliquely references African Americans' historical experience. The persecution and violation of feminine desire, the breaking up of families, and the denial of personal autonomy are fresh memories for African Americans. Mardou's difficulty in choosing supportive loyalties—selecting who to love—is a symptom of persecution and, too, the complex effects of late capitalism. And to recall Brian Philip Harper's point, the phenomenon of fragmented subjectivity that characterizes the postmodern era was not new to oppressed peoples in the United States or anywhere else.[25] The Beats were keen to the psychic costs of the era's markets, politics, and inevitable wars. Their art and social practices were an affirmative response to dehumanizing forces. Despite the trivializing moniker, the film's Blabber Mouth Night marks important cultural symptoms of race and gender relations and emulates the Beats' insistence on honest personal disclosure for the achievement of positive intimacy. At the same time, via Arial Lavalina's persona, the film warns that too-concentrated subjectivity may isolate individuals, preclude strong community ties, and stave off imagination.

Art as a Community Barometer and the Mind's Path to the Body

In addition to tableaus of jazz and rituals of interpersonal disclosure, the film uses painting and dance in a scene at the Poet and Painters Mission to epitomize the intersection of cultural cross currents that shaped the Beat generation. An anonymous down-home blues riff on acoustic guitar sets the opening tone of the scene. Most of the people lie on cushions talking. An entire interior wall is reserved for painting. A bearded man in suspenders paints with broad strokes and hot orange colors. A young boy-child sporting a black hat sits on the painter's shoulders like a hip cherub-muse knowing secrets of creativity. Roxanne sits on the floor, works the mural, and talks to Julienne who asks, "Don't you ever get tired of painting your own face?" "Why should I?" she replies. Commenting on the serendipitous rewards of art making, she adds, "It smiles at me from time to time." Roxanne walks off before the anonymous bearded painter works downward. His brush sweeps over Roxanne's self-portrait. Surely the audience is startled at the apparent offense. But Roxanne is not offended. The mural, like jazz performance, is collaborative and at the service of immediacy. The mission's wall is dedicated to the act of painting and not to a particular representation. The bearded painter's gesture signals the culture's move away from valuing the abstract individual action, demonstrated earlier in the decade by the likes of Jackson Pollock and Willem de Kooning, to a celebration of collaborative actions articulated in texts such as *Visions of Cody* or the film *Pull My Daisy* (1959). *Visions of Cody* incorporates dialogue transcribed from five days of recorded conversations, while *Pull My Daisy* was the important result of cooperative, improvisational efforts among David Amram, Robert Frank, Allen Ginsberg, Jack Kerouac, Larry Rivers, and others. The shift could be seen and heard in other inclusive and participatory activities such as happenings and free jazz, which were structured to focus attention on the present, encouraged egalitarian relationships among participants, and blurred definitions between art maker and audience. At the Poet and Painters Mission meanings arise in the process of action. This scene shows the transformational power of collaborative art; a wall supersedes its sheltering purpose to both constitute and measure, like a barometer, change in a community.[26]

Following this painterly activity and in keeping with the scene's stress on the appearance of spontaneity, a dance movement begins and shows, in the film's most explicit terms, the convergence of African and European culture. The dimming of the room's main lights signals the beginning of the dance. The bearded painter descends the ladder to watch as a black man switches on a handheld spotlight. Another black man cues the commencement of a violin sonata with a hand-drum beat. It is appropriate that African Americans inaugurate this emblematic event for a feature film audience. Cuing and lighting are gestures of agency that here suggest the sources for the revitalization of Western culture. The man with hand drums in his lap will provide rhythmic accompaniment for the sonata. Roxanne rises to her feet. The interlocking of hand-drum rhythms, piano harmonies, and violin melody enable Roxanne's movement. Hands stretched overhead, she performs a ballet dance that combines erotic hip gyrations with delicate pirouettes, aggressive approaches to the camera and sudden retreats to less intimate distances. She bows her legs, pumps her hips, and arches backward touching blonde hair to the floor. She springs up erect, alert as an owl. Her arms extend horizontal while her fingers dance delicately, and her shoulders shift left then right. The camera registers the audience's rapt attention. Julienne comments, "When she dances, she doesn't know where she's at," while Roxanne's shadow gambols on the walls. As the musical tension builds the camera pans the room and passes the drummer whose gleaming white teeth affect savage pleasure. Here the film exploits primitive clichés. Julienne's comment suggests Roxanne is madness in motion evoked by the strange musical fusion. The drummer's white teeth do not signify the servile happy Negro, but the triumph of original energy. Sensually provocative dance is no longer relegated to a sideshow on film in which African Americans perform the spectacle of the lindy hop or the "primitive" dances of Katherine Dunham and her troupe. African Americans have returned white youth to their bodies. But Roxanne's dance also undermines primitive stereotypes. Contrary to what Julienne thinks, and given the tenor of her exchanges with him, she knows exactly where she is. Julienne separates thought from emotions and kinesthetics, as does the film itself.[27] In so doing both Julienne and the film disqualify their own judgments. Roxanne's movements are skillful products of mind and body. They necessitate awareness, intelligence, and control. Shocked as they may be, the film's viewers can sense this.

In conclusion, I have shown how a Hollywood feature film adopted a Renaissance comedy form and traditional mimetic notions of drama in order to erase the issue of interracial love in Kerouac's novel and to close off its destabilizing openness. MGM's trivialization and censorship of the novel was part—beginning with the *Howl* trial—of a larger mass media trend of cooling the surface of conflicts issuing out of the social and aesthetic worlds of the Beats. Kerouac's personal, indeterminate, extraordinarily vulnerable prose breeched the invulnerable look of media surfaces shielding the discipline of the consumption/military economy in the United States. Yet Kerouac's prose kept close kinship with subordinate energies present in the liberal arts and social forms of the time. These forms and values sympathetic with the Beat generation bled into the film's surface. Kerouac, other artists, and critics near the creative foment of the period winced and despaired at popular media's portrayals of beatniks. Yet, in their despair, they missed the force of their influence on mediated images of print, television, and film: especially the capacity of active audiences to scrutinize them and use them well. There is irony here because Kerouac's earlier prose in *Visions of Cody* sizzles with the conviction of vernacular intelligences and their ability to incorporate mass-mediated images for their own purposes: to make simulacra of simulacra. Is it too obvious to say it was naive to think mass media systems would convey images that conformed to the Beats' needs and felt experience, or that these systems would be sympathetic to renegade innovators? As I suggested in the first chapter, Ginsberg not only accepted his complicity with the media, he exploited it. He plotted the shape of his own spectacle. He understood the Burroughs bromide, "all resisters sellout." Kerouac's disposition was ill-suited to dancing with media machines. In most such encounters he drank to disguise his vulnerability and became a fool. He thought his surrendering film rights to MGM for fifteen thousand dollars was a shameful act.[28]

Yet, short of fascist control, media are also complicitous with their subjects. The fact that MGM agreed to make *The Subterraneans* speaks to the Beats' original charisma and the interests of a growing younger culture in new expressive opportunities, social relationships, and identity possibilities. Media executives, directors, screenwriters, and set and costume people directly serve the interests of ownership and investment. The Beats serve these interests, but obliquely. They seek to reconfigure capital's dispensation, to align it with the subordinate interests of alternative social forms. Sometimes producers, directors, screenwriters, choreographers, and music directors help them and at some risk. Moreover, the very culture of a film set, the sum of its diverse participants—actors, musicians, technicians, gaffers, gophers, janitors, extras—is a vital social world coming to bear on its product. The meanest of film-set functionaries brings something personal to the outcome of a film. It is reasonable to speculate that anonymous people working on this film were keen for the best jazz, painting, and poetry in the Bay Area. Did not their attitudes, if not their knowledge, seep into the film? MGM's *The Subterraneans* is a complex business of overlapping and competing interests. The film's art, its confessional tableaus, and some of its dialogue are all borrowed from the egalitarian openness present in jazz, literature, dance, painting, happenings, and intimate, mixed gathering places.

Active audiences could test and explore in their lives provocations in the film that were sympathetic or disparaging to Beat generation writers. It is true that such critics as Theodor Adorno and Max Horkheimer would despair that these testings are useless, that all constituents—even resisting individuals—are complicit in the propagation of a false reality. And Jean Baudrillard, too, who replaces despair with indifference, insists participants conform to the preeminent postwar reality as simulation.[29] I acknowledge these critics' insights, but their acquiescence to determinism seems unhelpful. With respect to Adorno and Horkheimer, the freedom they surrender seems a function of their despair in the face of capitalism. Outrage precludes thinking a way through it. The Beats stood at odds to an academia that had decided what was right, what the standards and possibilities were. They committed themselves to making an art that measured the fullest possible spectrum of their experience. Their work seemed to say that freedom had to do with being as mindful of experience as possible in order to discover what is not taught and what is not conventional knowledge and what we struggle against—awake or dreaming. This kind of sensitivity opened the Beats to new forms, and new identifications and performance with others; capital's conventional forms of speech, its representative surfaces, would have them do otherwise. The Beats had lured capital into new symbolic territory for the making of new caricatures. But members of a nascent, youthful counter-culture (in part, the film's audience) used caricatures as a wedge into the unfamiliar. The film imparts some truth in its assertion that the middle class craves security, that it needs caricatures in order to avoid the burden of imagining others as human. But significant numbers of an audience smell ruses when they see stereotypes. They sidestep safety and follow the scent to new ideas, new social bonds, and new art.

Allen Ginsberg, dressed for his day job as a marketing researcher, at Alta Plaza in San Francisco, 1954, the year he moved to the city and before he wrote "Howl."

ruth weiss serving drinks at the Cellar, a popular North Beach venue for poetry and jazz. She was among the first poets to combine poetry and jazz there and in the Bay Area. Allen Ginsberg is sitting on the floor.

A young, creative, and charismatic Bob Kaufman in San Francisco, 1954.

ruth weiss taking her poetry to the streets at the Grant Avenue Street Fair in the late 1950s.

The evocative book cover on Bob Kaufman's *Solitudes Crowded with Loneliness,* 1959.

ruth weiss, hip publicity photo, 1960.

Omar Tanguay sits out at piano while Dick Partee blows his saxophone during a session at the Coffee Gallery, 1958.

Allen Ginsberg, completely absorbed in the performance, reads at San Franciso State, November 22, 1955.

A local jazz combo puts out the groove at a Venice Beach cafe. Rhamat Jamal, drums; Abdul Karim, piano; Everett Evans, bass; Paul Freidin, alto saxophone; and Jerome Lindsay, trumpet.

ruth weiss weaves her poetic web with koto player Michiko Kimura (not pictured) at the Exploratorium in San Francisco, 1972.

4

READY FOR BREAKFAST

Doing his bit to dispel the anxiety of influence, Jack Duluoz, fictional narrator of *Visions of Cody,* chose the literary guidance of a teenager over T. S. Eliot.

> "Obviously, an image which is immediately and unintentionally ridiculous is merely a fancy"—T. S. Eliot, *Selected Essays,* 1917–32 . . . when little Cody Pomeray was sixteen, and was just beginning to learn the things that would eventually lead him through the mazes of the mind growing to all kinds of realizations that when a thing is ridiculous it is subject to laughter and reprisal, and may be cast away like an old turd . . . a thing gone dead. There were no images springing up in the brain of Cody Pomeray that were repugnant to him. They were all beautiful.

This passage, taken from *Visions of Cody* (1972), attacks high art authority and icons. It dismisses narrow opinions about beauty. Instead, it defers to the unprejudiced mind of a sixteen-year-old boy. *Visions of Cody* was dangerous to aesthetic hierarchies. Its forms and content rose from lowly origins to stare down high modernism. On the surface it seemed to signal the eclipse of high modernism by an uppity college dropout. Less ostensibly, *Visions of Cody* indicated not so much the eclipse of high modernism as flamboyant trespassing of its borders and bridgings of its moat by diverse, self-determined, marginally enfranchised individuals and groups performing a variation on Woody Guthrie's contemporaneous lyric: this culture is your culture and mine. Although Kerouac disdained the institutional trappings surrounding a canon, he admired many of the works canonical lists enfold: Dickinson, Faulkner, Joyce, Melville, and Proust, for example. Kerouac draws from these resources, but as significantly, he draws from the often-scorned worlds of the lowly commoner, the mundane, and the realm where they register—"all images springing up in the brain." Ideally, nothing is refused; rejected things are celebrated.[1] Whereas T. S. Eliot's Prufrock is ashamed to speak of "lonely men in shirt sleeves, leaning out of windows" to anyone but himself, narrator Jack Duluoz insists on the importance of peopled red-brick environs in towns and cities across the country; among them is Cody Pomeray, Duluoz's lonely, shirt-sleeved, leaning-toward-everything American hero. Nothing is repressed; everything is in colloquy with everything else.

Visions of Cody is important, in part, because it early marks a cultural leveling through the mingling of high and low and refined and crude. It inscribes democratic values by way of its radical egalitarian writing. In particular, it attempts to achieve ethnographic authenticity and juxtapose it to narrative conventions. *Visions of Cody* conforms to the protean energies dispersing through other arts such as jazz, painting, and film and through socially explicit democratic actions emerging then and in the coming decades.

Had *Visions of Cody* been published in 1951 when it was written, readers, critics, sociologists, and politicians might have observed a postwar "slackening" or, as I prefer, opening, much earlier than they did.[2] Publication of *Visions of Cody* was untenable in 1951, however. The Cold War was crystallizing. It was a time of walls and rigid decorum and strong opinions about what was proper. The widespread need to contain dissent loomed large in the House Un-American Activities Committee (HUAC) deliberations and censorship battles of Hollywood and book publishing. Moreover, in the academy the clear standards of new criticism dismissed the vernacular energies coursing through *Visions of Cody.* Six years would pass before the publication of *On the Road* (1957). The prospects for publication of *Visions of Cody*—Kerouac's experimental rewrite of *On the Road,* which he much preferred—were slim, indeed. Nevertheless, *Visions of Cody* is an early-morning pronouncement of postwar cultural health. It testifies to a period when artists and activists devoured their vernacular breakfasts and entered high culture's ring, where they contend for legitimacy to this day. I am writing about *Visions of Cody* because it presents a ringside view of the emerging battle.

Although the much-discussed postwar leveling, helped by the pervasive growth of mass media and electronic technologies, has seemed new, it is not unprecedented. Insurgent vernacular energies have infused popular cultural forms such as subversive and romantic adventure literature and blackface performance since the early 1800s.[3] These forms, like the later, subordinate modern expressions of romanticism, Dada, surrealism, jazz, film, radical politics, and situational constructs of uncertainty and relativity, not only worked through and helped constitute popular culture but also rocked stable hierarchies and gave reactionary elites something interesting to attack. The populism evident in the work of many U.S. artists and personalities—Charlie Chaplin, Samuel Clemens, Kenneth Fearing, Susan Glaspell, Emma Goldman, Langston Hughes, DuBose Heyward, Ira and George Gershwin, Carl Sandburg, Gertrude Stein, John Steinbeck, Walt Whitman, William Carlos Williams, Thomas Wolfe, and Richard Wright—indicated the insurgent influence of vernacular expressions. These artists celebrated *uncultured* arts and mores, though they doubtless refined their rougher edges. And while Kerouac was not interested in refinement, differences in this respect from his predecessors were more in degree than kind. Nevertheless, Kerouac's work marks a period when previously submerged, disparaged, or unnoticed vernacular expressions were about to make a huge public splash.[4]

The work of art is valuable only insofar as it is vibrated by the reflexes of the future.

—André Breton

Kerouac took liberties and, therefore, formidable risks in writing *Visions of Cody*. Working-class pride, avant-garde libertinism, and vernacular traditions and arts nourished his experimental stance. These influences combined with Kerouac's intuitive awareness of the growing presence of simulacra as a preeminent means of signification in the culture are my focus. Kerouac's apprehension of the simulacrum liberates his prose and informs its experimental crossings of aesthetic and cultural boundaries. His prose adopts the focus of painterly sketchings and the speed of a cinematic camera. It imitates advertisements and movie and television production practices. An extended portion of the novel displaces authorial prose with tape-recorded transcripts, followed by prose imitating the transcripts. These are full-blown simulacra. Moreover, the simulacrum permits Kerouac to adopt a writing style informed more by jazz improvisation than schoolroom grammar. Finally, the freedom of the simulacrum compels Kerouac to revise the stature of the lost main character of *On the Road* (1957) into the American hero of *Visions of Cody*. The importance of all of this is that *Visions of Cody* helps us to situate historically the implications of postwar mass media and consumer society.[5]

Aside from the tumultuous beauty of much of the prose in *Visions of Cody*, the work provides answers to serious questions that confronted it. What happens to a culture when it is increasingly characterized through the rivalry of commodified aural and visual images? How do individuals and groups handle the proliferation of commodities? How free are they in their use of them? What effects do these mass media have on social relationships between individuals and groups? What becomes of a culture's roots and lore—the stuff of its identity and art? *Visions of Cody* meets Breton's criteria for artistic value. It is a reflex of its future and a timely forecast of our present.

The history of western art since the Renaissance shows that independently minded artists need not have waited for the arrival of the era of mechanical reproduction to flout the aura of the masterpiece, to make adversarial gestures toward its conventions and traditions—the stuff of its ideologically constituted separateness. They only needed romanticism.[6] The advent of mechanical reproduction has made the practice accessible to more people, however, and therefore more pervasive. The copy of the work of art clutched by consumers' hands, penetrated by their eyes, heard by their ears in their particular life circumstances potentially leads to what Walter Benjamin called a "tremendous shattering of tradition."[7] Consumers and artists persuade the copy to go prodigal; they encourage it to mock, to bite, or to ignore completely the hand that once fed it. From tradition's point of view, even high-quality reproductions are prone to run errant into the pejorative world of simulacra. The simulacrum is a populist tool and serves the people. It adapts itself to the individual and becomes personal. It seeks intimacy and can achieve it on the fly. It is an improviser, even a free one. How free? That is contestable. Freedom is always negotiating with what is always resisting it. Freedom struggles in the crucible of the shifting interests of copies, traditions, and peoples' imaginations. Kerouac, through *Visions of Cody*, puts simulacra through their paces.

all the movies we'd ever been in.

—Jack Duluoz, thinking of being with Cody

Benjamin has noted that established technologies exhibit in crude form the qualities of the technologies that supersede them; as they begin to exhaust their functional possibilities, they anticipate their successors. Hence, Dada was painting anticipating film. But I will invert this logic to say that film anticipates the vitality and visual complexity of Kerouac's prose. The advent of the film enhanced visual acuity. The camera led the human eye along to roam the shapes and textures of objects changing in a fluid environment. Through slow and accelerated motion, the film teased the eye's desire to apprehend the depth of objects and the subtleties of their movement and inertness. In short, the film heightened the keenness of things—inanimate things and the animate expressions of bodies.

Movie watching was a primary activity of Kerouac, and it is a primary activity of Jack Duluoz, who makes liberal use of his movie house experience. He favors B movies—the cruder icons, the slickless, less staged, more improvised, and closer to the working-class streets productions of W. C. Fields and the Three Stooges. These low-budget films were like emperors that knew their pants were down. They had no great concern for artifice and concealment of production processes and machinery. Duluoz identifies with moving images and transforms them to his own narrational ends. But even more, B movies informed Kerouac's aversion to artifice. They exemplified one of film's noblest benefits, "that everyone and everything looks what it is" according to the work of the senses. Similarly, Kerouac's prose sought to give: "right there, the vision, what you get, what there is."[8] And "what there is"—no need for contrived drama and special effects—dazzles. Open your senses to Hector's,

the glorious cafeteria of Cody's first New York vision when he arrived in late 1946. But ah the counter! As brilliant as B-way outside! Great rows of it—one vast L-shaped counter—great rows of diced mint jellos in glasses; diced strawberry jellos gleaming red, jellos mixed with peaches and cherries, cherry jellos top't with whipcream, vanilla custards top't with cream; great strawberry shortcakes already sliced in twelve sections, illuminating the center of the L—Huge salads, cottage cheese, pineapple, plums, egg salad, prunes, everything—vast baked apples—tumbling dishes of grapes, pale green and brown—immense pans of cheesecake, of raspberry cream cake, of flaky rich Napoleons, of simple Boston cake, armies of eclairs, of enormously dark chocolate cake (gleaming scatological brown)—of deepdish strudel, of time and the river—of freshly baked powdered cookies—pyramiding glazed desserts made of raspberries, whipcream, lady fingers sticking up—vast sections reserved for the splendors of coffee cakes and Danish crullers—All interspersed with white bottles of rich mad milk—Then the bread bun mountain—Then the serious business, the wild steaming fragrant hot-plate counter—Roast lamb, roast loin of pork, roast sirloin of beef, baked breast of lamb, stuff'd pepper, boiled chicken, stuff'd spring chicken, things to make the poor penniless mouth water—big sections of meat fresh from ovens, and a great knife sitting alongside and the server who daintily lays out portions as thin as paper. The coffee counter, the urns, the cream jet, the steam—But most of all it's that shining glazed sweet counter—showering like heaven—an all-out promise of joy in the great city of kicks.

But I haven't even mentioned the best of all.

He keeps going like this. But it is difficult to imagine that Hector would not have been flattered, or that he could have purchased better copy from advertising experts, or that he could hire a gifted film producer to make a spectacle of his counter more mesmerizing than Kerouac's typed page. Of course Hector would censor the parenthetical and the classist remarks about the penniless watering mouth and the dejected "poor Cody, in front of this in his scuffled-up beat Denver shoes, his literary 'imitation' suit." No Chaplinesque irony permitted (although one could argue here that Kerouac is parodying Chaplin-like irony itself). And lose that line about *kicks:* what, the idea of associating respectable middle-class patrons with hipster decadence, excess, and addiction. The main point, however, is that this prose shrinks the pupil with its light. It fluidly accumulates its effect, growing it delight by delight into a kind of culinary clerestory of abundance. Kerouac is here both modern consumer and artist; any imagined line between the two has blurred. He consumes Hector's spread with his eyes and reproduces it with a typewriter. But his prose is infused with the simulacral effects of film, which enhance ocular attention and open new paths of correspondence among the senses. This passage celebrates the autonomy of the senses and implicitly technologies that amplify them. It celebrates not greed but the consumer/artist's transfiguring power.[9]

If films have helped teach Kerouac to attend closely to the world and its content, the "Joan Rawshanks in the Fog" section of *Visions of Cody* shows that this was not an uncritical attention.[10] It was an attention he turned back on the sophisticated apparatus of the Hollywood film. This vignette presents Duluoz in the mien of a participant-observing journalist or ethnographer watching a film being made in the affluent Russian Hill neighborhood of San Francisco on a cold foggy night. The set is organized around a past-prime female star (apparently Joan Crawford) accomplishing, as directed, three tasks for the camera: she must cry; she must run up a hill; she must fiddle with her keys in a kind of panic before opening the door to a house. Kerouac notes the size of the undertaking and the immensity of resources and human effort concentrated on the task. It's like the scenes of "great airplane disasters or train wrecks." "A thousand eyes" of neighborhood spectators watch the proceedings, but they watch under tightly controlled conditions. Duluoz is especially attentive and involved with the consumer/spectators of the film set. Their watching is as directed as the surrounding automobile traffic (controlled by leased police), the positioning of the klieg lights, and the angle of the camera.

The crowd's movements conform to the needs of the set, which resembles an occupation: "there was no backway out, the audience, the crowd had been . . . surrounded and looped in and forted in by this invading enemy." Authority resides with the young director, a lollipop in his mouth, talismanic for inspiration, which he communicates through an alphabet of commands and gestures to an obedient crew. The director's gestures make physical contact with Joan. He draws her head down by a scarf around her neck to make her listen good, suggesting the convention of maltreatment for stars "on the way out." The director's occupying authority derives from an official arrangement with the property owners described as portly gentlemen—bankers and businessmen who understand the prerogatives of property, here, secured by the police, as they watch the set. Thus the structure of movie-making mirrors the structure of fascism as an efficient, utilitarian schematic of mastery.

The structure is rigid and therefore vulnerable. Vulnerability is reflected in the fact that each take, "a vastly planned action," is repeated three times. It is impossible to forecast what impurities might seep in to corrupt the director's prefabricated idea of the image. Though it strives to be hermetic, the film set is permeable to willful individuality leaking in and out in all directions. The Hollywood film set tends to be inorganic and inflexible. It does not accommodate improvisation. The whole enterprise is deluded. Thinking itself rooted in solid ground, it floats on a volatile chaos. Volatile substance consists in the suppressed anger of technicians who appear as a bent-over proletariat and a hemmed-in, impatient spectator overheard yelling, "I'll be damned if I don't go home *between* scenes!" Duluoz adds that as far as anyone knew, no between-scenes breaks had been scheduled. Yet someone had the "democratic social intelligence" to remind everyone they did not have to stand and freeze. They could leave when they wanted and contumaciously bump the klieg lights on the way out.

The idea of democratic social intelligence develops further. Individuals in the crowd take affirmative and disparate actions. Spectators not engaged in observing the set enact subplots of their own "subsidiary love affairs." The movie house has long been a ritualized space for spectators acting out their own romantic dramas. But here, in the confines of a production set on a cold, foggy night, kliegs watching, gathered people are aware of themselves and each other. Talking and touching is going on. Minds are engaged. Senses open. No iconic dress of the movie theater cues behavior. This suggests that spectators initiate and sanction cinema rituals, just as they spontaneously enjoy one another. They are not an unconscious mass.

Moreover, if the movie theater explicitly designates every spectator a voyeur, spectators designate themselves as critics. One might think that the machinery of a movie set would befuddle and dissuade spectator criticism, but it doesn't. It stimulates it. For example, the chronicler and spectator Duluoz and Mrs. Brown disagree over the leading man. To Duluoz he seems like an empty shell and a meanly fawner. He thinks it would be horrible to be married to such a man. Brown disagrees and imagines that the leading man has many children, loves his wife, and paints her in the backyard under the sun. Teenage girls criticize the leading lady "in loud voices for everyone to hear, that her make-up was very heavy, she'd practically have to stagger under it." Comments like these show that audiences understand that conventions of the movie set are dedicated to the production of takes, that is, lies. Just as they sense varying levels of alienation between themselves and their work, they understand that Hollywood film actors live in a heightened relation of alienation to the *art* they make. This is the heart of the fascination.

Spectators know that Joan is paid to do as directed and to help the camera be convincing about things not her own. They know she weeps tears she otherwise would have saved for other purposes. They notice or speculate discrepancies between cinematic personas and actors' off-camera situations and point them out, be they embarrassing or admirable. They interrogate their entertainment, test it against their experiences, and they are entertained in the doing—aroused. They hone these discerning skills for life. And if they believe a given lie, a given myth, or idea, it is their own—and no martinet production company's—to keep or at the moment of disillusion, discard. From this perspective the Hollywood spectacle is the spectators' objectified servant. Plot, film mechanics and techniques, and actors' shanks are subject to spectators' scrutiny. Thus, Duluoz reflexively and ecstatically concludes, "it isn't that Hollywood has won us with its dreams, it has only enhanced our own wild dreams, we the populace so strange and unknown, so uncalculable, mad, eee . . ." Duluoz is not under Hollywood's spell—its mystifications, its fogs. Rather, Kerouac's pleasure crests as the writerly process leads him to the mystique of the populace where ideology and the symbolic dissolve into virtual if not realized *jouissance*—plentitude of bodily joy. Kerouac's pleasure is the pleasure of his own body evoked as he reads and writes the populace. Yet he implicates spectators in the same pleasure as they, too, make their own meanings from mass-mediated culture. Whether they conform or resist the spectacle's desire, the meanings and the pleasure of making them belong to themselves. Such meanings can be salubrious; they can disavow unhelpful actions and lead to intelligent ones. They can also be dangerous. *Jouissance* vaporizes ideology into undifferentiated space, a space beyond good and evil. As intelligibility returns, however, it may associate mutable pleasure with pathological ideology and reinforce it. Perhaps this is the dreadful moment when certain of the masses validate maniacal voices and follow them.[11]

The regimented production practices of 1950s Hollywood mirror its idea of a fixed singular public. Fixated on formulaic technique, Hollywood sets press technicians into rote tasks of recapitulating cliches—"fufoonery and charaderees," and therefore "the Death of Hollywood is upon us." Kerouac was looking for a film styled after his prose. He was looking for an agile camera unburdened by the universal vision—the pan-vision. The pan-vision worked to the extent that it was embedded in the perspectives and wishes of a dominant, more homogeneous moviegoing public. But after the war, public division and fragmentation into groups increased. Like many of these stratified groups, Kerouac believed Hollywood was manufacturing toxic fogs. By 1960 the studio system had collapsed.

I wish I had ten personalities, one hundred golden brains, far more ports . . . more energy.

—Jack Duluoz, *Visions of Cody*

Multiple visions riddle their way through *Visions of Cody* via the lawlessness of simulacra. One could believe it the result of one hundred brains, each with multiple ports and ample energy. The novel delivers splintering shots to the husks of literary conventions and structures of craft. Narrational experiments convey multiple voices and perspectives that cohere by simulacral association around Cody—the epic hero of an unofficial America. Disparate loric strands intersect and overlay like a Jackson Pollock all-over to give mythic substance to an unlikely hero—the center and unity of the novel.

Cody Pomeray is a hero from the "bottom of the world, where raggedy Codys dream, as rich men plan gleaming plastic auditoriums and soaring glass fronts on Park Avenue." Taking myths to be ciphers and tapping into lore of the Americas, the novel renders Cody a hero on par with "Simon Bolivar [and] Robert E. Lee," the kind of hero "young Whitman" personified and sang about, like "young Melville . . . rough and free." Cody keeps company with the "presence of champions, the Pensacola Kid, Willie Hoppe, Bat Masterson . . . Babe Ruth . . . Old Bull Balloon . . . Jelly Roll Morton . . . Theodore Dreiser." He finds trouble, raising Cain. He finds solace with the Three Stooges.[12]

No metaphor can adequately demonstrate the substance or the significance of what Kerouac has done with the Three Stooges tableau. I believe it an unprecedented treatment of a most ordinary contemporary experience. The narrator Duluoz proceeds to tell the story in an oral fashion as if he were talking around a dinner table or in a night club—perhaps on a stage—or as Kerouac wrote to Cassady on January 8, 1951 about his newly found writing style; it is like "you and I were driving across the old U.S.A. . . . no mysterious readers, no literary demands, nothing but us . . . 'telling eagerly the million things we know.'"[13] He is relaxed and full of spontaneous excitement: a bit of a ham. The story proceeds as a free-style reminiscence of one of the best "jazz tea-high" visions he'd had of Cody.

Briefly, the story begins when he and Cody were walking along a San Francisco sidewalk on a workaday afternoon. It was an afternoon much like afternoons of his childhood on Moody Street in Lowell when Duluoz and his friend G. J. would stagger and bump and knock each other around like the Stooges did on over 200 ten-minute movie shorts.[14] Duluoz cannot remember the name of one of the stooges, "the bushy feathery haired one," but he says Cody can, who as a kid also saw the shorts in countless B movies. That Cody and Duluoz grew up with the images of the Stooges is an important detail. They are kinsmen. Their minds are comprised of similar rudiments. Duluoz narrates a braid of intertwining memories. You can distinguish among the strands, but they are mutually porous and form a single filigree of Duluoz's and Cody's experience. This weave of Cody, Duluoz, and the Stooges associates with plural constituencies. It jumps with "wild tenor cats" in Little Harlem. It mixes with "shuffling audiences of whole Mexican and Arky families" and homeless street dwellers. It contains dreams inspired by Chinese communities across the country. The text returns to the "rewardful" (because after work) afternoon in San Francisco. Cody and Duluoz feel like classical, Homeric heroes—"only American." Chirico-like red brick factory chimneys and Velasquesque shadows haunt the streets in this prose. As they walk, unaccountably Duluoz and Cody begin talking about the Stooges. And suddenly Cody is imitating them: "and he did it wild, crazy, yelling in the sidewalk right there by the arches and by hurrying executives . . . I saw his . . . rosy flushing face exuding heat and joy, his eyes popping in the hard exercise of staggering, his whole frame of clothes capped by those terrible pants with six, seven holes in them and streaked with baby food, come, ice cream, gasoline, ashes—I saw his whole life . . . all the movies we'd ever been in." Three times throughout, like a refrain, Duluoz speculates: "supposing the Three Stooges were real?" As he and Cody walk, he writes, "I saw [the Stooges] materialize on the sidewalk . . . and Cody was with them, laughing and staggering in savage mimicry of them and himself." Cody and Duluoz are fellow stooges on life's streets. Duluoz recalls seeing the Stooges at a B movie in an unfamiliar city "goofing on the screen and in the streets that are the same streets as outside the theater." This is a strange moment. Movie shorts and life experiences mingle as real. This mingling supersedes knowledge that the Stooges are "photographed in Hollywood by serious crews like Joan Rawshanks in the fog" and that "as Cody says, they've been . . . bopping mechanically . . . the style of the blows . . . the symbol and acceptance of them also, as though inured in their souls . . . in their bodies." Cody and Duluoz accept the mechanically executed symbol. In geste they have become simulacra of the Stooges because of Cody's profound imitation. Duluoz explains below,

> I knew that long ago when the mist was raw Cody saw the Three Stooges, maybe he just stood outside a pawnshop, or hardware store, or in that perennial poolhall door but maybe more likely on the pavings of the city under tragic rainy telephone poles, and thought of the Three Stooges, suddenly realizing—that life is strange and the Three Stooges exist—that in 10,000 years—that . . . all the goofs he felt in him were justified in the outside world and he had nothing to reproach himself for, bonk, boing, crash, skittely boom, pow slam, bang, boom, wham, blam, crack, frap, kerplunk, clatter, clap, blap, fap, slap-map, splat, crunch, crowsh, bong, splat, *BONG!*

The medium sends its messages, but audiences, like artists, shape them to useful ends; this is the novel's ethnographic demonstration.

Here Cody's Stooges kick the lid off the trash can that would contain his impetuous charisma. They foil the disdain, shame, and violence of enfranchised classes. Who would have imagined such interpretive power in popular audiences? Kerouac is a consummate audience, therefore, the unfettered power of simulacra infuses his prose.

Enter free jazz. The narrator, Jack Duluoz, knew the New York City jazz scene. He knew the music stores, including Manny's, where hipsters and Symphony Sid hung out, and where Lee Konitz bought reeds for his alto and Arnold Fishkin strung his bass. Duluoz had rarer knowledge. He followed Konitz and Fishkin to a "mystery . . . though I still say it must be a music school," where Konitz and Fishkin sat at the iconic feet of Lenny Tristano.[15] Tristano was a blind musician trained in European musics at the American Conservatory of Music in Chicago. Jazz was his wedge into new musical territory. By 1949—with his students Konitz, Fishkin, Warne Marsh, and Billy Bauer—Tristano had made "Intuition" and "Digression." These are the earliest recordings of what is now called free jazz.

There was a mystique about Tristano because he did not perform much. But his students (excellent musicians) did. Kerouac had important contacts in New York City's jazz world—including Gerald Newman, who recorded evolving jazz in clubs throughout the city (especially Harlem) in the 1940s and 1950s. Kerouac frequently accompanied Newman; they were good friends. Kerouac had an instinctive ear for recognizing little-known musical talent—including Tristano. He introduced his friend and accomplished jazz musician Tom Livornese to Tristano in the 1940s.[16] According to Billy Bauer, Tristano's sextet performed one free piece every evening of an engagement at Birdland.[17] There is a good probability that Kerouac heard Tristano's free pieces in recorded form or perhaps live. Conceivably, they influenced his prose. Regardless, the relative simultaneity of Tristano's free jazz experiments and Kerouac's prose experiment in *Visions of Cody* begs examination.

Some critics suggest that Tristano's approach to free composition resembles the European innovator Anton Webern much more than it resembles Ornette Coleman's.[18] This is wrong. It confuses the concepts of atonality and freedom. Coleman, Tristano, and Webern skirted tonal music, but Webern ranks among the most systematic atonal composers of this century. Tristano played jazz because he was an improviser. Like Ornette Coleman's works, Tristano's free compositions were spontaneously composed, collective improvisations.

It seems that Tristano is often overlooked, in part, because he harbored reservations about bebop. He greatly admired Charlie Parker's playing. They reportedly had a performance date set, but Parker's death intervened. He revered Bud Powell's playing, too, but reacted against the tendency in inexperienced bebop players to run notes together indiscriminately without regard to their place in the structure of the harmony or the solo itself. To foil this he had his students learn solos by Louis Armstrong, Lester Young, and Roy Eldridge. He had them study Bach's pieces, which also feature well-constructed extended single lines. Tristano's influences included Earl Hines, Teddy Wilson, Nat King Cole, Art Buckner, and especially Art Tatum; and he had no interest in obscuring this fact. Unlike many bebop players he did not need a revolution. He was no moldy fig, but he loved the New Orleans–rooted classic jazz. He modernized the polyphonic implications of New Orleans jazz, and Bach's contrapuntal etudes, fugues, and concertos helped him do it. At the same time his music was as harmonically complex as the most challenging bebop. Tristano's music was marginal; it flowed between the cracks of swing, classic jazz, and bebop. For convenience some called it cool jazz. Certainly, he influenced cool players, but unlike some of his students he never identified with the California scene. Critics called him cool because he was not a blues-based player or teacher. He seems to have avoided blues forms and blues-inflected tones as did his student/associate horn players. Moreover, his tunes frequently changed meter, which made it difficult to find a compatible drummer. When he played with drummers, they played light, in part, because it was

embarrassing to be caught playing convincingly in the wrong meter. Consequently, the punch and the heat associated with bluesier,
harder bop could not be heard in his compositions. Cook and Morton say that he wrung jazz dry of emotion. To the contrary, Konitz,
Bauer, Fishkin, Brown, and others say Tristano insisted jazz conform
to the rhythms of feeling. In 1950 Tristano told John S. Wilson in
Down Beat, "it would be useless for me to play something I don't feel.
If I played something that I'd have to impose on myself, I wouldn't be
playing anything good."[19] I am with the latter opinions. Tristano did
not wear his emotion on his forehead. He kept it personal. He was
marginal because his music was sophisticated and often experimental. His constituency was small and not loud enough to be heard during a factional time in jazz history. Oversimplification and dogma
characterize factional times. Tristano's music was too sophisticated
for either.[20]

After recording "Marionette" and "Sax of a Kind" at a session on
May 16, 1949, drummer Denzil Best left the studio to play a gig.
Tristano decided to use the remaining studio time to record some
"experiments" similar to the ones he had conducted with his students at his own studio. They discussed the order of instruments and
ran tape. According to Arnold Fishkin there were four takes but only
"Intuition" and "Digression" survived.[21]

Let us be clear that neither Tristano's recordings nor Kerouac's
novel are equal to improvisation. The recordings and the novel were
made by means of improvisation, but they are products—the result
of processing equipment, selection, editing, naming, packaging, and
marketing. Moreover, there is the caveat that what I am going to say
has always, already been said. Language about freedom is not particularly open or particularly free. Artistic freedom has to do with escaping anything that would describe it. In the absolute sense it has
to do with the realm signified by words and phrases such as *death*
and *nonbeing* or *total being* and *life*—paradox. Improvisation, too,
traffics in various levels of consciousness designated by the same

oxymorons. What improvisation retains by way of form, by way of control, and by way of medium proscribes its freedom. Kerouac's prose unfolded at various levels of improvisation. He sought to write in the way jazz soloists played, which was the way Cody—"this strange angel from the other side . . . of Time"—seemed to live. The idea of free jazz is a theoretical body of knowledge that obscures as much as it illuminates. It can describe a recording. It can guide musicians to freedom's threshold, but it cannot tell us what freedom is like. Musicians, other artists, and audiences may get there, but they cannot speak about it while there. Cody and Duluoz study performing musicians. They sense when a musician is free. They hear and feel "IT." Sometimes improvisers return with improvisation's goal: something new. "Intuition" and *Visions of Cody* are not freedom but freedom's token.[22]

The piano, saxophone, guitar, and bass proscribe musicians' freedom to the extent that musicians are bound to the ideology and technique informing instrumental design and function. Jazz has always challenged the musical technique and theory that crystallized in the Enlightenment. Some experiments in free jazz have set out to subvert and destroy ideologies of music as a means of weakening their extensions into the social structure. Neither Tristano nor Kerouac seems to have had these goals in mind. They absorbed the arts of the past, recombined their usable elements, drew upon their contemporary experience, imagined, improvised, and made an art of the present. As Ray Smith indicates in *Dharma Bums* on the 6 Gallery, he was looking for a renaissance.

With respect to "Intuition" and "Digression," only the order of instruments was predetermined. The recordings show Tristano begins first. On "Intuition," Konitz, Fishkin, Bauer, and then Marsh follow. The same order unfolds on "Digression," except that Bauer precedes Fishkin. The description below will focus on "Intuition" because similar features constitute both compositions. I will describe the piece in detail because I want to convey to the reader how the musician's specific actions reflect their intense focus in the moment and how the tension between competition and cooperation among the players results in the spontaneous expression of multiple voices. The ensemble of multiple voices undermines longstanding practices in which the ensemble and individual players submit to the rules of harmonic progression and instrumental arrangement. Kerouac concerns himself with a similar problem, as I will demonstrate. Just as Tristano and the other players call the compositional voice into question, Kerouac, too, drastically undermines the validity of the controlling narrative voice.

Intuition

Tristano's opening has complete authority and autonomy for twenty-two seconds. Chromatic figures dance around a descending chromatic bass line, which initiates the piece. There is a rest. The right hand swoops up and loops back, halting at a chord that calls a new key. From there, the left hand begins a new descent through sparkling right-hand chromatics. This could be a sophisticated opening for most any standard. By the end of the next measure you know this is no standard. The piece operates across a fluid time scheme and it is harmonically lawless. Unorthodox key changes occur on strange beats and off beats within an odd number of measures. In general, however, the bass and melody (the left and right hand) make tonal shifts together. Each tonal shift is a kind of zone of comprehensible consonance and dissonance—more appropriately, an unstructured blending of the categories. By no means do these zones conform to the diatonic order of major and minor scales.

Tristano is a colorful, fleet fish to watch. But he shares the water with the others, who fall into the music successively to build up a complex graceful anarchy of sound. Each musician is free to initiate or follow a gesture, a direction, or a theme, and all do at various points in the composition, although Tristano seems to have the most influence in the denouement of the piece. Tristano's personality was influential, but his dominance also has to do with the historically determined hierarchy of instruments. As a chordal instrument the piano encourages the subordination of melodic instruments, which, practically speaking, cannot help but convoy along. For this reason Ornette Coleman's *Free Jazz* (1960) sessions excluded the piano. When the players are not initiating their own moves, they are responding to the others' moves. For example, Konitz begins with a chromatic entry into Tristano's harmonic area. Tristano stops his linear movement. He swims in place for a measure in order to accent—on two alternating chords in bebop style—Konitz's fluid acrobatics. Tristano resumes with the laying out of disjunctive chords. His movement has a crablike velocity; it is getting somewhere, but it is a back-and-forth getting there. Every chord takes a different angle that points to an alternate direction the piece could take. Konitz reels off sixteenth-note arpeggios that clash and harmonize with Tristano. Presumably, Konitz follows Tristano by ear. It is possible that Konitz or any of the other players within eyeshot of Tristano's hands visually gauge his harmonic vicinity. Konitz's flourish packs enough forceful dissonance, however, that it is also possible he is trying to take over, which does not happen. After thirty-three seconds Fishkin enters the mix by walking up and down a ladder of half steps. Tristano pauses to enjoy Fishkin's footwork. He alternates the two chords punched earlier while Konitz takes another round of arpeggios. Konitz's arpeggios transmute into a movement of slow sustained notes as Bauer speeds through his own arpeggiated entry. The composition is now a dense polyphony of Bauer's sixteenth notes, punchy bass, legato saxophone, and slow, low-end piano melody. There is no way of knowing what will happen next. Tensions vibrate through the bizarre movements of the several loosed voices.

Bauer, who also commands a chordal instrument, makes a startling and influential move against all of the countervailing currents except Tristano's ascending chromatic bass line. Bauer simultaneously joins and alters Tristano's ascent in two ways. First, he deploys three different chords over the bass line in three successive staccato ascents of three half steps. In rhythmic terms he imposes three sets of triplets over Tristano's rising legato quarter notes. Second, he extends the third triplet by two half steps. The fifth step becomes the crescendo of the piece. Bauer has the foreground. From here he initiates a descent of warped waltz-time arpeggios. Tristano, impressively, is with him; right-hand chromatics flutter around Bauer's slow-motion chaos of spin-falling figures. Tristano's bass line revolves around Bauer's descent like a dizzy shark. Konitz pauses. Listening, he seems to consider his next move. Fishkin is back on his ladder adding low-end coloration. Indeed, though Fishkin's playing is reserved by later standards, he has crossed a threshold. He has overthrown the bass's bondage to time. Here, like the other instruments, the bass contributes melody and color. Fishkin does not keep the pulse, he intuits it.

Sixty-five seconds have transpired. From here all of the players collude to arpeggiate individually through various tonal zones, although no two players are in unison. Each player regulates his own alterations of speed, timing, and syncopation. Marsh enters during this section of the piece. He moves slowly through the chords. The distinctive tone of the tenor saxophone cuts through. There is a fugue-like quality to the piece. At one point the ensemble follows Konitz's bizarre counterpoint of rising and falling intervals. His is a subtle, seamless, yet still dramatic move that changes the entire sound-scape. Like Bauer earlier, Konitz fertilizes a small seed planted by Tristano, which, apart from Tristano's intentions, grows into a lush patch of sound.

Extending for two minutes and twenty-five seconds, "Intuition" packs complexity. It is an experiment. There are moments of uncertainty. Various players hesitate. At points they look for leadership. At other times they vie for it. The melodic players compete with harmony's hegemony. The ambivalent tension between harmony and melody is a cord that free jazz later cut. The players seek independence from the piano but more than not end up deferring to its suggestions, as objects yield to gravity. Nevertheless, the piece is remarkable. It demands the players' maximum attention, agility, and quickness. It permits invention. Each musician is free to compete with and challenge ingrained restraints, and they do, some more than others. Thus, the piece is an open forum. Rules suspended, the musical field is level. Theoretical and practical musical relationships are open and vulnerable to challenge and change. Whatever a player's individuality, it is accepted. Here, multiple perspectives congenially mingle.

If "Intuition" reveals and undermines the constraints of common forms and prescribed instrumental roles, similarly, *Visions of Cody* tests and finds wanting conventions of narrative voice. The singular narrative voice is shown to be a restrictive device and is undermined throughout the text through parody, ellipses, and word stoppages at mid-syllable, through abrupt shifts of perspective and subject matter, sudden insertions of Dadaesque drawings, and through the free-associational technique, which reveals the activity of the mind itself as a multiplicity of voices. These multiplicities constantly intrude upon the writer's attempt to articulate a world in much the same way that unorthodoxies intrude upon musical conventions in "Intuition." Rather than suppress them, the musicians and Kerouac insist on their value.

Kerouac believed jazz provided the best model for realizing the benefits of spontaneous intelligence. Jazz ensembles successfully negotiated tensions of tradition and invention, cooperation and competition, community and individuality. Jazz performance realized the expression of multiple voices and perspectives. Even a single bebop soloist seemed to approach the musical subject from a variety of perspectives—as Kerouac put it, "from every angle." So diverse and vast were the strains of jazz that a talent like Lester Young could synecdochically become "the greatness of America in a single negro musician." Whether or not Kerouac heard "Intuition," the parallels with his prose are too precise to ignore. Through spontaneous improvisation, Tristano's experiments extended the implications of bebop's and other jazz styles' vast multiple reserves. The license of simulacra allows Kerouac's text to follow jazz's patterns; the text builds up a complex web of intersecting and overlapping materials in the constitution of its Cody—its America.[23]

I noted earlier that *Visions of Cody* marks a postwar proliferation of simulacra that permits, even encourages unprecedented crossings of aesthetic boundaries. Kerouac has studied the technologies of image making. We have seen how his prose (and its consumer audiences) transfigures images' effects and meanings. *Visions of Cody* responds to the culture's growing maelstrom of competing claims of shifting signs. The novel also attends to images that mainstream presses, advertisers, broadcasters, and Hollywood neglect. In the "Frisco: The Tape" section, Kerouac uses the mechanical reproduction capability of the tape recorder to assist and supplement his attention and to experimentally question the very act and substance of narration.

Unable to post one hundred attentive brains around the West End Bar, frustrated by futile attempts to take in all of the action, Duluoz parenthetically confesses, "(I can't think fast enough) (do need a recorder, *will* buy one at once)." When he arrived in San Francisco in December, 1951, Kerouac recorded five days of activity at Evelyn's (Neal Cassady's wife, Carolyn's) and Cody's (Neal Cassady's) apartment. The tapes became more than a simple mnemonic device. The "Frisco: The Tape" section mirrors and perhaps exaggerates the unstable and circumscribed process of narration. The transcripts capture monologues, streams of thought, and conversations about Bull Hubbard (William Burroughs); jazz artists such as Billie Holiday, Chu Berry, Coleman Hawkins; Irwin Garden's (Allen Ginsberg's) failed plans for romance with Cody in an improvised bed that collapsed at Bull's marijuana farm in Texas; the problems of writing and police harassment. But they also record breakdowns in conversations, the unreliability of memory, unpredictable shifts of thought, sudden insights, interruptions, and intrusions endemic to the narrational process. These transcripts displace the writer in order to show the artifice of narrative. They attempt to render a more authentic record of life by exposing narrative's fragmented, haphazard processes.[24]

Just as "Intuition" is not free of longstanding musical biases, the tape section in *Visions of Cody* is not free of narrational controls. In direct and oblique ways Kerouac supplements what would otherwise be a transcript of decontextualized, disembodied voices. He tells us where the recordings take place and who is speaking (he changes the names to be consistent with the novel). He points out other limits of the technology by noting when the tape runs out or the equipment breaks down. The transcript includes many parenthetical additions that describe significant contextual matters as well as characters' actions, gestures, and mannerisms. For example, Duluoz and Cody frequently discuss transcripts of previous nights' recordings: "([Cody] pointing to words on manuscript)" (144). These occasions become platforms for elaboration, confirmation, or contradiction of previously discussed topics. During a party, the recorder running, the transcript notes, "(Cody dancing to classical music)" (147).

Though he is not explicit about it, Kerouac does have an agenda for the content of the recordings. He directly influences the trajectory of the taped dialogues through his questions and comments. He also selects the tape footage to be used and determines its placement in the text. Clearly, Kerouac seeks a way of capturing Cody's inspired speech, which he constructs in the other sections of *Visions of Cody*, and which became part of the legend of Dean Moriarty (Neal Cassady) in *On the Road* (1957). Ritual conversational props are on hand: jazz, alcohol, marijuana, and Benzedrine. On the third night (other nights, too, but less so), they blow on flutes and piccolos between turns at speaking (151–170). The purpose of all of this is to facilitate the release of rhythms of thought and speech. The results are uneven. Cody is self-conscious in the presence of the tape recorder (138); in addition, Kerouac is trying to call up Cody's specific memories of his father, Old Cody; Bull Hubbard and June (Burroughs's wife, Joan Vollmer); Irwin Garden; and Huck (Herbert Huncke). Kerouac's interest in specific topics may interfere with free-floating speech. Perhaps, too, the drugs are not helpful. Cody expresses considerable frustration in not being able to recall or articulate his thoughts spontaneously and clearly (129–135). The fact that Kerouac includes large sections of tediously fragmented and at times offensive transcript substantiates his commitment to a kind of ethnographic authenticity and the ethic of spontaneity, come what may.[25]

The placement of the "Frisco: The Tape" section is telling. It follows Section 2 of the novel, which consists of highly charged, limpid prose much in the vein of *Town and the City* (1950). Section 2 imagines Cody's childhood. He prefers living with his vagrant, wine-loving father to the securities of domesticated in-laws. As a boy Cody impressed young men such as Slim Buckle and Tom Watson, who taught Cody pool and gave him some fatherly guidance. We see the development of Cody's precocious auto didacticism, athleticism, his car-driving ability, and his charisma. He moves from small-town boy to urban man. All of this occurs against the symbolic backdrop of neon light and red brick, which indicate the modern urban emotional spectrum—the "center of the grief and . . . ecstasy" (87). Substantial portions of the fourth night's transcript concern this period (170–181). On the fourth night's transcript, Cody and Duluoz discuss Old Cody's job at a Denver barbershop, his Model T that he drove well into the 1930s, his wine drinking, and his itinerant movement from flop house to flop house. Cody and Duluoz discuss the moment when Cody began to consider poets more significant than philosophers. The content of the transcript reflects Kerouac's desire to confirm concrete details about Cody's childhood and to learn new ones. Cody seems dispassionate as he speaks of these matters.

Repeatedly rehashing the past is no kick. In contrast, the prose of Section 2, infused by Cody's heroic qualities, kicks (47–92). The relationship between Section 2 and the tapes helps crystallize the relationship between conventional writing and its subject matter. The former turns memories' ambiguous emotions and images into a compelling streamlined contrivance of contextualized emotions, syntactical rhythm, and symbology.

Memories are not crystal. The transcript shows Cody and Duluoz scrutinizing a letter from Cody's father. They critique the letter's imprecision, but their own scrutiny seems unreliable. Cody admits that he and his father rarely agree on matters of the past. For example, Old Cody believes he and his then twelve-year-old son traveled 14,000 miles crisscrossing the country in boxcars. Cody insists the distance was closer to 1,400 miles when he was just six years old (172–173). Troubled by this and moved by the letter's sense of loneliness, Cody and Duluoz formulate a plan to bring Old Cody to San Francisco. The plan has two benefits. One, Cody's father will be in the salubrious company of family and grandkids. And two, Cody and his father can compare memories, which will enlarge the material available for Duluoz's narrative purposes.

Thus the "Frisco: The Tape" section is a fascinating experiment that uses the mechanical device of the tape recorder to reveal in all of its nakedness the mechanical artifice of narration. It explodes its pretense to seamlessness and objective truth. The tapes prove useful mnemonically. Along with the tedious, fragmented, ambiguous, and offensive sections, they include intelligent and entertaining moments of extended speech. Yet the tape section, as spontaneous and unedited as it is, is subject to narrational conventions. It demonstrates the threshold between meaning and nonmeaning—comprehensible narrative form and incomprehensible formlessness. Kerouac uses the device of mechanical reproduction in order to capture unadulterated forms of speech and life. He is compelled to narrativize and impose form on it, however, a gesture that correlates with the postmodernists' retrospective feeling that by the middle of the twentieth century there are no longer any grounds—authentic realities—only texts. But Kerouac also contradicts the postmodernists. He returns the origins of the simulacral break to its evolution from speech, to the beginning of writing itself. There never were any grounds, only simulations. Long before poststructuralism, *Visions of Cody* interrogates the institution of writing itself. It exposes its wont to define and contain—to rule.

Kerouac does not conclude his novel with "Frisco: The Tape." He preceded "The Tape" with the sketches of Section 1 and the conventional prose of Section 2 about Cody's childhood and adolescence. He follows it with "Imitation of the Tape"—a timely addition and an early marker of a cultural moment comprised of accumulating levels of simulation. Having starkly reduced writing to its rudiments in speech and syntax with "The Tape," Kerouac revels in the liberty of his "Imitation" (249–398): his response to the tyrannies of narrative convention. This section includes the "Joan Rawshanks in the Fog" and "Three Stooges" vignettes. It is filled with references and alternate accounts—pastiche and parody of W. C. Fields's B movies; comics; A. P. Hill's U.P. news reports; dream, marijuana, peyote, and road trips; radio programs such as *Gangbusters* and *Dragnet;* mythic lore of Doc Holliday and the Hurricane of 1938; historical constructs of the U.S. Civil War and the Boer and Spanish Wars; literary masters such as Homer, Shakespeare, Melville, Proust, Joyce, Hemingway, Duluoz's own writings (including grade school compositions), and the tape dialogues.

Kerouac supplements these alternate accounts with replications of the form of the transcripts but not the precise content. He tests his ability to create the inflections and grooves of natural conversation and speech, which he hears as uncalculated and immediate. Unlike high critics, however, he does not disparage such speech, especially when it sounds ridiculous. Below, dialogical play flouts high critical smugness.

Jack: Nicholas Breton—a brief poem—not too well known—this is my tale and descantation hear you now, I dedicate to you . . . Nicholas Breton was a deafmute too, because of the couched meanings, and so, a neighbor relative of Cowens . . . in old Dervishoor. Thyme?

Cody: Well said lad—figuratif, dedicatee, dove

Jack: Roaned, spavined, lorned, de-horned, hoof and Mouthed

Cody: Leaking, drooly, bloody, follypolly, wounded

Jack: Made to wring the meaning, made to roam the void Made to sing demeanors to the meeters of the

Cody: You mean this is the pit of night, the moonsaw?

Jack: The moonsaw's come, the rainy night is milk, red eyes sea,

Cody: Can't decide? Have no bones? Ick up stone? Or stick an own?

Jack: Crick alone, turtle dove alone, moan alone, pose alone.

Cody: Nonsense be, as nonsense was; or nonsense is a trapeze

Jack: Nay a hole beneath it . . . upon the void afloat (310)

Spontaneous speech, even incomprehensible speech, is freer speech. If you cannot dissolve structures of narrative and language, you can, at the least, mix and personalize the codes. This is an essential human activity to be celebrated. Some of Kerouac's imitation dialogues are private, but they evoke the defiant pleasures and warm, rhythmic vocalisms of shared community that concludes the earlier "Frisco: The Tape"—the paragon of the quality of community he is after:

(TAPE CONTINUES WITH COLORED REVIVAL MEETING ON RADIO)

Preacher: (*Screeching*) WE KNOW HOW TO PRAY!

People: PRAY!

Preacher: MEANWHILE HE TOOK CHANCE ABOUT JE-SUS ONE DAY

People: OH OH!
A voice: BLEST IS THE LORD, WUNNERFUL!!
Preacher: AFTER AWHILE THEY KEPT UP ON PRAYIN
People: YEAH!! . . .
Preacher: JEEEE-EE!
People: JEE-EE!
Preacher: ZUS!! I SAID AFTER WHILE!!
People: AFTER WHILE!!!
Preacher: JEE-SAS!
Women: JEE-SAS!
Preacher: I WALK IN THERE—
People: I WALK IN THERE!
Preacher: I WILL!!
People: I WILL!!
Preacher: I HEARD THE WAY HE WORKS—
People: OH-OOO!
Preacher: AFTER AWHILE HE *TOLD* HIM!!
  CRASH! BOAA!
Preacher: —AND WHILE HE TOLD—
People: YEAH. HEAH!!
Preacher: —SIGHT!—
People: YES!!
Preacher: I HEEEARD—I HEEEEEEEEEERD—I HEERD A MAN MAY
  DO WORKS
People: MOTHER!
  MOTHER!
Preacher: I GOT MY SURANCE!
  BUT THEY CAN'T DO IT!—
  I HEEEEEEEEEEEEEEEEERD! (246–247)

For Kerouac, the *jouissance* of community—whether a tight jazz ensemble or a freewheeling religious service—evokes his feeling for a *jouissance* of text.

Finally, pushed by the momentum of all that precedes it, the "Imitation" section revises conclusions about Cody in *On the Road*. *On the Road* was fast-picaresque, a now enduringly vital, but ultimately conventional work—"just a horizontal account of travels on the road," wrote Kerouac. He continues to say that *Visions of Cody* adds a "vertical" dimension to the "study of Cody's character and its relationship to . . . 'America.'"[26] Verticality is the operative mode of simulation. It permits the buildup of strange resemblances and of the crisscrossing identifications infusing the remarkable action of Cody's life. The horizontal trajectory of Dean Moriarty's life in *On the Road* burned "like fabulous yellow roman candles exploding like spiders across the stars," then vapored out (8). *On the Road* leaves Moriarty returning to the ruins of his domestic life in a "ragged . . . motheaten overcoat," carless, alone on the street, his image shrinking through the rear window of a Cadillac (309). When Sal Paradise (Jack Duluoz in *Visions of Cody*) looked westward, he saw a sentimental, nearly pathetic image of Moriarty. His future consisted in "the forlorn rags of growing old" (310). To everyone but Sal Paradise, Moriarty was a beat, nowhere good riddance. Paradise, his friend Remi Boncoeur, and their girlfriends were going to an Ellington concert and Moriarty's destination, Fortieth Street, was in their direct path (308–309). Boncoeur would not even allow Moriarty in his Cadillac. In contrast, in *Visions of Cody* Duluoz writes, "I see Cody's face occupying the West Coast like a big cloud"—not a loser but a hero, a "King" (342, 398). Cody inspires an unofficial mythic present because he conveys a diversity of vernacular performance and identity. He also inspires Kerouac's spontaneous or free prose, his method.

On December 23, 1950 Cassady sent Kerouac a 13,000-word letter telling the story of "Christmas of 1946 Denver." It was to be part of the autobiographical novel Ginsberg and Kerouac had been encouraging Cassady to write. Most of the letter was lost, but City Lights published part of it in *The First Third* (1971). Though Cassady did not think the letter important, Kerouac responded three days later,

"I thought it ranked among the best things ever written in America. You gather together all the best styles . . . Joyce, Celine, Dosty & Proust." Unlike the spare Hemingway and the selective, lyrical Fitzgerald, Cassady "hides nothing; the material is painfully necessary . . . the exact stuff upon which American Lit is still to be founded." It was "kickwriting . . . what kicks you and keeps you overtime awake."[27] It also included the mundane stuff of life most novelists avoid. "Don't undervalue your poolhall musings, your excruciating details about streets, appointment times, hotel rooms, bar locations, window measurements, smells, heights of trees." High modernism disparaged the contents of Cassady's life. Kerouac turned it into fast metaphysical contemplation.[28] The letter confirmed the trajectory of Kerouac's literary instincts. It transformed his lingering stylistic ambivalence and confusion into fierce commitment. Less than a year later, on October 9, 1951, while he was writing *Visions of Cody*, Kerouac wrote Cassady to say, "from now on just call me Lee Konitz."[29] Cassady pushed Kerouac across the threshold. Jazz had transformed the mumbo jumbo of its diverse rudiments into a new art of the Americas. Kerouac forged the literary counterpart. His writing was a simulacrum of jazz.

Jazz conveyed the cultural resources of the Americas. Not even the mythic metaphor of the Mississippi River could contain the sources of this "conglomerating music of the world" (329). Drawing toward the end of his novel, Kerouac presents Lester Young, among jazz's most skillful, inventive, and sensitive musicians, as the epitome of America's creative energy:

The greatness of America in a single negro musician—Lester is just like the river, the river starts in near Butte, Montana in frozen snow caps (Three Forks) and meanders on down across states and entire territorial areas of dun bleak land with hawthorn crackling in the sleet, picks up rivers at Bismarck, Omaha and St. Louis just north, another at kay-ro, another in Arkansas,

Tennessee, comes deluging on New Orleans with muddy news
from the land and roar of subterranean excitement that is like
the vibration of the entire land sucked of its gut in mad midnight, fevered, hot, the big mudhole rank clawpole old frogular
pawed-soul titanic Mississippi from the North, full of wires,
cold wood and horn.

Lester blows . . . and now Americans from coast to coast go
mad (392–393).

"What?" Duluoz asks rhetorically. "This had no effect on Cody?"
(393). Let the alluvial metaphor for the transmission of culture displace the later rhizomic one.[30] To know one's cultural resources, "this
is the mark of the hip generation" (393). Cassady lived out the implications of these resources. Kerouac, through *Visions of Cody*, gave
them voice through the manifold associations of a single epiphanic
insight he had in Mexico: "I saw him with eyes of fire or on fire and
saw everything not only about him but America, all of America"
(297). The vision sounds overblown, but the text excavates the shaping power of vernacular lore whose roots extend into eras long before
the colonial invasion. For Kerouac's Duluoz, who on the surface is
enchanted with Mexican kicks, excluded history matters. He believes
himself a citizen of a borderless America: from the "race of the Iro-
quois pushed out of every place in the western hemisphere" (333).
He sketches a dream he had in a baggage car: "America's last hope.
Bring on the Mexican heroes. I am the blood brother of a Negro
Hero. Saved! And so all of the fellows are workers . . . The workers
have become so intelligent. (Tony the Mex, I know him well . . . I'm
a reporter for United Press. But he loves me; I don't have to be U.P.)"
(367). The dreamer knows that like a journalist or an ethnographer,
he is an outsider. Yet, press pass or not, he is accepted in communities of labor and color. Kerouac's romanticism makes the point that
America's excluded voices comprise its spine, its heart, and its
best art.

The visions of the novel do not amount to a one-sided romanticism, however. Dionysian energies exact as much destruction as they permit creativity. That Bull Hubbard (William Burroughs) put a bullet through the head of his wife for kicks is an indelible memory in the minds of Cody and Duluoz, and the horror of the event is accented by their own misogyny. Both Cody and Duluoz let their passions overrule their commitments to women, wives, and children. Cody is a virtuoso thief—on at least one occasion as maniacal as Ahab. His ability to lift automobiles is matched perhaps only by Charlie Parker's ability to move through chord changes (364–371). The escape motif, via road trips, art, sex, tea, Benzedrine, or junk, lingers like fog over the streets where Cody and his coterie gather, but this should not obscure other meanings. Cody and company are in solidarity with other outsiders surveyed in the book, including the American Indians, African Americans, and vagrant families on the road reminiscent of Steinbeck's fictional Joads, not to mention street folk passing their days in U.S. cities and small towns. Some of the street folk have frozen personalities, some are eccentric or insane, and some of them are children (Cody was one of them). All of them are alone.

These are not America's sinners, however, but symptoms: "The sins of America are precisely that the streets . . . are empty where their houses are, there's no sense of neighborhood anymore, a neighborhood quarter or a neighborhood freeforall fight between two streets of young husbands is no longer possible . . . Beyond this old honesty there can only be thieves" (261). The narrator identifies early a central issue of the postwar years—the effects of an exploding consumer culture that encourages people to know themselves through their nonessentials. For all of the resourcefulness and independence Kerouac saw in common folk, he also saw the potential for decadence in a society where people are too busy with work, consumption, and personal security to mix with each other, particularly those different from themselves. Shoppers have paranoid visions; they mistrust strangers, the poor, and nonconformists and learn to script them as thieves, nuts, molesters, dope fiends, indolents, Communists, and later beatniks. Consumer culture advertises the streamlined American dream, but the escapist veneer of Kerouac's prose exposes the dream as a destructive cycle of mass addiction that threatens to annihilate individuals' genuine participation in life. The American dream is an unstable illusion. The novel celebrates a fragmented and plural society that is comprised in as many dreams and visions as there are individuals. On October 6, 1950, Kerouac wrote Cassady in the tone of a pundit: "The modern young writer is now faced with the problem of many voices in America."[31] Such is the vertical knowledge building up the very structure of *Visions of Cody*.

Many postmodern critics (and other kinds of critics) have followed in Kerouac's wake without acknowledging that he commanded a boat that could even float. *Visions of Cody* demonstrates the urgency of the question of how the novelist or writer can speak for multiple voices. Having realized that their authority straddles tenuous assumptions—subjectivity and objectivity, truth, purity, science—even the most precise kinds of writers now think about the question Kerouac raises. Writers of cultural studies (this one included), ethnomusicology, and ethnography now pay more attention to how the strategies of their craft may cast shadows over the realities they seek to discover. In his introduction to the important essays in Writing Culture: The Poetics and Politics of Ethnography (1986), James Clifford says "writing and reading of ethnography are overdetermined by forces ultimately beyond the control of either an author or an interpretive community. These contingencies—of language, rhetoric, power, and history—must now be openly confronted in the process of writing."

Clifford goes on to narrow the line between poetry and prose and ethnography. "'Poetry' is not limited to romantic or modernist subjectivism: it can be historical, precise, objective . . . it is just as conventional, and institutionally determined as 'prose.' Ethnography is hybrid textual activity: it traverses genres and disciplines." Clifford concludes by saying that the essays he is introducing do not claim that ethnography—and by implication cultural studies—is "'only literature,'" but that the essays themselves insist "it is always writing." Through the "Frisco: The Tape" section and the "Imitation of the Tape" section in *Visions of Cody* Kerouac exposes the determinants of writing and reveals its processes. He throws all of Clifford's contingencies—language, rhetoric, power, and history—into the mix. He emerges with a romanticized, pluralistic America, but he is remarkably transparent about how he got there.[32]

Visions of Cody ultimately celebrates the health of the culture—eats it for breakfast. Instead of measuring the boom in babies, the novel gauges and exploits the postwar boom in simulations and their mediating technologies. The freewheeling ethic of simulation permits the novel to mingle aesthetic ideals with vernacular ones. Vernacular intruders rearrange the furniture of revered domains of Homer, Shakespeare, Joyce, and Proust—"my remembrances . . . written on the run instead of afterward in a sick bed."[33] Kerouac's populism issues passports to disdained places such as indigent Mexican towns, hustling streets, train station restrooms, red-light districts, jazz jam sessions, and peyote vacations. It enlists the tape recorder to help authenticate in ethnographic fashion the novel's subjects, only to transmute them through liberated imitation. Penciled sketches take on the sumptuous movement of cinematic ones. The diverse resources of jazz help shape the form of *Visions of Cody*—its method and pluralism. Though blotted with culturally entrenched racialisms, the novel portends and unequivocally celebrates the African Americanization of U.S. culture, the Americas, and the world. Kerouac inscribes the dawn of a future when simulational technologies will help expand the near invisible stylistic influence of an oppressed minority into the look, sound, and movement of a far-flung popular culture.[34] Convinced of vernacular intelligence, *Visions of Cody* shows how audiences study the whirl of shifting signs hurled at them, make distinctions, personalize and use them well, like artists. It brooks no space for passivity and complacency, and suggests there is little time for being a victim. Unlike Dean Moriarty in *On the Road,* the novel coronates the protagonist Cody Pomeray as "King" because he is an agent for neglected cultural energies that matter. weiss and Kaufman were such agents; they emerged from the socio-economic and cultural shadows that Kerouac could only visit through the simulacral layers of B movies and his own vagabond travels as a chronicler and a dreamer of Cody's vernacular triumphs. Kaufman's vernacular, too, triumphs, but he negates narrative visions. weiss also shatters narrative surfaces like glass. She sets the broken pieces afloat in ineffable spaces. Ginsberg and Ferlinghetti combined their own narrative voices and made them accessible through free association, satire, shock, and rhythm. They took poems and personality to the market place, which travestied and caricatured both but lured audiences and changed the culture. Ferlinghetti and Ginsberg became market place savants and entrepreneurs for new voices. They helped fulfill what Kerouac's *Visions of Cody* forecasted, namely that vernacular culture would triumph through its adoption of postwar capitalism's premier means of signification: simulacra. Questions of multi-national capitalism's sustainability in abeyance, *Visions of Cody* is one of the most optimistic, serious works of its century.

5

HOWL OF LOVE

In Chapter 1 I described how the public surface of "Howl," its effective, sensational pitch, radiated fanfare and was a magnet for pillory. I suggested that the myth of the first reading of "Howl" at the 6 *Gallery* obtained its enduring charisma from radical social and political energies emanating from the bebop jazz scene in Harlem in the early 1940s. The first section of this chapter will expand the subject of Ginsberg's politics in *Howl and Other Poems*. Especially, I will show how not only jazz but other creative and insubordinate vernacular experience—such as association with avant-gardist friends, local Communist politics, hip urban street life, personal mysticism, and what might be called an affirmative culture of madness and the insane—helped chart the poems' political selflessness. The second section of the chapter explores *Howl* and the jazz of John Coltrane from 1955–1964 and how correlations of substance and style in the works of the two artists culminate in a shared politics in *Howl* and *A Love Supreme* (1964); it is a politics unattached to dualities and therefore untethered to dogmas. Yet it interfaces all stories, feels life's conditions, and understands life's stakes. This politics does not pit one against the other. It does not exploit differences but cheers them. It does not exclude, withhold, or deny; it validates the common interest. Its pluralism is immanent, tough, and generous over ensuing years. It is a politics of love.

We have seen that the rising edge of a new vernacular lore cycle informed the contents and styles of popular culture in the 1950s. Intriguingly, these vernacular styles perform in ways akin to Deleuze's and Guattari's view of desire, theorized not as an oppositional lack but as productive, creative, and uncoded—always a free-flowing movement of plenty that in every direction seeks to associate, mix, and connect.[1] The working principle of this chapter is that from 1950–1965 desire wore style for clothes. In Ginsberg and Coltrane style is not mere pastiche. Like Deleuze's and Guattari's desire, its productivity out-maneuvers rigidities. It can destroy them, but more often it makes them supple and puts them to use. Such an entity, be it desiring force or style, is unavoidably political. In *Howl* and *A Love Supreme*, style is a special kind of knowledge that partakes of vernacular sources and the spectacle. It dazzles and shocks and critiques just as it gives. These qualities constitute the works' "line of flight"; their radical politics of love is a salubrious weapon embedded in the style of both works.[2]

Acquainted with Madness

Allen Ginsberg planned to be a labor lawyer when he entered Columbia University in 1943. His mother Naomi Ginsberg had groomed him for the vocation. She was a supporter of the Communist Party U.S.A. and took him to party cell meetings. Later, she would become sympathetic to Trotsky. At the meetings, Allen Ginsberg acquired knowledge of and passion for class struggle and social justice. His father had also been sympathetic to labor and justice issues but not to Stalin. Louis Ginsberg was a Socialist. The relationship between Communists and Socialists in the United States, despite times of tenuous cooperation during the Popular Front years, has been fraught with mistrust expressed through harsh rhetoric. The Communists accused the Socialists of being bourgeois and the Socialists accused the Communists of being Stalin's toadies.[3] Political conflicts certainly complicated the Ginsbergs' marriage. Early in the marriage, however, they seemed to accommodate each other's ideological differences with perspective and affection. Sadly, these differences would become moot.

In 1929 Naomi Ginsberg had her first serious psychological breakdown, which would recur often. She was institutionalized during much of her life and during most of her son's adolescence. Still, Allen witnessed many of her breakdowns, which were poorly timed and lacked respect for the sensitive nature of a child. Terrible images of her suffering remained with her son. He memorialized them in the poem "Kaddish," which he worked on from 1957 to 1959.[4] The poem was a tribute to his mother after her death in 1956, but it brooked no platitudes in its confrontation with the painful past. The poem is filled with the guilt, fear, and confusion of everyday life with Naomi. Her raging paranoia was juxtaposed with her kindly affection, mandolin playing, tragic idealism, and love of freedom.

Ginsberg's concern with madness came to the fore before he wrote "Kaddish." "Howl" was in large part dedicated to the subject. The poem was written as a gift to Carl Solomon, whom Ginsberg met during his own eight-month stint in 1949 at the Columbia Presbyterian Psychiatric Institute. The third section of the poem exclusively addresses Solomon.[5] This autobiographical history is a useful frame for looking at Ginsberg's choice of vocation and the spectacular language and passion he brought to it. Ginsberg, the poet, did not see madness in a way that conformed to its accepted history. For example, madness was not medieval surrender to or possession by the devil. Nor was it simply antireason or separation from reason, and therefore an assault on the rational faculties and civil society—in short, criminal, as eighteenth-century scientists and philosophers had couched the term. Nor was Ginsberg's madness what it was for Goya in the nineteenth century and Grosz during the early part of the twentieth; for them, madness opposes the world and holds it culpable.[6] Ginsberg's madness was not a condition but a process, deportment, and knowledge—a style. Madness meant possible destruction, yes, but it was also a freedom ride—"my queer shoulder to the wheel"—through the psychic colonies staked out by powerful institutions and social habit.[7]

Ginsberg made connections with the vernacular streets he hyped, where much more was happening than the television set showed. "Howl" unfurled a collage of vernacular, if spiritualized action. Its multiplied densities included hip angels and the warped musical wheels of the shopping-cart homeless; Communists protesting nicotine fogs of capitalism; the addicted, cruising black American streets "for an angry fix," anarchists voting for infinity; hot jazz musicians blowing America's raw mind of love; and promiscuous heterosexual males sweetening a million vaginas at dusk. There's more: poverty meditating on jazz and road-demons of cars and motorcycles traveling to the speedway crucifixion; Dadaists throwing eggs, demanding their brains be disconnected; hydrogen bomb protesters riding psychedelic airplanes among the intellectuals of war; boxcar vagabonds rattling across snow in the patriarchal night; visionaries who drove across the country in seventy-two hours on a rumor that someone, anyone, had a vision; zealous jazz fans who believed the holy "bop apocalypse!"; promiscuous homosexuals rammed up the ass by hallowed motorcyclists; inspired poets out to remake the impoverished prose of Homo sapiens. All of these modes of conduct from the streets, difficult to commodify, swarmed fabulously together on Ginsberg's page, just as they teemed through the night and underground of the country. *Howl and Other Poems* traced their lines from obscure corners, invisible territories, and ghettos in order to implicate the United States in a new reality; madness was in the house. Throughout this work mad vernacular styles claim the country.

America I've given you all and now I'm nothing.

—Allen Ginsberg, "America"

It is useful to distill selves down to two core emotions: (1) when puffed up, pride; (2) when beat, pity. It is not typical of the former to permit desire's release. New art, new social relations, and new politics make few friends of personalities or nations—specifically, the poem speaks to "America"—clogged with pride. The poem's voice enjoys unrewarded self-pity for the first six of the poem's eighty lines: long enough to open up. Then by way of instantaneous, wily artifice, it adopts the pose of the seducer's tease: America, "when will you take off your clothes?" Self-pity approaches emotional nudity. Ginsberg sheds his pity and runs naked as a child through the jazz ghetto in "Howl." In "America," he is naked and passing out flowerpots, marijuana, and sunshine to the inhabitants of twenty-five thousand asylums, to prisoners in prisons, and other underprivileged. Multiple associations of ill repute inform the substance of his then-unpublishable literature. Nevertheless, Ginsberg peddles his strophes. One strophe for the price of one Ford car and two strophes for two. Ginsberg is a factory of strophes looking for a mostly young, underserved, nearly invisible mass-consumer market. The poem "America" does not stop with the insubordinate, vernacular present, however; it also mixes with a vernacular, political past.

America free Tom Mooney
America save the Spanish Loyalists
America Sacco and Vanzetti must not die
America I am the Scottsboro boys.

In the lines above, "America" pulls up history by the roots and assembles traces of its radical positions and actions. Three controversial imperatives build up to the contemporaneous, 1950s indicative style of shocking identity: "I am the Scottsboro boys." The poem's historical traces are not abstract. They are the elements of personal biography: "America when I was seven momma took me to Communist Cell meetings . . . the speeches were free everybody was angelic and sentimental about the workers it was all so sincere you have no idea what a good thing the party was." The programmatic speeches, slogans, communal rituals, and egalitarian interactions of the local cells comprise not the truth but the lore—the active substance of Ginsberg's experience of U.S. Communism in this section of the poem. Indeed, from the 1920s through 1945, such slogans functioned as signposts orienting communities to their purposeful moment in the revolution: "FREE TOM MOONEY! AND LIBERATE THE SCOTTSBORO BOYS!" or "THE SCOTTSBORO BOYS MUST NOT DIE! NEGRO AND WHITE WORKERS UNITE!" or "SAVE DEMOCRACY IN SPAIN AND SAVE DEMOCRACY AT HOME!"[8] Communists, Socialists, liberals, and other concerned citizens took to the streets in order to manifest a popular front of justice in the face of a mainstream politics of entangled racism, ethnic bigotry, right-wing demagoguery, and market interests. Ginsberg's identification with nine African American boys dubiously accused of raping two white women on an Alabama freight train is a rare creation. He stared into the eyes of the other and saw Narcissus.[9] A brief recounting of the Spanish Loyalists issue is instructive about the politics of this kind of identification.

The cause of the Spanish Loyalists has been the international left's Aristotelian tragedy. Officially, it is the story of men and women freedom fighters crushed by fascism and the neglect of the free world. This summation is correct but not complete. Because it is also true that the International Brigades, as they were called—a 40,000-strong global contingent of volunteers—were not infallibly noble; recent findings in Soviet archives and testimony by a few of the surviving volunteers have exposed corruption in the ranks: political machinations, desertions, betrayals, murders. The corruption was largely a result of Comintern ideological enforcement via the paranoid opportunism of Stalin.[10]

The Spanish Loyalists (also known as the Republican government) were a coalition of Republicans, Socialists, Communists, and anarchists. They were popularly elected in Spain in 1936. The election was terribly divisive, however. The losers formed the Nationalist Party: an alliance of the Falange fascists, the Carlist right-wingers, the Monarchists, the military, and the Catholic Church. The Nationalists refused to permit implementation of the Republican reform program, which attacked entrenched privilege in Spanish society. In July 1936 Generalissimo Francisco (Franco) led an army revolt in Spanish Morocco, which began the Spanish Civil War. From the beginning, Italy and Nazi Germany sent infantry, planes, tanks, aviators, and technicians to aid Franco. Britain, France, and the United States maintained a noninterventionist policy. In fact, they preferred the rising fascist axis to a leftist revolution, no matter how democratic. Nevertheless, in all three countries, liberals, Socialists, Communists, and others demanded in vain that action be taken to help the Republic. The Soviet Union, with its own totalitarian goals cynically in mind, alone aided the Loyalists. Nevertheless, the Communists International (Comintern) was able to recruit idealistic volunteers of many political persuasions from over fifty-three countries to help fight fascism; they were called the International Brigades. The American contingent called itself the Abraham Lincoln Battalion (ALB).

The ALB was illegal in the United States. It was illegal for Americans to fight in a foreign army according to an 1818 federal statute. When the State Department discovered that volunteers were signing up to help the Loyalists, they ordered all passports stamped *Not valid for Travel in Spain*. Meanwhile, Texaco and Standard Oil were shipping 3 million tons of oil to Franco on credit under the category of tourism. Moreover, under the guise of neutrality, the United States had placed a damaging trade embargo against Spain's legitimate government. The volunteers went to France first. From there they climbed over the treacherous Pyrenees into the war zones. Twenty-seven hundred volunteers comprised the ALB. Approximately one hundred of them were black, and all of these were Communists. More blacks volunteered, but the party convinced them that they were needed more stateside than overseas. Officially, the Communist Party did not tolerate racism or Jim Crow, but actually weeding out racism from party ranks would require more than the issuing of an order. We know from Ralph Ellison's critique of Communist politics in *Invisible Man* (1947), from Irving Howe, and most recently from the revelations Mary R. Habeck and her coauthors have culled from Soviet archives that the Communist Party often exploited race for publicity in ways that opposed the interests of African Americans whose rights it championed. In addition, it seems that the ALB was, itself, democratic only insofar as the volunteers appeared apparatchik.[11] Still, hypocrisy aside, the Communist Party has since 1919, its first year in the United States, proved its willingness to advocate the rights of African Americans. It was perhaps the only community in the country where African Americans could work with whites, not for them—mingle with whites and feel like human beings. African Americans had seen white Communists take to the streets to protest the treatment of the Scottsboro boys and Tom Mooney the same. Black men and women saw the struggle of the Spanish Republic as part of their own struggle against long-term systematic inequality. They had a pan-African consciousness as well, which made them eager to fight the Italians, who had invaded the independent nation of Ethiopia in 1935.[12]

The International Brigades hyped itself as a multicultural and multinational brigade that fully enfranchised and integrated its minorities. Although it was illegal, the ALB was the first integrated fighting force in the United States. Of the available testimony by African Americans, though there were racial tensions, not one testifies that their role in the force was anything other than matched to their talents and skills. When the war ended, many dreaded the prospect of returning home to second-class citizenship in the United States. Among the ranks of the brigade were African American pilots, nurses, mechanics, interpreters, machine-gun commanders, cartographers, and mortar instructors. African American Oliver Law was among the best-known men in the battalion. Law began his tour in Spain as a machine-gun commander. After one hundred and twenty days of fierce fighting at Jarama, he made captain. Subsequently, he was promoted to commander of the entire Lincoln Battalion and the Canadian, Cuban, and Irish volunteers that joined in with it.[13] The official story has described Law as a genuine hero. His leadership has been a conspicuous symbol of ALB egalitarianism. A few ALB survivors lately demur. They say the Comintern had control of the ALB and that Law was rashly promoted for propaganda reasons. They say he was inexperienced and dangerous to the troops he commanded. Worse, some say he was a coward. One rumor reports that rather than having died from an enemy bullet to the stomach in July 1937, the official version, he was fragged by friendly fire. But these are recent accusations. They complicate the history of the ALB but have little bearing on Ginsberg's grass-roots sense of the cause of the Spanish Loyalists. The point I want to make is that if we put in abeyance its martial aims and consider the intentions of the volunteers themselves, the ALB, like mixed jazz ensembles, enacted a new social reality.

Given his exposure to the local cells and his knowledge of the Loyalists' issues, Ginsberg was likely familiar with the progressive stance of the ALB. In his early years he knew egalitarian principle; "America" shows that his association with local people who struggled to live it made an indelible impression. The voice of the poem "America" is not sorry for its association with Communism. It does not apologize for its celebration of people who took vernacular flight from the rigid lines crushing them. I say vernacular because the appeal of Ginsberg's experience of Communism was not based on its opportunist leadership nor its top-down conspiracy to overthrow the U.S. government. It was most certainly not based on the sharp edges of its ideology and programmatic rhetoric. Ginsberg never joined the party, but he respected many Americans who did, of whom Robert A. Rosenstone writes,

> they were vitally interested in short-range goals for which Communists agitated on specific issues . . . in the thirties . . . [They were] not [interested] to build barricades in the streets or to storm Capitol Hill. Rather they joined the party because it defended Negroes like the Scottsboro Boys or Angelo Herndon, because it organized the unemployed or industrial unions, because it objected to anti-semitism in the United States and Germany. This phenomenon could occur because CP journals . . . such as the *Daily Worker,* rarely spoke in the language of Marxist-Leninism. Violent revolution, class struggle, the dictatorship of the proletariat—none of these reached the pages of the *Daily Worker.* The goals of the party perceived by Americans joining were more often those of "general social improvement and bettering of conditions than as specifically socialist aims." Most typically . . . a party member would say . . . "I joined the party when it moved a widow's evicted furniture back into her house. I thought it was right. That's why I joined."[14]

Action—practical, egalitarian, and compassionate—became the attractive feature of local Communism. Memory of such actions inform the politics of Ginsberg's poems. Let us take an intratextual excursion of *Howl* before I return to the imperatives in "America."

For part of the time that Ginsberg penned *Howl,* he kept a job loading and unloading buses for Greyhound, where he wrote, "the wage they pay us is too low to live on." He concludes, "I am a communist."[15] These lines come from the poem "In the Baggage Room at Greyhound," which Ginsberg wrote on May 9, 1956, the night he quit the job. He quit because he obtained another job as a yeoman-storekeeper with the USNS Pvt. Joseph F. Merrell. At $5,040 per year, the new merchant-seaman job paid well. By July he joined a new ship, the USNS Sgt. Jack J. Pendleton, and delivered parts for an early warning radar system for three months in the Arctic Circle and assembling cargo from various military depots.[16] These jobs financed Ginsberg's trip to Tangier and Europe later in the year. Unless he was a spy, such employment indicates that Ginsberg had no allegiance to the post-Stalin regime of the Soviet Union. Instead, Communist language in "Greyhound" is born of the lore of committed sympathy with workers, despite the fact that the poet is about to quit his job and leave them behind. In "Greyhound" the workers shepherd people's comings and goings. In this poem Greyhound employs a sardonic porter wearing a red cap; Joe, with his hysterical breakdown at the customer-service counter; Sam hobbling in the basement; and the "Negro operating clerk named Spade dealing out with his marvelous long hand the fate of thousands of express packages." Later, the poem continues,

> Yet Spade reminded me of Angel, unloading a bus,
> dressed in blue overalls black face official Angel's workman
>   cap,
> pushing with his belly a huge tin horse piled high with black
>   baggage,
> looking up as he passed the yellow light bulb of the loft
> and holding high on his arm an iron shepherd's crook.

"Greyhound" begs reasonable, contemporaneous questions. Is the U.S. work ethic as strong as its hype? Why can't a vital worker be paid adequately while owners and stockholders (who often do not work) build up wealth? What is the relationship between investors and the symbolic and real value imposed on the labor of cynics, limpers, neurotics, black people, maverick poets, and others without clout? "Greyhound" charts a flight through the symbolic mire that designates marginality and assigns the indignity and hardship of an inadequate wage to those who work. Everyday the unity and ethical quality of work is crushed by the skewed distribution of profits. This is not melodrama but "tragedy reduced to numbers." Yet tragedy produces truths that the market obscures. Tragedy slants a knowing eye at capitalism's dualistic assumptions. It flings the inefficiency of a modernized humanistic tradition into the market's production of otherness and inequitable hierarchies. The Greyhound operation is not a utilitarian profit center but a sacred space: God's "rickety structure of time," with racks in the baggage room to keep everyone and everything together—all attended to by shepherds and a black angel. Initially, Ginsberg's imperatives in "America" suggest a kind of shell shock; stunned bewilderment radiates from the absurd past. According to conventions of linear time and psychology, the poem's voice is stuck in the trauma of history. It is trapped in the madness of an appalled reflex: "Save the Spanish Loyalists." Was this insane babble? Or was it the subversion—through the symbolic resurrection of the struggle to save the Loyalists—of history structured as a succession of finalities? My reading is that history's traces—the remnants of *causes célèbre* in "America" and "Greyhound"—do the work of America's unfinished business. This is not business to be finished by Communist Party leadership, which so frequently sabotaged justice for the sake of short-term notoriety. It is the vernacular business of people writing letters and articles, going to the ballot box, and marching in the streets. Just enactments in behalf of Sacco and Vanzetti, Mooney, and others effect their presence through Ginsberg's poems. In ways small and large readers feel and sift their momentum and propel it into the future.

Ginsberg's poem "Sunflower Sutra" does not perform across an externalized object such as the United States or Greyhound. Here, lore traverses the self. The term sutra is a Sanskrit word that refers to late Vedic wisdom literature (500–200 BCE). Sutras frequently combine narrative of the Buddha's life and aphoristic wisdom. "Sunflower Sutra" combines narrative with an unschooled, nontraditional variety of aphorism—after the manner of spontaneous poesy. The voice of the poem does not purport to be the Buddha: the enlightened one. Simply, it assumes that illumination, like the light of the sun, disperses itself to anyone who is in the open to receive it. And those who receive it share it. The wisdom of "Sunflower Sutra" is the wisdom of one's vernacular substance—the self flying out in all directions through style.[17]

"Sunflower Sutra" is set in a Bay Area shipping yard strewn with obsolete, industrial debris. Ginsberg clearly narrates the tale. Kerouac is with him. The depressed mood of both men mirrors the waste surrounding them and therefore calls for the wiliness of bums. Ginsberg, Kerouac, and others among the Beats learned wiliness from friends such as Herbert Huncke, the larcenous, homeless, freezing junky and gifted raconteur, who showed up at Ginsberg's door in 1948. For warehousing Huncke and his swag, Ginsberg was confined to the Columbia Psychiatric Institute for eight months in 1948 and 1949. Huncke conveyed the mien of a foreigner in his own land. He was a citizen of the streets. John Clellon Holmes said, "We went to Huncke . . . because of the life he had lived—he was a source—even more, a model of how to survive." Neal Cassady, too, was an artiste of cunning survival. The biographer William Plummer writes of Cassady's early resourcefulness when he would join his father, "big Neal in several thousand-mile jaunts through the West, hitchhiking, riding the rails, frequenting hobo jungles in California, selling homemade flyswatters in Nebraska. He would sleep in cardboard cartons in boxcars and sleep in a rolltop desk on Larimer Street. He would learn his first con-man tricks, notably how to affect the waif look so to better cadge nickels for his father and cronies to convert into wine,

canned heat (denatured alcohol), even bay rum." Thus, the style of
those who are said to have no style, the style of the desperately re-
sourceful, cracks the gloom pressing in on Ginsberg and Kerouac.[18]

In "Sunflower Sutra" style disperses the self from the inside out—
scatters it like Coltrane scattered modes to God in 1964. Upon seeing
the sunflower, memories from Ginsberg's seminal past flash bright,

> —it was my first sunflower, memories of Blake—my visions—
> Harlem
> and Hells of the Eastern rivers, bridges clanking Joes [sic]
> Greasy Sandwiches, dead baby carriages, black treadless tires
> forgotten and unretreaded, the poem of the riverbank, con-
> doms & pots, steel knives, nothing stainless, only the dank
> muck and the razor-sharp artifacts passing into the past—

By the standards of analytic observation, Ginsberg's William Blake
visions in 1948 were evidence of a psychotic break. By Ginsberg's
standard, the visions were the anointing flight of the poet. Ginsberg
had just masturbated and was lying on his bed when he believed he
heard Blake recite the poem "Ah Sunflower." For several days afterward, he felt overwhelmed by the feeling of the unity and intelligence of life. The feeling so saturated him that he no longer needed
to pine for Blake's "sweet golden clime." Ginsberg said, "I suddenly
realized that this existence was it! The spirit of the universe."[19] The
universe excluded no ridiculous sandwich of Joe's nor the blight of
obsolete and forgotten commodities, and neither could poetry. Psychotic flight made Ginsberg a body—alive to the cut of the trashed
artifact's presence in the culture: its poetic necessity. Ginsberg halts
the passing into the past. He stanches the consumer economy's modern Lethe.[20]

The personal lore of the former New York vision effects an extraordinary trope on the Bay Area sunflower that extends for 400 of
the poem's 674 words. This trope smears temporal distinctions between the former and present sunflower visions. It smears spatial

differences. Inside becomes outside and outside becomes inside; subjectivities become objectivities and vice versa. It begins in the middle and scatters toward everything else in every direction, but not at first. The initial appearance of the sunflower is as a black absurdity. Upright in the light of the sunset, it appears

> bleak and dusty with the smut and smog and smoke of olden
>   locomotives in its eye—
> corolla of bleary spikes pushed down and broken like a bat-
>   tered crown, seeds fallen crackly out of its face, soon-to-be-
>   toothless mouth of sunny air, sunrays obliterated on its hairy
>   head like a dried wire spiderweb,
> leaves stuck out like arms out of the stem, gestures from the
>   sawdust root, broke pieces of plaster fallen out of the black
>   twigs, a dead fly in its ear.

A few lines later, he continues, "all that dress of dust, that veil of darkened railroad skin, that smog of cheek, that eyelid of black mis'ry." It is a beaten down Negro of a sunflower. It is the caricature of an oppressed, forlorn, nappy-headed African American—a kind of brutalized sharecropper peering over blighted fields or, perhaps, a Scottsboro boy denied even the status of a sharecropper. Here is the objective view, which by stroke of a pen becomes subjective: "Unholy battered old thing you were my sunflower O my soul, how I loved you then." The sunflower traverses history's effecting of present souls: Ginsberg's, Kerouac's, and anyone else who will hear—ultimately, America's soul. A pluralism of style unglues history's sticky tangle. Style explodes modernity into the opening of the unity of life. It blazes into ash the lines of separation and confinement. It turns selves to bodies and bodies to everything else:

> —We're not our skin of grime, we're not our dread bleak dusty
>   imageless locomotive, we're all beautiful golden sunflowers
>   inside, we're blessed by our own seed & golden hairy naked

accomplishment-bodies growing into mad black formal
sunflowers in the sunset, spied on by our eyes under the
shadow of the mad locomotive riverbank sunset Frisco hilly
tincan evening sitdown vision.

The "Sunflower Sutra" shoots its lines in all directions, including
the East, in order to loose blackness and madness from their confinement. Blackness and madness are the beneficiaries of style's accomplishment, which is not a goal but the process of growing; in another poem, "the kindly search for growth."[21] The search for growth
is not an entrenchment of roots but rhizomatic. It grows scattershot
into the coming decades—associating and mixing, continually. The
new lore cycle's coming round spun through Ginsberg's art and John
Coltrane's, too, in his own passionate search.

Jazz's short history is a history of the search for growth. Jazz's
eclecticism and its constant motion toward the other is perhaps the
predominant characteristic of a music whose development has always confounded attempts to essentialize it.[22] Jazz neither abandons
its vernacular sources nor does it shy from association with the most
contemporaneous influences: be they vernacular or formal. Jazz is
not stifled by tyrannies of high and low aesthetic categories. Much of
the discussion about postmodernism has centered on the observance
of collapsing boundaries between high and low art. Modern jazz occupies a fault line of this collapse. It has helped spin the motley
threads of African American gesture and lore into the fabric of multiple canons, revered and not: Piet Mondrian's rhythmic geometrics
(1940s); Jackson Pollock's action paintings; Robert Frank's photography; Nicholas Ray's rebels; Marlon Brando's method; Elvis Presley's
sound and his pumping hips; and as we have seen in another chapter,
Roxanne's, too, in the film *The Subterraneans*. My point is that jazz—
its attitude for openness, its love of spontaneity, its virtuosic discipline, its frequent displays of genius, its wont for risk, its refusal to
stop growing—compelled a similar quest for skillful freedom across
the cultural spectrum.

John Coltrane and Allen Ginsberg were contemporaries. There is no direct evidence that they knew one another or that they were familiar with each other's work, although, certainly, on the latter count, they probably were. Both men made New York City their home, where they were in the vanguard of creative activity. In the second half of this chapter I will present important background and analysis of Coltrane's musical development in the 1950s. In this way I will draw into focus—allowing for differences between the media—the remarkable correspondences of style and politics between the two artists' works, *Howl* and *A Love Supreme*. I have already discussed in Chapter 1 how socio-political energies embedded in bebop style rippled across the lines of time, class, and color into "Howl" and its audience. Coltrane, too, honed his chops on bebop, individualized its complex meanings, upped its intensity and range, and in the end exhausted its potential in order to develop new styles of jazz. In 1955, when Ginsberg wrote "Howl," Coltrane was still building his knowledge of bebop and perfecting his technical skills in the Miles Davis Quintet.[23]

Davis originally wanted Sonny Rollins in his quintet, but he was not available. Davis settled for Coltrane more out of instinct than objective criteria. At age twenty-nine Coltrane had not yet distinguished himself as an important player. Davis's was a working quintet that in addition to Coltrane on tenor saxophone featured Paul Chambers on bass, Red Garland on piano, and Philly Joe Jones on drums. The group played the clubs and cafes in New York City for almost two years. The consensus among critics then was that it was the best jazz act of the mid-1950s, except for Coltrane. Critics said his playing was derivative of Sonny Rollins and Dexter Gordon at best and jumbled and uncertain at worst. In Coltrane's occasional hesitation and fumbling, however, Davis heard an emerging originality. By 1957 originality's silence and occasional muddle would become, to repeat Ira Gitler's well-worn but apt phrase, "sheets of sound."[24]

The group made five albums, four of them in two recording sessions in 1956: *Workin'*, *Cookin'*, *Steamin'*, and *Relaxin'*. Barring outrageous mistakes, Davis kept the philosophy that the first take was the best take. This corresponded to Kerouac's and Ginsberg's belief that the first thought was the best thought, which did not always mean that the first word on the page was the best word on the page, of course.[25] Immediacy of emotion was paramount to the styles of both art forms, as was skill. Kerouac, Ginsberg, and many other Beat-associated writers honed their chops writing thousands of then-unpublished pages of letters, stories, poems, plays, and novels. They read and studied other writers, and they talked incessantly with each other about writers and writing and jazz. Like the best jazz players, they spent years of days and nights woodshedding. Few people practiced more than John Coltrane. He never embraced the concept of maturity. He exploded every musical plateau on which he could have legitimately halted his growth. Moreover, many audiences, peers, and critics would seem to have preferred that he not only stop growing but return to musical territory long gone by. Because it was a working band, the Davis Quintet was tight. In the studio Davis called the tunes just as he called them on the stage. According to Gitler's notes for *Steamin',* there were no second takes in either of the two sessions, in which the band made all four albums I've mentioned.[26]

Coltrane knows his changes on the Davis sessions, but his execution is sometimes irresolute on tunes such as "Surrey with the Fringe on Top" and "Four." Even Coltrane said about this period with Davis, "The standards were so high, and I felt like I wasn't really contributing as I should. Why he picked me I don't know. Maybe he saw something in my playing that he hoped would grow." Indeed, after the Prestige sessions with Davis, Coltrane would apprentice fruitfully with Thelonious Monk and kick his drug habit. By the time he recorded *Blue Train* with his own group in 1957, his tone was searing the air with the precision of a jet plane. On *Blue Train,* he does not just make changes. He paints each chord in full and signs it. He shows each chord a canvas unto itself, a world of sound-color whose boundaries exceed diatonic principles and the conventions of tenor saxophone. And he plays many chords. For example, in a transcription of "Moment's Notice," Coltrane's solo straddles two keys and alternates sixteen and twenty-two bar choruses of twenty-six to thirty-three chords at 252 quarter tones/minute. The chord connections are unusual, too, in that they are designed to harmonize with a repeating note in the song's melody. The technique would bloom into fuller expression in his later work with pedal points and modes. It also foreshadows the development of his music's deeper purpose of suggesting everywhere accessible centers (nothing is marginal) around which everything passes. Coltrane's innovations as a composer rival and complement his forward thinking as a soloist. Bear with me for two metaphors germane to Coltrane's style as a tenor soloist and that of his contemporaries, Dexter Gordon and Sonny Rollins.

Dexter Gordon's solos were narrative in style. They conveyed the momentum and inevitability of a well-told story; they were Aristotelian in the way they began ponderously, built up, and accelerated to an emotional peak. Then they would unwind gracefully. On the other hand, Sonny Rollins developed motives. He would play a poignant phrase and then manipulate it. He would juggle its parts in a playful, continuously inventive way chorus after chorus. Even when he took his solo afield of the motive, as he always did, he would preserve its suggestion, still, in a phrase or a note, mothering its implications, usually, by way of rhythm. Artful story-telling and motivic development alone did not satisfy Coltrane. On *Blue Train*, for example, he composed some of the most indelible melodies in the jazz cannon. But as a soloist on the same record, he pressed jazz harmony beyond its limits with unprecedented rigor and passion. The style comes to its apotheosis in the 1959 recording of "Giant Steps."[27]

Since its release in 1960, "Giant Steps" has been emblematic of total harmonic competence. The piece was a flight of new logic—an assemblage—the epitome of harmonic innovation in jazz. We do not know how many takes Coltrane allowed for "Giant Steps," but it took two sessions two months apart before he got a version he was willing to release. The tune proceeds from beginning to end in continuous modulation—not through the typical bebop intervals on the circle of fifths, but through alternating modulations of major thirds and augmented fifths. The predominant structural element consists in the II–V–I progression (often with chord substitutions) circulating in thirds. Coltrane's solo of mostly arpeggiated chords results in a seamless and highly unusual linking together of distantly related keys. Each measure of each chorus includes two chords and the pace is supersonic at 285 quarter-beats per minute; he's running over 100 chords/minute.[28] The solo packs to maximum density each fleet chord. The operative principle of the solo in "Giant Steps" is to eliminate selection, to utilize—within the considerable scope of the piece's structure—every conceivable harmonic resource. Now Ginsberg's poetry can intervene in my discussion.

On the surface, Coltrane's musical conception, at this point in his career, seems remote from Ginsberg's conception of poetry and jazz, and it is, but it is also similar. For example, we have known since the publication of *Howl: Original Facsimile* (1986) that the poem underwent retakes. First thoughts were best, but the thoughts of "Howl" were refined through several revisions. An important difference between Coltrane's and Ginsberg's art lies in the underlying economic, legal, and social practices of jazz and of poetry. For example, *Howl* was improvised in the making, but the poems are now autonomous entities, finished, and copyrighted. Similarly, Coltrane's recording of "Giant Steps" is finished and copyrighted. Unlike the recording, however, the composition "Giant Steps" is unfinished and in the process of becoming. The piece's innovative harmonic patterns may remain the same, but soloists can also improvise on the piece in a virtually infinite number of ways. Moreover, they can alter the melody and substitute chords that change the harmonies. "Giant Steps" is now part of a creative community and its audience in a way that *Howl* is not. As a compositional frame, "Giant Steps" continues to function as a tool for the development of both musical skills and innovation in jazz. While *Howl*, too, may function to inform and enhance reading and writing skills and spur imaginative work, it is not an improvisational vehicle for soloing poets.[29]

The poem "Sunflower Sutra" appears to disregard the rules of poetic meter, rhythm, and form, as well as those of syntax and grammar. But more accurately, Ginsberg does not as much dismiss conventions as subordinate them to serve his poem rather than stifle it. On the other hand, "Giant Steps" seems to reflect fastidious adherence to rules of harmonic form. But in fact, virtually every measure of "Giant Steps" is a violation of the rules of diatonic harmony as well as the customary modulations of bebop. Both works seek new linkages and combinations among available elements. "Sunflower Sutra" perceives interconnected relations between the image of the sunflower, the self (and memory), and the physical world—the other. Coltrane's composition perceives new relations among chords and musical tonalities. "Giant Steps" crystallizes these relations in a dense and lucid form. Similarly, "Sunflower Sutra," thick and clear, assembles its elements at about the poem's midpoint as

> those blear thoughts of death and dusty loveless eyes and ends
>   and withered roots below, in the home-pile of sand and saw-
>   dust, rubber dollar bills, skin of machinery, the guts and in-
>   nards of the weeping coughing car, the empty lonely tincans
>   with their rusty tongues alack, what more could I name, the
>   smoked ashes of some cock cigar, the cunts of wheelbarrows
>   and the milky breasts of cars, wornout asses out of chairs &
>   sphincters of dynamos—all these
> entangled

Coltrane and Ginsberg share the exhaustive impulse.

Nevertheless, the Ginsberg of *Howl* is in a different place from the Coltrane of "Giant Steps." Unlike Coltrane, Ginsberg does not invent an alternative schematic for ordering his lines. His lines are as free as wind, while Coltrane's lines expertly parley the obstacle course of unique structure. Still, Coltrane was in two places at the same time. In 1959, while he was headlining his own recording projects that swept the breadth of harmonic plausibility, he was also back with Miles Davis exploring an alternative musical horizon through the window of modes.

By the end of the 1950s, many jazz musicians became weary of the dictatorship of harmony (and rhythmic regularity). They had tired of kowtowing their solos to the authority of chord changes and the measured line. "Giant Steps" had taken jazz harmony to the wall of complexity and virtuosity. The wall yielded to what became known as modal jazz and its close relative free jazz. Miles Davis was looking for an opening, and he found one, early. He was among the first to experiment with modes. And he was the first to popularize them with the release of "Milestones," the sole modal track on his 1958 album of the same name.[30] With the release of *Kind of Blue* in 1959, fame came to Davis and his sextet. In the two recording sessions for *Kind of Blue* the Davis sextet distilled the complexity of bop harmony down to the rudiment of a chord (mode), or a few chords. Suddenly, it seemed as if the horizontal plane of melody had risen up to flatten the towering edifice of harmony. In effect, modal jazz simplified jazz harmony and opened up new freedoms for the improviser.

Rudimentally, a western mode is a series of seven notes whose central tone is the tonic note of any chord from a major scale. For example, the second chord of the F major scale is G minor. The notes that comprise the G minor chord and variations on it derive from the Dorian mode, which always begins with the second note of any major scale and builds up from there (GABbCDEF). The Dorian mode on G is the basis for one of two sections of Davis's "Milestones." The second section of the tune is based on the Aeolian mode on A (ABCDEFG): the sixth degree of the parent scale of C major. To go from over one hundred chords/minute on "Giant Steps" to nearly six minutes of alternations of the two chords on "Milestones" was quite a consolidation, but it set forth new challenges. Soloists could no longer depend on the chord progression to help guide improvisational variety and listener interest. Modal jazz sprung improvisational lines from the clutch of traditional harmonic changes, but now the burden of musical interest fell on players' ability to produce compelling melody from the mode and its tonal zone. Like Ginsberg's poems, Coltrane could now construct solos made of lines as long as he chose or as long as his breath or the end of a measure (if there was one) would permit.

"Milestones" is tightly structured by two modal themes. The first theme opens and closes the tune. It also intervenes to separate Davis's solo from Coltrane's and then Cannonball Adderly's on alto saxophone. The rhythm section—Red Garland on piano, Paul Chambers on bass, and "Philly" Joe Jones on drums—maintains and initiates transitions between the two themes while the horns improvise. Davis's solo beautifully shapes the contours of the mode. But Coltrane and Adderly adventure outward by extending their melodies into the mode's chromatic implications. Their melodies broach the western frame.[31] Everyone on the session was up to the challenge of making simplicity compelling. Modal jazz became progressively more open and free.

The Davis sextet's "Flamenco Sketches" on *Kind of Blue* is instructive. The *Kind of Blue* sessions included Adderly and Coltrane. Bill Evans handled piano, except for on "All Blues," which featured Wynton Kelly. Paul Chambers played bass, and James Cobb was the drummer. Preliminary work for the sessions was famously minimal. According to Bill Evans's notes, Davis independently conceived and drew up the "sketches" for all of the tunes only hours before recording in New York City on March 2 and April 22, 1959.

The plan for "Flamenco Sketches" (incorrectly called "All Blues" in the notes) was "a series of five scales [modes], each to be played as long as the soloist wishes until he has completed the series." With respect to all of the tunes, Evans added, "and I think without exception the first complete performance of each was a 'take.'"[32] There was no opening or closing theme on "Flamenco Sketches." A four/four pulse guided the rhythm. The improvised melodies comprise virtually all aspects of this spontaneous composition, and they determine the modal transitions. This fact underscores the extraordinary paradox about Evans's playing on the session. In the previous chapter, I showed how Lenny Tristano's piano work, for the most part, controlled the collective direction of his free ensemble experiments "Intuition" and "Digression." Rather than try to reinvent the function of the piano in jazz, Ornette Coleman excluded it from the ensembles for *The Shape of Things to Come* (1959) and *Free Jazz* (1961). The paradox of Evans's playing lies in the simultaneity of its delicate reserve and diamond-edged clarity. The piano does not push or pull. It follows the melodies of the horns. Even Evans's solo follows the modal concept. He subordinates the bop procedure of using the left hand to accent or comp the single-note melody of the right hand. Evans begins to integrate the movement of both hands into a continuous and spacious melodic line through all of the modes. His playing was unprecedented and very influential. It helped save the piano for the future of jazz.

Coltrane's playing is distinctive from that of other soloists. Ekkehard Jost astutely observes that unlike the solos of Adderly, Davis, and Evans, Coltrane's solo transitions, through the modes of "Flamenco Sketches," understate the harmonic principle of modulation. Paul Chambers's suspensions act to signal Davis's transitions. Adderly and Evans, on the other hand, twist—in conventional modulatory style—the notes of their melodies through the portal of each mode. But Coltrane shifts into new modes through a kind of "kinetic cumulation, interrupting the relatively calm melodic progress of his improvisation with interpolated 16th and 32nd figures."[33] Coltrane understates the harmonic links between the modes by foregrounding rhythm in the shift to the new mode. Thus, perhaps because he knew harmony best, Coltrane saw modes as a window into new musical relations in which melody, timbre, and rhythm dissolved the chordal scaffolding hemming in jazz. His lines were now as free as Ginsberg's. More than any other player on the jazz scene, Coltrane would develop modes throughout the first half of the 1960s. He and the other members of the John Coltrane Quartet took modal jazz to its fulfillment in *A Love Supreme* (1964). In *A Love Supreme* the symmetries of politics and style with Ginsberg's *Howl* come to the fore.

In order to develop the principles of free modal composition, Coltrane had to find players to help him do it. By 1960 drummer Elvin Jones and pianist McCoy Tyner agreed to play in the quartet. These three played with a variety of bass players including Steve Davis, Reggie Workman and Art Taylor; but mostly, they played with Jimmy Garrison. This was the core group—John Coltrane's Classic Quartet, 1960 to 1965. The group worked with a number of other musicians in its live performances such as those at the Village Vanguard (1961) and on special recording projects like the Africa/Brass sessions (1961). Multi-instrumentalist Eric Dolphy was a frequent collaborator, and Archie Shepp contributes a second saxophone at the end of "Psalm," the fourth and last section of *A Love Supreme*.

Just as "Giant Steps" can be seen as a pioneering fulfillment of harmonic organization in jazz, *A Love Supreme* is the consummation of the free modalism that the quartet had been pioneering. The quartet's various free modal practices can be heard on a range of recordings such as *My Favorite Things* (1960), *Olé* (1961), *Impressions* (1963), and *Crescent* (1964). In the period between 1960 and 1965, the content and pacing of every performance (studio or stage) of the quartet was open to the free play of emotion and spontaneous gesture. It is untenable to show a progression of development. Again, one of Jost's observations succinctly obtains. After *My Favorite Things,* the group "constantly moved back and forth between stylistic innovation and already proven procedures."[34] The quartet functioned as flight: innovation without iconoclasm. From the shards and flotsam

of African American blues and from African timings, oriental intervals, and European theory and instrumentation, *A Love Supreme* as-
sembled a new species of suite. Its innovations resounded with a
popular need for social growth through a creative, new commerce of
differences. No doubt, some of this popular need expressed itself as a
fetishistic compulsion to possess god; in some cases, as with *Howl, A
Love Supreme* became talismanic for participation in a fashionable
holiness. But as style, like the poem "Howl," *A Love Supreme* opened
wide.

Bebop was the mother of this openness because it had absorbed
and conveyed, at times ambivalently, social and stylistic traits of earlier, vernacular African American musics and rituals. These traits included polyrhythmic relations with the beat and the use of notes out
of the scale. In addition to openness, African American musics esteemed verity, community, and participation. Such qualities were
manifest in the gatherings of the field hollerers, the spirituals singers,
the polyrhythmic dances on Congo Square, the religious services of
plantation African Americans, and the blues performances at clubs
up North and juke joints down South. They were present in the late
seventeenth-century expansion of Creole society to Northern cities.
In places such as Philadelphia and New York City free and slave
blacks mixed with whites in plebeian "afterhours conviviality." They
were present at New York City's Catherine Market in the 1820s and
later. At the market young whites watched blacks dance for eels and
absorbed and imitated their moves in order to share their complex,
defiant affirmation. Such historical elements, even as they were eventually couched in the fiercely black exterior of bebop, have always
preferred association to isolation. They produced agreeable mixtures
of difference in early blackface performance and later, jazz. To be sure
these mixtures eventually took on the spots and then the blight of
ruling ideologies of prejudice, but their original disposition was not
to withhold or deny but to open, grow, and give. Through hybrid

popular rituals artists and audiences negotiated their lives' terms. Wheel-about dance moves, altered notes, interlocking offbeats, and the tricky codes of vernacular talk and song assessed the terms of domination and charted life through them. Such elements obliquely cycled through bebop's modern style. Bebop derived pleasure through confounding the *ofay*, yes, but it also embedded a veiled invitation heard by whites and blacks alike, that is, the composers of *Howl* and *A Love Supreme*.[35]

Both works derive from improvisational practices and require the ceremony of sustained aural attention.[36] Performances vary. For example, Lewis Porter heard a live recording of one of the last performances of *A Love Supreme:* July 26, 1965, Antibes, France. Porter writes, "Coltrane's solos differ entirely in detail from but are structured similarly to those on the authorized LP. It is a valuable document because it allows us to confirm our impressions that most of the suite was improvised over the barest of sketches. None of the instrumental solos duplicates those on the authorized version in any way."[37] Necessarily, Ginsberg's public readings are not so improvised. From reading to reading, however, the poems differ in tone and mood, points of emphasis, rhythm, audience participation, and even content—all subtle means of improvisational reading, even composition. For example, at the Town Hall Theater at Berkeley on March 18, 1956, Ginsberg read the following published lines from "Howl," which spoke of the best minds of a generation,

> who distributed Supercommunist pamphlets in Union Square
> weeping and undressing while the sirens of Los Alamos
> wailed them down, and wailed down Wall, and the Staten Island ferry also wailed,

And whether prepared or impromptu, he adds, "and Bird was wailing the most at Birdland!" The Berkeley audience lamented approvingly.[38]

who talked continuously

—Allen Ginsberg, "Howl"

Both *A Love Supreme* and *Howl* comprise rudiments of oral culture.
For example, the entire first section of "Howl" takes the shape of oral
prophecy with its breathlike, incantatory rhythms which circled out
from and back to their anaphora—the orienting starting place at
the pronoun *who*. The days and nights that the Beats spent talking
and singing and listening to calls and answers of jazz became the aural glue of their community. From the pronominal *who*, the word-
sounds of "Howl" shoot forth an oral dance of ecstatic pain—con-
versationalists,

> yacketayakking screaming vomiting whispering facts and mem-
>   ories and anecdotes and eyeball kicks and shocks of hospitals
>   and jails and wars,
> whole intellects disgorged

Oral communication succeeds when it touches the body and mind.
Talk and song, rhythmic movement and gesture sear the eyes and
ears in order to grasp the body. Breath—the speaker's and the
reader's—measures the poem's time. The ebb and flow of breath
helps guide punctuation and, too, furthers the poem's irregular, measured elapse through the placement of consonant and vowel sounds:
the constituents of the poem's hold and release, its tension, its rhythmic groove of attack, syncopation, and accent. Similarly, the modal
principle underlying *A Love Supreme* allows the Coltrane quartet
(when it chooses) to supersede standardized rhythm. For example,
part four of the suite, "Psalm," is a musical transcription of the words
to Coltrane's free verse poem "A Love Supreme." Its melody is un-
measured. Each note of the melody corresponds to a syllable in the
poem. Thus, like "Howl," each musical note or syllable of "Psalm," its

duration and emphasis, is a function of breath and immediate desire rather than standard rhythmic division.[39]

The rhythms of "Howl" are uniformly motley as are the flows of combinations of words. Indeed, returning to the theme of madness, word flows in "Howl" cut a path of triumphal insanity. To the institutionalized Carl Solomon, the poem says

> I'm with you in Rockland
> where we wake up electrified out of the coma by our own
>   souls' airplanes roaring over the roof they've come to drop
>   angelic bombs the hospital illuminates itself imaginary walls
>   collapse O skinny legions run outside O starryspangled
>   shock of mercy the eternal war is here O victory forget your
>   underwear we're free.

"Howl" liberates sound-images from meanings. Of course, just as nets swipe butterflies from their flight, interpretations snatch words from theirs. Certainly, I am a butterfly catcher, if only to let the butterfly go after saying an important thing. Both "Howl" and *A Love Supreme* show that social, psychological, and artistic bondage result from "imaginary walls." Art can imagine a loving freedom even as it calls cold realities to account.

Social and Political Tumult

"Howl" helped bring social and political heat in the United States to a high simmer. Eight years later, *A Love Supreme* intruded upon a time when the heat had reached a boil—a time of wailing and diminished but not depleted optimism and rage. Since World War II the momentum of social change had been building. Strong feelings of disaffection had been wrapped up in jazz since the formation of bebop in the 1940s. Coltrane's biography correlated with bebop. Af-

ter a brief stint in the navy band in Hawaii in 1945, Coltrane returned to his draft-interrupted studies at the Ornstein School of
Music in Philadelphia. He made a living playing swing and rhythm
and blues, but bop was his style of choice. He not only learned the
changes, he learned hipness, which like the changes and since he was
from North Carolina, took some time. He learned the hip musical
skills and the hip look—the shades on the stage—the talk, and the
junk. In 1949 he made tenor in Dizzy Gillespie's last big band, where
he played with the hippest musicians in the country. Ernest Hemingway believed that courage was grace under pressure. Hipness was
close to this. It meant style under threat of capricious menace. It was
a flight through the material realities of truncated citizenship. It was
a flight that the Scottsboro boys were too young and too geographi-
cally remote to have learned. But hipness was not an enduring flight.
It charted a path to its own wailing wall. Coltrane hit that wall in
1957. It yielded when he kicked his habit that year, a habit that invites
reflection on Coltrane's life experience and the extraordinary musician he became.[40]

Acquainted with Loss

For a while I don't think he had anything but that horn.

—Coltrane's high school friend David Young

John William Coltrane was born in Hamlet, North Carolina and
grew up in High Point in the same state. As an African American boy
growing up in the South he was privileged. He was middle class, lived
in a segregated neighborhood of black business people and pro-
fessionals: doctors and dentists and teachers and clergy. He was an
only child and received a good education. His father John Robert

Coltrane owned a "pressing club" (tailor and dry cleaning business) where his mother, born Alice G. Blair, also helped out. The Blair and Coltrane families were a close and supportive group, and they both lived in High Point. Coltrane's grandfathers were ministers in the African Methodist Episcopal church, where Reverend William W. Blair was quite prominent. Reverend Blair was also a community activist and an effective leader in establishing solid public schools in the area for black children. Coltrane said of his grandfather, "He was the dominating cat in the family. He was most well versed, active politically. He was more active than my father . . . a tailor. He just went about his business. But my grandfather was pretty militant, you know. Politically inclined and everything. Religion was his field. So that's where—I grew up in that."[41] Coltrane's mother had musical talent, too. She sang and played piano, but she does not seem to have ever taught John. Alice's sister Bettie married into the Lyerly family. They had a daughter named Mary Lyerly, "Cousin Mary" on the title of one of Coltrane's tunes. Coltrane and Mary were very close. Every Saturday they went to the movies together, and they both loved roller-skating. Coltrane said she always "was like a sister to me." On the *Giant Steps* album sleeve, he referred to her as "a very earthy, folksy, swinging person."[42] John and Mary were both excellent students. When John was in the seventh grade in the years 1938–1939, however, the sturdy pillars of both families began to crumble.

Within a twelve-month period Coltrane lost his Aunt Effie and his grandmother on the Blair side, both grandfathers, and his own father, who died—like his son twenty-six years later—of stomach cancer. These losses were devastating. As Mary said, "All of them passed at the same time . . . we had them all . . . and then all of a sudden they were all gone, with only months in between. John couldn't even remember what his father looked like. He would say to me, 'Mary, what did Daddy look like?' I would talk to him and I would tell him what he looked like."[43] There were no photographs. Coltrane was close to his mother, and he depended on her love and support very much, but she was only one person and could not fill the void that the others had left. Coltrane's grades fell. The family's economic status plummeted. But Coltrane's internal engine drove him toward music, and from the start of eighth grade (the first year of high school in High Point) until the end of his life he pursued a musical career relentlessly.

Musical Education

For economic reasons, somewhere between 1942 and 1943, Coltrane's mother left High Point for Philadelphia. She ended up in Atlantic City, New Jersey because she found work there. It was also near her older sister, who had recently fallen ill and needed her. The Coltranes had been renting their North Carolina house to boarders, and John stayed with them until he finished high school at age sixteen on May 28, 1943. Acclamations were given out to the best students. John was praised as the "Most Musical." In June of 1943 he left High Point for Philadelphia. He got a job in a sugar refinery and enrolled at the Ornstein School of Music, where he took saxophone lessons and studied music theory.

While growing up in High Point, church music had certainly been among the musics saturating Coltrane's ear. Compositions such as "Alabama" (1963), "Spiritual" (1961), and A Love Supreme (1964) indicate he was quite familiar with black preaching.[44] In elementary school a woman named Julia Hall played piano and led the children in singing assembly songs such as marches, spirituals, and hymns. In the 1930s Coltrane and his cousin Mary would visit the local park, where a dance floor had been installed. They listened to swing blasting from phonographs and watched the dancers. The cousins also attended swing band concerts at the Kilby Hotel. Cab Calloway, Duke Ellington, Ella Fitzgerald, and Jimmy Lunceford were among those said to have passed through town. In the fall of 1939 the Reverend

Warren B. Steele, who had been a World War II military band member and performed in a local chamber group, started a community band of wind and percussion instruments. Coltrane, age thirteen, joined up. He started on alto saxophone and was soon switched to clarinet. The repertoire consisted mostly of marches, but Coltrane was also learning to read music and how to run scales. He would buy sheet music of popular songs such as "Blue Orchard" and learn to play them note for note. He held rudimentary jam sessions in the basement of his house. When he entered high school he became a founding member of the band at William Penn High School, which was lead by Grayce W. Yokely. Yokely said of Coltrane, "I remember John being a very fine little boy, a very conscientious type child. He was interested in wanting to learn, and he always showed great potential for music . . . [He] showed great interest in wanting to get everything just right. He was a very rhythmic fellow, and he paid attention."[45]

In 1940 Coltrane discovered Lester Young and decided he would play saxophone. He started with the alto sax and according to childhood friend Rosetta Haywood, "He kept that saxophone with him all the time, and you could hear him all the time . . . practicing by himself." Coltrane practiced well. He became an excellent reader and carefully mastered challenging tunes. He drilled scales and studied their relationship to chord progressions. Thus when he arrived at the Ornstein School of Music, he was ready for a challenging teacher, and he found one: the multi-instrumentalist Mike Guerra. Guerra was a sophisticated musician and popular teacher. In the 1940s he attracted the likes of Gerry Mulligan, Stan Getz, and others. In addition, nightclubs, first-rate musicians, and tight swing bands made Philadelphia one of the most progressive music scenes in the country, and Coltrane's ears were wide open to its sounds. By 1945 Charlie Parker and Dizzy Gillespie had spread bebop fever to Philadelphia's young generation of musicians, which included Benny Golson (one of Coltrane's best friends), Jimmy Heath, "Philly" Joe Jones, Lee

Morgan, and many others. By 1944 Coltrane was playing professionally, mostly stock arrangements, for big bands. He also played popular tunes in small combos. He joined the segregated musicians union
and on August 6, 1945, the Navy drafted him, where among other
duties, he played music for the Melody Masters in Hawaii. Although
the armed services were still mostly segregated, a July 1946 article in
a navy paper in Oahu called *The Mananan* reported that the Melody
Masters were cracking racial codes: "This last of Manana's bands, has
done much to break down the racial barriers around the island.
Lovers of fine swing are not prejudiced against who gives it to them,
and the Melody Masters gave fine swing. Playing for dances all over
the 'rock,' these music makers left a fine opinion of themselves and
they also left pleased audiences." The article added that the band had
been under a lot of stress. With the war winding down, the armed
services were downsizing and decommissioning, which made it difficult to hold the group together. The article credited Coltrane as
the cohesive influence: "Much of this 'carry on' spirit can be attri-
buted to Coltrane who sought to keep the band together in the wan-
ing hours."[46]

Coltrane rejected segregation. During his first few years in Philadelphia he made one or two trips back to High Point to visit family
and friends, but after 1945 he never returned. He was becoming
an artist. His music demanded freedom. Love of personal freedom
caused Coltrane to dislike performing for segregated audiences in the
South. Philadelphia was far from color blind, but it was not Jim
Crow. And like other cities such as New York, Los Angeles, and San
Francisco, the music environment was socially and creatively an
open canvas. The new bebop style had shaken the city, and Coltrane
felt the tremors. The navy band played swing, but Coltrane's practicing and after-hours jam sessions explored and mapped the frontiers
of modern jazz.

After the navy, Coltrane performed for a living, and with the help
of GI benefits resumed his formal music education. He returned to

Ornstein to study with Mike Guerra for a few months before moving on to Granoff Studios in the fall of 1946, where he continued, probably, until the early 1950s. Granoff was one of the largest music schools on the East Coast. It competed with Juilliard in New York and the Curtis Institute in Philadelphia. Dennis Sandole, a legendary guitarist and teacher, took Coltrane under his wing. According to Sandole, his student took two classical lessons per week (most students took one) and was "superbly prepared for each one. He was superlatively gifted, you know. I mostly teach a maturing of concepts, and it involves advanced harmonic techniques you can apply to any instrument. Coltrane went through eight years of my literature in four years." Sandole also exposed Coltrane to what the former called "exotic scales—scales from every ethnic culture." Coltrane absorbed the principles of Nicolas Slonimsky's influential *Thesaurus of Scales and Melodic Patterns,* but he also partook of Sandole's *Scale Lore,* an unpublished book that differed from Slonimsky's in that it was less analytical and more aural in approach; it adhered to the virtue of Miles Davis's bromide, "if it sounds good it is good." The book utilized elaborate chromatics of seven, eight, nine, and ten-note scales. It embodied an open and eclectic outlook, which enhanced Coltrane's own searching inclinations, his constant pursuit of new sounds, form, and technique. Coltrane hand-copied the book's useful pages and evidently remained close to Sandole for many years.[47]

Professionally, Coltrane picked up considerable freelance work in Philadelphia in swing and rhythm and blues bands and a few bebop combos. He also began to take touring jobs. His first gig on the road was with Joe Webb's rhythm and blues outfit, featuring the singer Big Maybelle. Bebop's influence was seeping into a number of progressively oriented big band outfits, and Coltrane landed road gigs with a number of them: King Kolax (1948), Eddie "Cleanhead" Vinson (1948), and one of his idols, Dizzy Gillespie, the following year. By now Coltrane was a productive artist, but he never stopped being a student. He flourished in the big bands—music communities that were learning, developing, and performing a new music. Kolax asked him to do some arranging and even recorded Coltrane's tune "True Blues." In Vinson's band he began playing his preferred instrument, the tenor sax. But Gillespie hired him for lead alto. The position required excellent reading skills but very little improvisation. Coltrane impressed Gillespie nonetheless, and when his big band folded in 1950, Gillespie hired him on the spot to play tenor in his small combo. Coltrane said he was attracted to the tenor saxophone because it opened "a wider area of listening." He continued, "on alto, Bird had been my whole influence, but on tenor I found there was no one man whose ideas were so dominant as Charlie's were on alto." Lester Young and Coleman Hawkins were two very different but very influential figures for Coltrane (and anyone else who picked up the tenor sax), as was Don Byas, Ben Webster, Illinois Jacquet, and Philadelphia local Jimmy Oliver. Coltrane also learned from his contemporaries Dexter Gordon, Sonny Stitt, and Wardell Gray, who had absorbed the tenor generation of Young and Hawkins but also Charlie Parker. Before Coltrane, they had devised their own sound. It was not until after the middle of the 1950s that critics finally stopped referring to Coltrane as a Dexter Gordon derivative.

During this period Coltrane was also enjoying heroin. Most everyone imitated Charlie Parker's musical habits, and too many people copied his drug habits. For complex reasons Coltrane was one of them; the habit diverted his attention and slowed him down. It was probably the most important reason he did not feel ready when the opportunity to play in the Miles Davis quintet arrived. Still he was able to do good work, and the opportunities kept coming. By the time he stopped using in 1957, he was making his own opportunities, leading his own bands, playing his own music, changing the sound of jazz, and pushing the music's freedom-loving, culturally open, and egalitarian meanings into deep spiritual territory that reflected and enhanced the social and cultural changes of his day. The musical odyssey had all along been a spiritual odyssey. Music delivered Coltrane from the void left by his departed loved ones and the cruel perplexity of the social and cultural scene.

More Political Tumult and Social Unrest

Some of the force of change teeming through the United States' postwar streets swept through the highest court in the land with the Brown vs. Board of Education decision in 1954. In 1955 Rosa Parks refused to sit in the back of a Montgomery, Alabama bus. In 1960 sixteen black and three white students challenged Alabama's intrastate busing practices. A mob of over a hundred whites met the students at the Montgomery Greyhound terminal and, with impunity, beat many of them. In February of the same year, students from Greensboro, North Carolina, Coltrane's home state, sat at a Woolworth store lunch counter waiting to be served lunch, but they were arrested instead. Two weeks after the Greensboro incident, segregation protesters marched in Orangeburg, South Carolina. The city stockaded 350 demonstrators. The Student Nonviolent Coordinating Committee (SNCC) became instrumental in spreading a rash of sit-ins throughout the South. In 1961 the Coltrane Quartet scheduled a benefit for SNCC at the University of California, Berkeley. By 1963 southern officials had arrested an estimated 20,000 persons for participating in indirect action. Though the demonstrators had been nonviolent, the local citizenry and in many cases the police responded brutally.

Many remember 1963 as a particularly ugly year. Ambushers murdered Medgar Evers—the field secretary for the NAACP—as he stepped out of his home in Jackson, Mississippi. President John F. Kennedy (who was only partially aware of the urgency of change, but who was generally viewed as moving in the right direction) was murdered. Two months earlier, on September 15, 1963, the Ku Klux Klan had murdered four black girls in an explosion that razed the church they were attending in Birmingham, Alabama. Coltrane responded by writing "Alabama," a piece of such beautiful lamentation as to make the terms of tragedy pale. These upheavals were overt symptoms of widespread injustice and inequality against African Americans. Although it was most conspicuous in the South, it was deeply embedded throughout the United States. Then as now, shocking inequality was evident in statistics of social welfare between the classes, but for minorities of color, the numbers were particularly grim. Not much changed in 1964, either. Civil rights workers continued to risk jail, beatings, and murder. The United States was escalating the conflict in Vietnam. To fight the threat of Communism, it would draft its poor and minorities to wage war on another poor minority on the other side of the world. In the summer of 1964 Harlem erupted with its worst riot since 1943. The spark was the fatal shooting of a fifteen-year-old black boy by an off-duty white officer. *A Love Supreme* intervened on these times.

A Love Supreme is perhaps Coltrane's most popular work. By the end of the 1970s it had sold over 1 million copies. By jazz standards, it was (and still is) a remarkably successful commodity. According to Eric Nisenson you can often find *A Love Supreme* in the record collections of those who, otherwise, care little for jazz.[48] The record became an amulet of divine favor. Like *Howl,* it also garnered international appeal. In the liner notes, Coltrane's letter to the listener and his free-verse poem to a nonsectarian God identified not only Coltrane's personal desire, but also tapped a widespread social aspiration to produce a love of social consequence. The idea of such a love helped inform the nonviolent actions sweeping the country. But by late 1964 that love was under extreme duress—buffeted and tested, as it had been, at every presentation of itself. It was no totality. Frustrated participants began listening to advocates of self-defense and black power for self-determination. After *A Love Supreme,* Coltrane's music, too, gave way to increasing disorientation and forceful complexity. Some radicalized whites and black artists and intellectuals, who were ready to fight if necessary, embraced it as the sound of militancy. My topic precedes Coltrane's later music and the full bloom of Afrocentric interpretations of it, however.[49]

Style and the Politics of Love

The skeletal form of *A Love Supreme* unfolds a wide sonic space. Its modal elements are not boundaries. They are like scenery that the quartet visits and leaves at will; they also help unify the suite. Coltrane unites the parts of *A Love Supreme* through the use of five notes drawn from the mode—a kind of cellular outline of the mode (an extended, variable motive) and in essence a pentatonic scale. Porter shows how the scale occurs throughout the suite's four sections in its "original form, in rotated forms, and transposed." The motive—a short musical phrase—is also a compositional vehicle for the piece. *A Love Supreme* introduces the new element of motivic ties between movements. For example, in "Acknowledgement" Coltrane plays a counter motive over the movement's principal theme, which is held down by the bass and later vocalized. His solo is thus a contrapuntal excursion to and from the motive and its parent mode. Coltrane saves one of the phrases of the improvisation and later redeems it as a theme—over a different rhythm and modal order— for the third movement, "Pursuance." The tractability of the suites' modal exploration is illustrated in a second instance in the first movement. Here Coltrane picks up the quartet's main theme and puts it through the simple harmonic rigor of all twelve keys. Concurrently with this, Tyner joins Coltrane's cyclic journey, while Garrison stands watch over the original mode. The result is a simultaneously static and mutating tonality that is the musical analog of the spiritual goal of centered awareness of constant change. In addition, Jones contributes to the tonal variety of *A Love Supreme* through his unsurpassed ability to lay out riveting, polykinetic color. And Coltrane, too, pushes out the breadth of the tonal spectrum of the piece by judiciously forcing vocal groans and cries and ecstatic screams through his horn. These are the tones of the body's most intense emotions. Both *A Love Supreme* and "Howl" testify to the inadequacy of diatonic harmony and the ideologies of correct technique, codified jazz, and formal poetic structures. At mid-century in the United States, the desire of mind and body set style's unruly agenda for an adventurous and skillful multiplicity.[50]

A motive in jazz consists in the recurrence of a few notes throughout a musical piece. "Howl" employs a similar device. For example, throughout the first part of the poem the pronoun *who* precedes a variety of strong verbs: "who ate," "who burned," "who vanished," "who broke," "who appeared." Thus a syntactical device becomes an aural and literal motivic variation that forwards the actions of the generation's best minds. As with Coltrane's musical lines, in "Howl" there are considerable variations in the range of development from one occurrence of the motive to the next. In Part I of "Howl," the trajectories of its generation's actions range from 18 to 165 words. Part II of "Howl" depends on the motivic effect of syllables in the emphatically expressed name of "Moloch!" Part III utilizes the motivic claim, "I'm with you in Rockland." And Part IV relies on the declarative syllables of "Holy!" Also, as does Coltrane, Ginsberg unifies "Howl" by introducing motive-like ties between sections of the poem. The syntactical device of the pronoun-verb of Part I becomes the variation of a possessive adjective-noun subject in Part II: "whose mind," "whose eyes," "whose love". These sounds counterpoint the primary motive in Part II of the sound of the name of "Moloch!" Part III presents another variation of the motive from Part I in order to counterpoint the former's primary motive. This time the syntactical variation takes one of three forms: noun-pronoun, "where you" or "where we"; noun-article, "where the"; or noun-noun, "where fifty". Finally, syllables of "Moloch!" in Part II mix with the "holy!" syllables of Part IV. Thus the adventurous aesthetics of *A Love Su-*

preme and "Howl" do not amount to artistic anarchy. Neither fairly sustains the designation of antiart, that is, antipoetry or antijazz.[51] To be sure, both works freely build up an original sonic chromaticity, but both Coltrane and Ginsberg unify their multipart works through familiar motivic and motivic-like procedures.

Thought waves—heat waves—all vibrations . . .
God breathes through us so completely . . .
so gently we hardly feel it

—John Coltrane, "A Love Supreme"

—must give

—Allen Ginsberg, "Song," *Howl and Other Poems*

Howl and *A Love Supreme* utilize a style that agreeably mixes differences; audible multiplicities gather. Sonic pluralism mirrors programmatic pluralism in both works under the ecumenical but still patriarchal sign of *Pater Omnipotens* in "Howl" and the he-God of *A Love Supreme.* The patriarchal designation, though presently anachronistic, reflects the tenacity of timeworn ideologies of social order. Moreover, the antidomestic bias of the Beats and much of the jazz community contributed to their contradictory attitudes and exclusionary actions toward women. Women were often held in contempt for their dependence and seen as a threat when they claimed their power and asserted their egos. Thus, then as now, with difficulty women won their autonomy, their creative freedom, and their dignity. Nevertheless, women such as Carla Bley, Hettie Jones, Lenore Kandel, Alice McLeod (later Coltrane), Diane di Prima, and ruth weiss helped generate the free energy of Beat writing and jazz just as they were discovering their own creative voices. They proved out the implications of works such as *A Love Supreme* and *Howl.* As they enjoyed the spontaneous procedures of performing new identities and creating their own uncensored art, they helped supersede patriarchy and disintegrated hierarchies through the leveling ideology of love.[52]

I conclude that *Howl* absorbed the modern vernacular disruptions of hip urban life, psychic breakdown, unsanctioned mysticism, and radical politics. Jazz, too, bore the meanings of these disruptions as they intruded upon many of the players, themselves, and jazz audiences. Jazz demonstrated that social and psychological dislocation could help generate a compelling style. *Howl* benefited from the demonstration. Ginsberg molded the strength of vernacular style into one of the most influential collections of poems ever written by a U.S. citizen. *Howl*, like its sources, was uncompromisingly candid in its perspective. It was intellectually clear and pessimistic and emotionally outraged over the toll of Cold War capitalism. At the same time, as I noted in Chapter 1, Ginsberg was an entrepreneur who sought his own fame and commodification. Hyped commodification was necessary in order for Ginsberg to throw *Howl* like a punch and then massage the bruise through humor, through free, spectacular lines, and through the poems' ultimate conveyance of tireless goodwill. *Howl*, through style, transmits a politics of candor and open conviviality among varied selves and bodies. Its poems peel away the veneer of capitalism's binary assumptions and prove the former's salutary convictions when they chant even Moloch's—"whose blood is running money"—holiness. *Howl* cannot withhold its weight of love; "the weight is too heavy."[53]

Of course, *A Love Supreme* emerged out of the very fabric of jazz's mutating history. Its eclectic elements of style—modes, irregular rhythms, motives, oral traces, vocalisms, oriental gleanings, and programmatic intent—sustain convincing resemblance with *Howl*. *A Love Supreme* and *Howl* absorbed the cultural moment and show that postwar style in the United States was a meeting place where different selves and communities opened up, mixed, and produced vital, compelling art. These works fibered the spine of disaffected and marginalized selves. People looked to *Howl* and *A Love Supreme* as emblems and sustenance for their own mode of independent, social, artistic, and political action, which for some, by the mid-1960s, became increasingly radical.

Unlike Ginsberg or, for that matter, Gillespie, Coltrane did not promote a flamboyant persona. Coltrane's gentle intelligence, instinctive warmth, and unassuming generosity with others lent credulity to the uncompromised but ultimately kindly intentions of his work. His personality was soothing to the naked volatility of the music's emotions. Consumers who were jazz fans and some who were not bought *A Love Supreme* in part because of Coltrane's benign persona. *A Love Supreme* was Coltrane's halo. Certainly, too, the aura of rebel spirituality helped the commercial success of *Howl* and the works of other Beat writers.[54] The Beat generation writers consistently cast jazz and its root musics, their demonstrations of style—African American culture itself—in sacred terms: "IT." *Howl* is one example of how the Beats sought to return to jazz what they had received from it. *A Love Supreme* proved jazz's reserves had not run dry. Both works continue to give.

CONCLUSION
THE HORN KEEPS BLOWING

Throughout this study we have seen that jazz eludes dogma. It defies attempts to fix its uses, parameters, qualities, and meanings; therefore, as I said in the Introduction, it is a healthy signifier of a vital music. A healthy signifier is a moving target that does not stop moving no matter how many times you shoot it. In other words, its terms are inclusive, mutable, and open. It transfigures foreign objects (even deadly bullets) into constituents, resources, and innovations. So John Coltrane incorporated Eastern modes and instrumentation for "India." And during his fusion period Miles Davis rocked his jazz with huge trap sets, overdriven guitar, electric piano, and signal-processed trumpet. Jazz does not often acknowledge its difference from anything. It sprawls beyond styles of music; it infiltrates and explodes them. It demonstrates that life is new every day.[1]

For the Beats, jazz suggested a style of writing, but it also outlined ways of talking that were from the heart, spontaneous, and conversational—call and response—as in the "Frisco: The Tape" section of *Visions of Cody.* The music accompanied a way of traveling in automobiles across vast distances and volatile terrain at tremendous speeds. Sometimes the Beats road-tripped a straight line to the destination like a musician speeding from a tonic to a dominant, then back to the tonic. At other times they cruised serpentine back-routes like Sonny Rollins curving through modulations, substitutions, and chromaticisms on the way to a familiar sonic place. Regardless, jazz was the sound of *On the Road*. Too, jazz mirrored a way of socializing. The point is related to talking, but like many jazz ensembles and venues, the Beats' social circles were usually mixed and open to the unfamiliar person: the stranger, the bum, black or yellow, white and brown, male or female, gay or straight. The music silhouetted human desire, itself unfettered, moving, mixing, associating, celebrating, and so overlapping notions of spirituality and creativity. Coltrane's poem "A Love Supreme" desires kaleidoscopic celebration. It reflects the way the suite itself collapses distinctions that separate:

> Words, sounds, speech, men, memory, thoughts . . .
> emotions—time—all related . . .
> all made in one . . .
> Thought waves—heat waves—all vibrations—
> all paths . . .
> ELATION.[2]

Coltrane's poem and music crystallizes the ongoing social and aesthetic transformations that jazz and Beat writers set into motion in the United States: blew 'em like wind. They pushed the culture toward creativity and social pluralism, and they are still pushing. The sixties were years of imaginative civil rights struggle. The peace movement bridged gender, race, and class boundaries. Rock 'n' roll and the interest in folk and roots musics brought diverse groups together. Everyone from Bob Dylan to the Beatles, from the Grateful Dead to the Doors grew from the seeds of the Beats and African American blues and jazz. And in the feedback loop James Brown funked up Miles Davis's rhythms while Jimi Hendrix and Carlos

Santana electromagnified his timbre. The result was a wider, mixed audience for jazz. Corporate and independent entrepreneurs, through technologies of simulacra, commodified this music for a massive youth culture much as they had commodified jazz and Beat poetry for smaller audiences the decade before.

Implicitly, the art of Coltrane, Ginsberg, Kaufman, Kerouac, and weiss sought to open up consciousness to a greater awareness of self, others, and things—life. Many people sought out alternative communities and spirituality. Environmentalism and women's and gay's civil rights activities seemed to be forms of transformation in keeping with the spirit of the Beats. Today Lou Reed, Patti Smith, Tom Waits, and the much younger Liz Phair, The White Stripes, Bright Eyes, Sleater-Kinney, and Fat Boy Slim cast a Beat shadow through discrepancies of rhythm, street-wise vocalizing, and vernacular collage. Black urban hip hop has crossed over every domain of class, race, and border much as bebop did in the 1940s. The trio Medeski, Martin, and Wood and the collaboration of Matthew Shipp and the Antipop Consortium have merged hip-hop beat with electric, free jazz instrumentalism. And poetry slams. And poetry jams.

In my own environs of Tampa Bay, there is the Irritable Tribe of Poets, a collective of approximately fourteen bards and seven versatile musicians. For the past couple of years they have been magnetically agitating at far-flung venues like the Viva La Frida, the King Corona Cigar Bar, and most recently at the Orpheum for the annual *Tropical Heat Wave* (2003), sponsored by the government-independent, noncommercial community radio station WMNF. Musical accompaniments span a functional range, from simple backdrop, to driving energy, to dramatic, sonic expression of spoken word. Stylistically, the music bridges folk to pop to jazz to jazz avant-garde to world eclecticism. Improvisation is the rule of all performance. The experimental jazzman Albert Ayler retrospectively said, "The scream I was playing then was peace to me." Rhonda J. Nelson, an Irritable Tribe poet, wrote a poem inspired by Ayler's quotation, "Albert Ayler

Is Missing." Before performing it at Skipper's Smoke House in Tampa, March 2003, Nelson passed a note to the band members with the following suggestions:

> Slurs of honking sax, Jaco's bouncing bass, rockets of samples, Jim [vocally] repeating my lines behind me. Retard at the end. Three slow triangle beats after last line: "Bells, Bells," to end song.

Nelson says, like Ayler, the band almost always gets it right:

> On this horn a man can shout and tell the truth
> This horn deserves bright leather suits.[3]

Ferlinghetti and City Lights still publish. Whole museum exhibitions feature the importance of the Beat Generation and jazz in the 1950s. Beat literature is prominently displayed in popular bookstores all over the country because youth are buying it. Documentaries and films about the Beats have been made and are in the making. Jazz history programs, though controversial, take up whole weeks of the Public Broadcasting System's airtime. Academies teach the music and high art venues hear it out. Jazz artists win Pulitzer prizes now. James Carter, Christian McBride, Brad Mehldau, Joshua Redman, and Jacky Terrasson reverently play the jazz traditions just as they develop their own musical voices through tone and rhythm. They show their freedom in the groove, touring and selling CDs all over the world. They are aware of their compromises, just as Duke Ellington, Benny Goodman, and Charlie Parker were intimate with theirs. Still the music cycles round from the humble beginnings of a favorite recording in the practice room to a career. The music globalizes and its values go with it, infiltrating unfamiliar cultures and disparate forms. Watch U.S. team sports analogically mirror black jazz style. Whole teams take the music's name as players demonstrate individual and collective virtuosity and cooperation, flash, precision, rhythm, and groove. The motley assortment of players, staff, audiences, even owners and entrepreneurs, despite the contradictions, come together. They use the spectacle as it shines their glory when they win and their blues when they lose.

Now millions use the technologies of spectacle via the microchip. Broadband conduits take web-surfing audiences and artists to anyone, anywhere and everywhere in real time. They trade culture. They write and speak, call and respond freely: "Blow as deep as you want," the Kerouac dictum.[4] They blow like a horn. Kerouac would have loved the web—an endless scroll of word, image, and sound. Desire is loosed in the medium. Structures of commodification sense peril and opportunity, much as they did when the Beats lured them in like a magnet. Enough. Peril and opportunity. Capitalist empires, oppressions, violent extremisms. The Beats, jazz, and improvised style still show us the opportunities. For the present generation, Nelson echoes the "braying oscillation . . . spacing that sound," the ambition "to reach peace."[5]

NOTES
CREDITS
INDEX

NOTES

INTRODUCTION

1. The following titles signal the oppositional drift of much of the positive criticism and historiography about the Beats. They include Stanley Fisher, *Beat Coast East: An Anthology of Rebellion* (New York: Excelsior Press Publishers, 1960); John Tytell, *Naked Angels: The Lives and Literature of the Beat Generation* (Boston: Twayne Publishers, 1976); Michael McClure, *Scratching the Beat Surface* (San Francisco: North Point Press, 1982); Gregory Stephenson, *The Daybreak Boys: Essays on the Literature of the Beat Generation* (Carbondale: Southern Illinois University Press, 1990); Steven Watson, *Birth of the Beat Generation: Visionaries, Rebels, and Hipsters, 1944–1960* (New York: Pantheon Books, 1995). From the beginning most critics have panned the Beats and their rebellion. An exhaustive accounting would constitute a book in itself but a few influential, representative examples include Norman Podhoretz, "The Know-Nothing Bohemians," *Partisan Review,* 25 (1958): 305–318; John Ciardi, "Epitaph for the Dead Beats," *Saturday Review* (February 6, 1960): 11–13, 42. Both articles see the Beats—Ginsberg and Kerouac are cited as the representatives—as manifesting conventional youthful rebellion and not serious resistance, and certainly not serious art. A more recent example is Ellen Friedman, "Where are the Missing Contents? (Post) Modernism, Gender, and the Canon," in which the Beats' work is seen as "infused neither with nostalgia for the unpresentable nor

with yearning for the not yet presented" but as reaffirming the master narratives, their hierarchies and stratifications. In Stanley Tractenberg, ed., *Critical Essays on American Postmodernism* (New York: G. K. Hall, 1995), pp. 146–147.

2. See Steven Best and Douglas Kellner, *Postmodern Theory: Critical Interrogations* (New York: Guilford Press, 1991), pp. 34–75; and Nicholas Dirks, Geoff Eley, and Sherry Ortner, "Introduction," in Dirks et al., eds., *Culture/Power/History: A Reader in Contemporary Social Theory* (Princeton: Princeton University Press, 1994), pp. 3–45.

3. The first quotation is from Dirks et al., *Culture/Power/History*, p. 3. Michel Foucault, *History of Sexuality*, vol. 1, trans. Michael Hurley (New York: Pantheon Books, 1978), pp. 95, 96; William Burroughs, *Naked Lunch* (New York: Grove Press, 1962), p. 205.

4. For a critique of cultural studies and its tendency to reify everything it analyzes, criticizing it, civilizing it, effectively killing it as culture, particularly music, see Charles Keil and Steven Feld, *Music Grooves* (Chicago: University of Chicago Press, 1994), pp. 227–237. For a fine treatment of the way black jazz musicians and intellectuals negotiated and challenged the musical, discursive and institutional practices of jazz, see Eric Porter, *What Is This Thing Called Jazz? African American Musicians as Artists, Critics, and Activists* (Berkeley: University of California Press, 2002).

Two recent studies on William Burroughs begin to move in the direction of a more nuanced cultural studies that guards against the overdetermined analyses that can result from a stringent adherence to cultural theory. See Timothy S. Murphy, *Wising Up the Marks: The Amodern William Burroughs* (Berkeley: University of California Press, 1997); Jamie Russell, *Queer Burroughs* (New York: Palgrave Publishers, 2001).

5. Chuck Kleinhans, "Cultural Appropriation and Subcultural Expression: The Dialectics of Cooptation and Resistance." Paper given at Northwestern University Center for the Humanities (November 14, 1994). Kleinhans lays out the cultural studies debate about the agency of artists and consumers in resisting dominant ideological and symbolic power. Also see Mike Budd, Robert M. Entman, and Clay Steinman, "The Affirmative Character of U.S. Cultural Studies," *Critical Studies in Mass Communications*, 7 (1990): 169–184. Budd and his colleagues feel that cultural studies practitio-

ners such as J. Fiske and L. Grossberg exaggerate the effectiveness of consumer agency in subverting the intended meanings of corporations. Sometimes yes, sometimes no. I think you have to look at each individual circumstance.

6. W. T. Lhamon, Jr. explains the rise of vernacular style to the surface of 1950s popular culture. Much of the style was African American and the Beats were among the first to flash its lights. See Lhamon, *Deliberate Speed: The Origins of a Cultural Style in the 1950s* (Washington and London: Smithsonian Institutions Press, 1990). For the phenomenon of white absorption and use of African American style (from the origins of blackface performance at Catherine Market in New York City all the way to hip hop), see Lhamon, *Raising Cain: Blackface Performance from Jim Crow to Hip Hop* (Cambridge, Mass.: Harvard University Press, 1998).

7. Kerouac, "Belief and Technique for Modern Prose," *The Portable Jack Kerouac,* ed. Ann Charters (ms 1954, New York: Penguin, 1995), pp. 484–485.

8. See Jack Kerouac, *On the Road* (New York: Penguin Books, 1957), p. 86. The preceding quotation is from Kerouac, *Visions of Cody* (New York: Penguin, 1972), p. 329. I will always specify the kind of jazz at issue: swing, bebop, modal, and free jazz, for example.

9. Eric Porter, *What Is This Thing Called Jazz?*

1 THE HORN OF FAME

1. Information about Seider from Thomas Albright, "Seider Ranked with the Very Best Jazz Musicians," *San Francisco Chronicle,* March 25, 1979. Interview with Robert E. Johnson, May 22, 2003. As I discuss in Chapter 2 the separation between lore and fact with regard to Kaufman and most of the Beats is much contested. He was an oral poet, yes, but Maria Damon's research shows that he also typed and handwrote his poems. See *The Dark End of the Street: Margins in American Vanguard Poetry* (Minneapolis: University of Minnesota Press, 1993).

2. *A Coney Island of the Mind* (New York: New Directions, 1954) is one of the best selling poetry books ever. On Rexroth, see John Arthur Maynard, *Venice West: The Beat Generation in Southern California* (New Brunswick,

N.J.: Rutgers University Press, 1991), pp. 52–54. Also see Maynard on Lipton's article "Disaffiliation and the Art of Poverty," *Chicago Review* (spring 1956): 54. For a review of the various Bay Area literary groups and their cross-fertilization, see Michael Davidson, *The San Francisco Renaissance: Poetics and Community at Mid-Century* (New York: Cambridge University Press, 1989). On Jack Spicer's views on the importance of the pop in art and his somewhat contradictory resistance to celebrity, see Lewis Ellingham and Kevin Killian, *Poet Be Like God: Jack Spicer and the San Francisco Renaissance* (Hanover, N.H.: Wesleyan University Press, 1998). Also see Spicer, *The Collected Books of Jack Spicer* (Los Angeles: Black Sparrow Press, 1975). These are the later book-oriented poems (beginning in 1957), but they convey a similar point.

3. Barry Miles, *Ginsberg: A Biography* (New York: Simon and Schuster, 1989), p. 197. I was unable to find Ferlinghetti's Emersonian note in Ginsberg's papers at Stanford University or in the City Lights Records at the University of California, Berkeley. This is surprising given how meticulous both men were about saving and maintaining correspondence. Miles's noting it could have been a momentous embellishment encouraged by Ginsberg, as happens in storytelling. On the other hand, Stanford had only recently acquired Ginsberg's papers. I am not sure that everything had been transferred. Moreover, some of the material may still have been in prerelease or preparation stage.

4. David Perlman, "How Captain Hanrahan Made 'Howl' a Bestseller," *Reporter,* 17 (December 12, 1957): 37.

5. "Big Day for the Bards," *LIFE,* 47 (September 21, 1957). Norman Podhoretz, "Howl of Protest in San Francisco," *New Republic,* 37 (September 1957): 34. "New Test for Obscenity," *Nation,* 185 (November 9, 1957): 34. Carolyn Anspacher, "'Howl' Trial Starts—Big Crowd," *San Francisco Chronicle* (August 17, 1958): 1, 6. See Perlman, "How Captain Hanrahan Made 'Howl' a Bestseller," pp. 37–39.

6. Hanrahan quotation from Perlman, pp. 37–39. Evelyn Thorne, 1957, Box 5, Folder 9, "Correspondence," City Lights Records, Bancroft Library, Berkeley, Calif. There are thirty-six such letters in this folder (hereafter City Lights Records).

7. Paraphrased from a documentary by Chris Felver, *Lets Go* (San Francisco: Cloud House Poetry Archives, 1983).

8. William Hogan, 1957, Box 5, Folder 9, "Correspondence," City Lights Records.

9. Gil Orlovitz, 1957, Box 5, Folder 9, "Correspondence," City Lights Records. Jim Morrison, "Break on Through," *The Doors* (1967, Los Angeles: Elektra/Asylum, 1988): 74007–2.

10. See Ellingham and Killian on the 6 Gallery, *Poet Be Like God*, pp. 56–62. Jack Kerouac, *Dharma Bums* (New York: Penguin, 1958), p. 13.

11. For Barthes's discussion of fighting bourgeois myth with antibourgeois myth, see *Mythologies*, trans. Annette Lavers (New York: Hill and Wang, 1972), pp. 131–137. Michael Davidson uses a different terminology, describing the 6 Gallery readings as an "enabling fiction." This terminology refers to the story's galvanizing function of providing a model for artists to look to for orientation and belief in themselves. It also implicitly refers to the fact that Kerouac first crystallized the story in the United States in his novel *Dharma Bums*, pp. 13–16. Davidson's designation is general. He does not examine the genealogy and content of the 6 Gallery readings. He mentions the event as one among several fictions that enabled the San Francisco renaissance—a much broader view of the Bay Area literary scene across several decades. The so-called San Francisco poetry renaissance is more or less namelessly subsumed into this larger movement, in contradistinction to the predominant sense that the Beats co-opted the San Francisco poets. See Davidson, *The San Francisco Renaissance*, pp. 1–31. Bob Kaufman, "West Coast Sounds—1956," *Solitudes Crowded with Loneliness* (New York: New Directions, 1965), p. 1.

Discrepancies among accounts of the 6 Gallery readings include: Barry Miles says a postcard that Ginsberg made to advertise the event is dated October 13, 1955. See Allen Ginsberg, ed. Barry Miles, *Howl: Original Facsimile* (New York: Harper & Row, 1986), p. 195. A facsimile of the postcard at the *Ferlinghetti, City Lights and the San Francisco Scene* exhibition reads, "8 PM Friday Night October 7, 1955," Bancroft Library, Berkeley, Calif., October, 1996. Davidson dates the reading on October 13. See *The San Francisco Renaissance*, p. 3; Richard Candida Smith dates it on the 13th. See *Utopia and Dissent: Art, Power, and Politics in California* (Berkeley: University of California Press, 1995), p. 160. Tom Clark also dates it on the 13th in *Jack Kerouac: A Biography* (New York, Paragon House, 1990). But Michael McClure puts the reading in December, 1955; *Scratch the Beat Surface* (San

Francisco: North Point Press, 1982), p. 12. Ann Charters dates it on the 7th: *The Portable Beat Reader* (New York: Penguin Books, 1992), p. 227.

Smith says that Ferlinghetti was one of the readers; *Utopia and Dissent*, p. 160. This is clearly an error. Smith apparently thought there were six readers and added Ferlinghetti. There were five readers. The sixth poet was the emcee Rexroth.

Ginsberg and Gregory Corso say that Philip Lamantia had renounced surrealism by the time of the reading, which does not jibe with the fact that he read poems by surrealist John Hoffman that evening; also, he was a contributing editor for *Arsenal: Surrealist Subversion,* and in a post-1956 reference to Ginsberg's aesthetics in the poem "Fud at Foster's" he exclaims "AND NO MORE REALITY SANDWICHES!!!" See Charters, *The Portable Beat Reader,* pp. 318–320. Corso and Ginsberg wrongly hype that Lamantia read his own poems after experiencing an epiphany of sorts, resulting from a trip to Mexico where he "took drugs, underwent visions, became catholic, became silent, and reappeared at age of 28 in native town to take part in the reading." See Allen Ginsberg, "Literary Revolution in America." Reprinted in *Howl: Original Facsimile,* p. 165; originally published in the literary journal *Litterair Paspoort 100* (Amsterdam, 1957).

12. Jack Goodman to John Allen Ryan, November 1955, quoted in Rebecca Solnit, *Secret Exhibition: Six California Artists of the Cold War Era* (San Francisco: City Lights Books, 1990), p. 48. See William Burroughs, *The Letters of William S. Burroughs, 1945–1959* (New York: Viking Penguin, 1993), pp. 314–315.

13. For Eberhart's quotations, see Richard Eberhart, "West Coast Sounds," *New York Times Book Review* (September 2, 1956): 314–315. For Jack Goodman's quotation see Solnit, *Secret Exhibition,* p. 5.

14. Ginsberg's twenty-page letter to Eberhart can be found in *To Eberhart from Ginsberg: A Letter About Howl 1956* (Lincoln, Mass.: Penman Press, 1976). According to Miles, the editor of Ginsberg's *Howl: Original Facsimile,* p. 158, the letter was sent to Eberhart on May 18, 1956. Eberhart's quotations from "West Coast Rhythms," p. 7.

15. See Michael Grieg, "The Lively Arts in San Francisco," *Mademoiselle,* 142 (February 1957): 142, 190–191.

16. The circulation figure and the other information cited above comes

from S. E. Gontarski, *The Review of Contemporary Fiction*, 10, 3 (1990): 8, 132–135. Gontarski edits the issue. Ferlinghetti's quotation is also from Gontarski: "Lawrence Ferlinghetti on Grove Press," ibid., p. 128. With respect to Don Allen's consultation with Ferlinghetti and Rexroth and their shaping influence on the "San Francisco Scene" edition, see Robert Allen's letter to Ferlinghetti: "We are seriously interested in including 'Howl' . . . in our S.F. issue of ER. G. [Ginsberg] tells me it is up to you . . . We will . . . state it is from the book you've published and will give your address . . . for interested readers. We both believe publication of it in our mag will create new interest in his work, as well as in that of the other poets included, and that it should stimulate sales of your book [*Pictures of the Gone World*] . . . R. [Rexroth] says he will say something about this, but I'd like to read what you have to say." Allen's letter, March 11, 1957, Box 4, Records. Ca. 1955–70, City Lights Records.

17. Ralph Cook, *The City Lights Pocket Poets Series: A Descriptive Bibliography* (La Jolla, Calif.: A. A. Laurence McGilvery / Atticus Books, 1982), p. 22.

18. Ginsberg's letter, "Correspondence," Box 4, City Lights Records, 1957.

19. Ginsberg had been a market researcher for various companies in New York and San Francisco. He also worked as a freelancer. This work ranged from testing public opinion about the Korean War to ascertaining peoples' feelings about slogans for toothpaste. See Miles, *Ginsberg: A Biography,* pp. 117–139.

20. By genealogy I mean to distinguish the 6 Gallery event from the oral tradition and literary-historical makings, and, at times, orchestration of the story via the ambitious Ginsberg and others. I'm referring to the genealogy of the story not in a linear, direct-begetting sense, but in the Foucauldian or Nietzschean sense—genealogy as symmetrical, diffuse, contradictory, and, at times, at cross purposes. I'm referring to the genealogy of the story and its mythological force in attracting audiences, believers, doubters, and interpreters. See Michel Foucault, "Nietzsche, Genealogy, History," in *The Foucault Reader,* ed. Paul Rabinow (New York: Pantheon Books, 1984), pp. 76–100.

21. Miles interprets this behavior of McClure, Harmon, and others as fierce competitiveness and jealousy. He says Ginsberg was dismayed by it.

My own feeling is that the Bay Area writers were independent-minded and dismayed over the popularity of the Beats more than they were jealous, but some of them at certain moments were jealous. See Ginsberg, ed. Miles, *Howl: Original Facsimile*, p. 213.

22. Weiss, telephone interview, October 17, 1996. See Ellingham and Killian, *Poet Be Like God*, pp. 288–290.

23. Here are some examples of letters Ferlinghetti received in response to the customs seizure and trial in 1957, Box 5, Folder 9, "Correspondence," City Lights Records: San Francisco resident Fred Burrous implored the help of God for "our city, country and children if we allow our public servants to invalidate the judgments of our greatest intellects." There is no indication that Burrous read *Howl*, but he esteemed Ginsberg because he esteemed W. C. Williams who wrote the introduction to *Howl*. He added that if the attorney general allows a trial, Americans will have "reason to hang [their] heads in shame before the world."

When Roger Jenkins read that the Customs Collector not only seized a shipment of *Howl* but burned a copy, he wrote, "I'm sending $5.00 to help defray either the cost of repaying the book or the newspaper notice concerning it." He added, "I've tried writing to Mcphee [sic], but I don't know what to say to people like him. If $5.00 isn't enough . . . let me know."

Jim Scheville sent this limerick to the *San Francisco Chronicle* editorial page:

The Juvenile Captain Hanrahan,
He ran and he ran and he ran
After delinquents uncouth,
He cried with a scowl,
"Lets Ban that book Howl
before poems corrupt all
our youth."

In the copy he sent Ferlinghetti he commented, "Sorry this had to happen. If there's anything I can do, please let me know." Neither the *Chronicle* nor Ferlinghetti published the poem.

The publishers Hill & Wang wrote, "We as publishers support your stand against censorship 100% and wish you success in ending attempts to suppress books and magazines on the Westcoast. I am enclosing a copy of the letter and sending it to Captain Hanrahan."

The trade publication *Publisher's Weekly* replied to Ferlinghetti with a query: "Many thanks for the notice about the customs seizure. Could you send us more details about the case. We would like to know dates and the names of customs personnel, what legal action are you planning and have you started it yet. Could you send any newspaper clippings about it? Full information will really do the job of bringing the matter to the attention of the trade."

Philip Booth, a professor at Wellesley College, wrote to the court: "*Howl* convinces me that it is a wholly legitimate work, and I am . . . shocked by its seizure." The writer goes on to say that if Macphee would ban *Howl*, "so would he have to include Moll Flanders, Clarissa, Ulysses, most 17th century poems and most of Shakespeare. The seizure of *Howl* seems . . . a direct threat and I . . . as a writer, a reader, and a teacher . . . protest against such an unwarranted seizure."

The editorial comment in the text comes from the *San Francisco Chronicle* (October 7, 1957): 18.

24. Kerouac's 6 Gallery story is in *Dharma Bums,* pp. 13–16. About the same time Rexroth wrote the "San Francisco Letter," which appeared in *Evergreen Review,* 2 (1957) and describes a renaissance, which includes mention of Robert Duncan, William Everson, and younger poets Ginsberg and Lamantia. Rexroth praises "Howl" but does not mention the readings at the 6 Gallery because he does not view it as the beginning of a poetry renaissance and even less a revolution. By 1972, however, Rexroth wrote differently about the significance of the 6 Gallery readings. In the *Evergreen Review* piece, Rexroth constructs the renaissance as ongoing since the end of World War II. At this time he was clearly ambivalent about the attention the Bay Area was receiving via the Beats. A reprint of "The Literary Revolution in America" can be found in Ginsberg's *Howl: Original Facsimile,* p. 165. For Ginsberg's letter to Ferlinghetti about the article, see "Correspondence," Box 4, City Lights Records, December 11, 1957.

25. On jazz-poetry in the Harlem renaissance, see Sascha Feinstein, *Jazz Poetry: From the 1920s to Present* (Westport, Conn.: Greenwood Press, 1997). With respect to the U.S. renaissance of the mid-1900s, I'm referring to Matheissen's influential *American Renaissance* (1941).

26. Quotations from *Dharma Bums,* pp. 13–16.

27. Ibid.

28. Kerouac, *The Subterraneans* (New York: Grove Press, 1957), p. 157; *On the Road* (New York: Penguin, 1957), p. 157.

29. Here I have used Chip Rhodes's *Structures of the Jazz Age: Mass Culture, Progressive Education, and Racial Disclosures in American Modernism* (London: Verso, 1998), pp. 178; 171–197. Also see David Levering Lewis, *When Harlem Was in Vogue* (New York: Random House, 1981); Ann Douglas, *Terrible Honesty: Mongrel Manhattan in the 1920s* (New York: Farrar, Straus and Giroux, 1995). For one influential Beat-era definition of the primitive, see Norman Mailer, *The White Negro: Superficial Reflections on the Hipster* (San Francisco: City Lights Books), originally published as an article in *Dissent,* 1957.

30. On the "social control buffer" and review of the origins of racism, see Theodore Allen, *The Invention of the White Race: Volume One, Racial Oppression and Social Control* (London: Verso, 1994), pp. 1–27. With respect to Darwinian social theory, I have in mind Thomas Huxley, *Evolution and Ethics* (1893); as for Freud, "Totem and Taboo" (1929); "Civilization and its Discontents" (1929). Also, a related influential text about the primitive, James Frazer's *The Golden Bough: A Study in Magic and Religion,* 3d ed. (London: Macmillan, 1911–1915). Neil Leonard documents the various publics' reactions to jazz. The musical establishment seemed universally appalled with jazz. The situation hit symbolic critical mass in 1927 when "the 400,000 organized in the National Federation of Music Clubs launched an effort to fight "'jazzing' of the noble compositions of the great composers." See Leonard, *Jazz and the White Americans* (Chicago: University of Chicago Press, 1962), p. 62.

31. Bob Kaufman, "Walking Parker Home," *Solitudes,* p. 5. Allen Ginsberg, "America," *Howl and Other Poems* (San Francisco: City Lights Books, 1956), pp. 31–34. Criticisms of Kerouac and the Beats: Norman Podhoretz, "The Know-Nothing Bohemians," *Partisan Review,* 25 (1958): 305–318. John Ciardi, "Epitaph for the Dead Beats," *Saturday Review* (February 6, 1960): 11–13, 42; Rexroth says, "Now there are two things Jack [Kerouac] knows nothing about—jazz and Negroes," Gerald Nicosia, *Memory Babe: A Critical Biography of Jack Kerouac* (New York: Grove Press, 1983), p. 568. In

"Kerouac's Subterraneans: A Study of Romantic 'Primitivism,'" (1994), Jon Pannish sums up Kerouac as a romantic racialist who trivializes black experience by failing to distinguish between outsiders who choose the margin and outsiders assigned to and confined to the margin. This echoes LeRoi Jones's (Amira Baraka) argument in *Blues People* (1963) about the prevalence of whites that did not make distinctions among outsiders. Yet Baraka believed Kerouac was one of few who had an ear for jazz. See LeRoi Jones, "Letter to the *Evergreen Review* about Kerouac's Spontaneous Prose," *Evergreen Review*, 1967. Reprinted in Charters, *The Portable Beat Reader*, pp. 349–354. Moreover, it seems to me that the entire narrative of *The Subterraneans* (1958) is concerned with the agency and implications of choice, that is, much of the narrator's stream of thought deals with the consequences and implications of a white man's bonding with an African American woman. To do so means Leo will have made the choice to be black, and for as long as he remains interracially yoked, irrevocably separated from the institutions of family and white privilege. Sascha Feinstein's *Jazz Poetry* (1997) credits the Beats with creating a wider audience for poetry and jazz and for facilitating its movement from obscurity to fad. But with the exception of Kerouac's recorded reading of "October in the Railroad Earth," she sees little merit in the Beats' work, again, because of its romanticism. Kerouac's quotations are from *Visions of Cody* (ms 1951, New York: Penguin, 1972), pp. 371, 373.

32. Kerouac, *Dharma Bums*, p. 85. As is pointed out by Stephen Prothero in the introduction to Carole Tonkinson's edited collection *Big Sky Mind: Buddhism and the Beat Generation*, Americans, rather than receiving Eastern teachings from masters and schools, have received them through books (New York: Riverhead Books, 1995), p. 120. Kerouac came to Buddhism via Thoreau's discussion of the Hindu *Bhagavad Gita*, which led him to Ashvaghosa's fourth-century *The Life of the Buddha* and then to Dwight Goddard's *A Buddhist Bible* (1932). The Beats' interest in Eastern ideas was enhanced by Bay Area poets' considerable knowledge of Eastern philosophical and mystical traditions. Rexroth was a skilled translator of Eastern texts: *One Hundred Poems from the Japanese* (1955); *One Hundred Poems from the Chinese* (1956). Philip Whalen and Gary Snyder translated Buddhist texts as well. They also studied Buddhism under Zen masters in Japan. There was, in

fact, a whole community of poets in the Bay Area who applied Buddhist principles to the practice of art and life including, besides the already mentioned, Lenore Kandel, Bob Kaufman, Joanne Kyger, Will Peterson, Albert Saijo, and Lew Welch.

33. See Thomas Owen, *Bebop: The Music and its Players* (New York: Oxford University Press, 1995), p. 42. Parker's comment is in Ross Russell, *Bird Lives!* (New York: Charterhouse, 1973), p. 212. Subsequent live recordings show that Parker did make the run again because as with countless other melodies, he memorized it.

34. Kerouac's notion of spontaneous writing mirrors jazz musicians' notions of spontaneous playing. For example, Paul Berliner's *Thinking in Jazz: The Infinite Art of Improvisation,* an analysis of 3,000 pages of transcribed interviews with jazz players, found that jazz musicians evaluate soloing ability, in part, according to the soloist's ability to be inventive spontaneously, to "apply general principles of solo formulation as they come to the player's mind. This attitude both maximizes the challenges associated with composing music in performance and optimizes the possibilities for conceiving imaginative ideas" (Chicago: University of Chicago Press, 1994), p. 268. Irving Howe, "Mass Society and Post-Modern Fiction," *Partisan Review,* 26, 3 (1959): 148.

35. Ginsberg, *To Eberhart from Ginsberg,* pp. 17–31; Kerouac, "Spontaneous Prose," in *The Casebook on the Beats,* ed. Thomas Parkinson (New York: Thomas Y. Crowell Company, 1961), p. 65; first published in *Evergreen Review,* 2 (1957). Dennis McNally, *Desolate Angel: Jack Kerouac, the Beat Generation, and America* (New York: Random House, 1979), p. 320.

36. Quotations are from Kerouac's "Spontaneous Prose," *The Casebook on the Beats,* p. 65.

37. See Eric Porter, *What Is This Thing Called Jazz? African American Musicians as Artists, Critics, and Activists* (Berkeley: University of California Press), pp. 54–100. Porter details a complicated response to bebop as it emerged into the wider public in 1945. As Jones indicated, many critics disparaged the music, but others championed the new style as a complex, intelligent high art, an accomplishment on par with the prestige of classical music. This kind of coverage helped bring respectability to jazz and black jazz

musicians that had previously been unknown. On performance theory see Judith Butler, *Gender Trouble: Feminism and the Subversion of Identity* (New York: Routledge, 1990).

38. Italics from Ginsberg's "Howl," in *Howl and Other Poems*, p. 21; On Kerouac's early response to Bop, see "Beatific: The Origins of the Beat Generation," reprinted in Ann Charters, *The Portable Jack Kerouac Reader* (New York: Penguin, 1995), p. 568. On Kerouac's following Newman around, see Nicosia, *Memory Babe*, pp. 124–125.

39. Steven Feld, "Sound Structure as Social Structure," *Ethnomusicology*, 28, 3 (1984): 406. Norman Mailer, *The White Negro*, section II, no page numbers. Though Charles Keil's *Urban Blues* deals primarily with urban rhythm and blues, I cite it because it was an early important demonstration of the relationship between social structure and music (Chicago: University of Chicago Press, 1966). James Lincoln Collier, *The Making of Jazz* (Boston: Houghton Mifflin Company, 1976), pp. 341–362. The quotation is on p. 342. Scott DeVeaux's more recent study, too, confirms the presence of the emotions Collier mentions, in the turn away from institutionalized swing. It was "a visceral reaction to things as they were, unpremeditated and impervious to rational argument. This state of frustration, anger and weariness was the necessary precondition for the emergence of bebop." See DeVeaux, *The Birth of Bebop: A Social and Musical History* (Berkeley: University of California Press, 1998), p. 248.

40. See Eric Lott, "Double V Double Time: Bebop's Politics of Style," *Jazz Among the Discourses*, ed. Krin Gabbard (Durham: Duke University Press, 1993), inset quotation, p. 244. Lott does not cite the origin of the slogan "Double V." Nat Brandt does in *Harlem at War: The Black Experience in WWII* (Syracuse: Syracuse University Press, 1996).

41. For early critical response to Bop, see Jones, *Blues People* (New York: William Morrow, 1963), pp. 180, 188–189. Also see Porter, *What Is This Thing Called Jazz?* pp. 54–100. For Gillespie and Clarke, see Dizzy Gillespie, *To Be or Not to Bop* (New York: Da Capo Press, 1979), p. 142. Also, Burton Peretti discusses the value and liabilities of jazz oral history and autobiography as empirical evidence (the interest of traditional historians) and as story/performance (the interest of folklorists and poststructuralists); Peretti,

"Oral Histories of Jazz Musicians: The NEA Transcripts as Texts in Context," *Jazz among the Discourses,* pp. 117–133. Gillespie's *To Be or Not to Bop* combines oral history and autobiography. To my mind the work reflects a wide and valid cross-section of perceptions about the bebop era that other oral histories, autobiographies, jazz histories, criticism, and biographies corroborate. Louis Armstrong was not the only jazz player upset about bebop. Natty Dominique thought the music was "nothing but a mess," and Mezz Mezzrow (a devoted "white-Negro" since the 1920s) called bebop "the music of tics . . . the agony of the split, hacked-up personality." See Peretti, *The Creation of Jazz: Race and Culture in Urban America* (Urbana: University of Illinois Press, 1992), p. 214.

42. Mailer, *The White Negro,* section II, no page numbers. The most superficial aspect of Mailer's essay is its linking of the hipster to the black sex myth. Here he exploits an old stereotype in order to create a white rebel. Baldwin thought Mailer had stooped pretty low, perpetuating prejudice, and said so; he seemed to forgive him, however, because of the great writing that had come before. See *Nobody Knows My Name* (New York: Dial Press, 1961), pp. 216–241. For Mailer's part, he felt no shame: when *Advertisements for Myself* appeared in 1959, he noted the *The White Negro* as the best thing he had ever done (New York: G. P. Putnam's and Sons, 1959), pp. 306–310.

43. On jazz and romanticism, see Alan Lewis, ed. Avron Levine White, "The Sociological Interpretation of Modern Jazz," *Sociological Review Monograph* 34 (London: Routledge & Kegan Paul, 1987), pp. 56–76. Lewis sees jazz operating on two levels: one, out of a black political consciousness; the other, out of a participation in the symbolic world of European-rooted romanticism. On zoot suits and antipatriotism, see Lott, "Double V Double Time," p. 245. I would add here that hipsters, jazz fans, and musicians by no means universally wore zoots, though Kenny Clarke, Gillespie, and Thelonious Monk often wore them. Many photos of Bop ensembles show musicians wearing conservative business suits, which is interesting because it suggests how bebop had thrown away show biz glitter and had inverted the square connotations of the "man in the gray flannel suit." Miles Davis wore Brooks Brothers suits exclusively. Bop musicians made serious business of art. Behind the shades lay the mystique of cutting-edge entrepre-

neurs, government spies, or high-crime operatives. On the other hand, Charlie Parker's erratic lifestyle was not conducive to fine dress or good hygiene. He mainlined his wardrobe, although he was known for wearing plaid flannel shirts (as was Kerouac, later). He looked good when he was not strung out or when someone else dressed him. For his information on zoots Lott uses Stuart Cosgrove, "The Zoot Suit and Style Warfare," *Zoot Suits and Second-Hand Dresses: An Anthology of Fashion and Music,* ed. Angela McRobbie (Boston: Unwin Hyman, 1988), pp. 3–22. According to Cosgrove the "zoot suit riots" in Los Angeles in 1943 stemmed in large part from the Latino population, who dashed around in zoots in considerable numbers. Smaller numbers of blacks and others wore zoots in Los Angeles; they were involved in the riots but to a lesser extent than Lott lets on. What is fascinating is that Latinos were hearing jazz as the sound of their positive opposition and identity, too.

44. For Alexander's quotation see David Meltzer, *Reading Jazz* (San Francisco: Mercury Press, 1993), p. 179. In 1995–1996, Berman's and Alexander's work received substantial attention in the Whitney Museum of American Art exhibit *Beat Culture and the New America 1950–1965.* For more, see Rebecca Solnit, "Heretical Constellations: Notes on California 1946–61" in the exhibit's companion volume, *Beat Culture and the New America 1950–1965,* ed. Lisa Phillips (New York: Whitney Museum/Flammarion, 1995), pp. 69–87.

45. Ginsberg, *Howl,* p. 9. ruth weiss, telephone interview, October 17, 1996; Paul Blake, conversation with weiss and Blake at the M. H. De Young Museum, October 12, 1996. Margolis's line, Steven Watson, *The Birth of the Beat Generation: Visionaries, Rebels, and Hipsters 1944–1960* (New York: Pantheon Books, 1995), p. 227. Bethune's comment is from Brandt, *Harlem at War,* p. 82. Her comments originally appeared in *The New York Times* (November 14, 1941).

46. Kaufman, "Walking Parker Home," *Solitudes,* p. 5. DeVeaux, *The Birth of Bebop,* p. 282. John Clellon Holmes, *Go* (New York: Random House, 1952), pp. 160–161.

47. John Clellon Holmes, *Horn* (New York: Random House, 1953), p. 165.

48. Lawrence Ferlinghetti, "I Am Waiting," *A Coney Island of the Mind*

(New York: New Directions, 1958), pp. 49–53. Pressures to conform to commercial requirements corrupted the communal ethic in African American music, and if there was a consistent complaint among jazz players who aspired to excellence, it was that they were bored. See Peretti, *The Creation of Jazz*, p. 172; and LeRoi Jones, *Blues People*, p. 181. Places like Monroe's and Minton's were bastions of experimentation, improvisation, and community, as was backstage, on the bus, or late hours in hotel rooms where jazz players could play and exchange notes freely. Accounts of the Beats' and associated poets' opposition to academic stiflement are legion, but for reference, see Charters' introduction to *The Portable Beat Reader*, pp. xv–xxxvi. On Dexter Gordon, see the monologue "On Bebop." *Dexter Gordon: The Complete Blue Note Sixties Sessions* (Hollywood: Capital Records, 1996): 7243. In the monologue Gordon also speaks of "the great leap forward." Bebop was the musical language, the talk, the clothing, the kind of "anything you could do" stunts players pulled to avoid the war, and how much fun he had. "I came up at just the right time," he says. In Ira Gitler's *Swing to Bop: Oral History of the Transition in Jazz in the 1940s,* players, forty years later, convey the excitement and enthusiasm that accompanied their commitment to the music. See Gitler's summary (New York: Oxford University Press, 1985), p. 86. On road trips, see Kerouac, *On the Road,* pp. 14–15, 112–115, 124, 133–135. Roland Barthes, "From Work to Text," *Textual Strategies: Perspectives in Post-Structuralist Criticism,* ed. Josue V. Harari (Ithaca: Cornell University Press, 1979), pp. 80–81.

49. Ginsberg, *Howl*, pp. 9–16.

50. Maynard, pp. 57–59. Ginsberg's gesture was not unprecedented. Helen Adam, Ida Hodes, McClure, Spicer, and others staged a reading of Duncan's play *Faust Foutu* at the 6 Gallery in January 1955, which became scandalous when Duncan stripped off his clothes "to represent the revealed nakedness of the poet." See Ellingham and Killian, pp. 60–61.

51. See Maynard, pp. 58–59, 121, 125–140. Lawrence Lipton, *The Holy Barbarians* (New York: Julian Messner, 1959).

52. McClure, *Scratching the Beat Surface* (San Francisco: North Point Press, 1993), p. 15. Kenneth Rexroth, *American Poetry in the Twentieth Century* (New York: Herder and Herder, 1971), pp. 161–162. Also see Charters, "Beat Poetry and the San Francisco Renaissance," *The Columbia History of*

American Poetry, ed. Jay Parini (New York: Columbia University Press), p. 584.

2 ON THE BRINK

1. Center and edge and margin and middle are problematic terms. There are probably few individuals, regardless of their socioeconomic station, who do not at certain moments feel excluded or marginalized and at other moments centered and secure. Feelings of alienation and despair or well-being cut across the boundaries of ideology and socioeconomic position. One's subjective sense of margin and center can vacillate with the speed of thought. I use these terms as a way to situate relationships among people relative to material conditions, social patterns, and the whole discursive field of social norms and aberrations. Malleable and permeable boundaries irregularly distinguish norms from deviance. The relationships are in flux. They intersect and overlap. They are not absolute or pure. Nevertheless, these terms help us map out the social and cultural positions of individuals and groups in ways that we can talk about them. Finally, the questions that cultural studies ask are often ethnographic questions. How do people generate identities? How do they conform to, resist, and transform their psychological and material environment? What borders do they cross? What cultural and material goods, habits, and innovations do they export and import across those borders, and how do they combine to affect the social and political space? All of these questions come to bear on the Beat generation and its art and social life. This chapter looks at Kaufman's and weiss's part in it.

2. Maria Damon notes the difficulty of sorting legend from fact in the Kaufman biography. Kaufman's Jewishness is remote as is the tale about his mother being steeped in voodoo along with Catholicism. According to Bob Kaufman's brother George, the most that can be said is that the brothers' paternal grandfather was part Jewish. The family was indeed Catholic, but without the voodoo affiliation. Bob Kaufman, however, and his wife Eileen encouraged the spread of the legend-like elements. See Damon, *The Dark End of the Street: Margins in American Vanguard Poetry* (Minneapolis: University of Minnesota Press, 1993), pp. 32–76. In addition, we will see that most of the material on weiss is autobiographical, which, as with all biogra-

phy, walks the delicate line between self-invention and history; it is also shot through with stylistic and aesthetic intentions, which even more blur categorical lines containing art, fact-based research, biography, and history.

3. Ferlinghetti's quotation is from his personal "Holograph Journal" in the Lawrence Ferlinghetti Papers, Bancroft Library, University of California, Berkeley, 1959).

4. ruth weiss, "Tale about Dori or Lioness with a Mane," *Gallery of Women* (San Francisco: Adler Press, 1959), no pagination.

5. Bob Kaufman, "Would You Wear My Eyes," in *Solitudes Crowded with Loneliness* (New York: New Directions, 1965), p. 40. See Ginsberg, "America," *Howl*, p. 31. Kerouac, *On the Road*, p. 17.

6. See Brian Philip Harper, *Framing the Margins: The Social Logic of Postmodern Culture* (New York: Oxford University Press, 1994), pp. 3–11.

7. Richard Candida Smith, *Utopia and Dissent: Art, Poetry, and Politics in California* (Berkeley: University of California Press, 1995), p. 201.

8. The ensuing quotations from this poem are in Kaufman, "Abomunist Manifesto," *Solitudes*, pp. 77–87.

9. On this notion that politics is war in times of peace, Kaufman sees what Michel Foucault later wrote about as the function of modern politics since the Renaissance and the entrenchment of the nation states. See Foucault, "Two Lectures," *Culture/Power/History: A Reader in Contemporary Social Theory*, eds. Nicholas B. Dirks, Geoff Eley, and Sherry B. Ortner (Princeton: Princeton University Press, 1994), pp. 200–221. Also, with respect to weiss's autobiographical writing and her account of fleeing the Nazis, see weiss, "ruth weiss," *Contemporary Authors Autobiography Series* (CAAS), ed. Shelly Andrews, v. 21 (Detroit: Gale Research, 1996), pp. 325–354.

10. See Kaufman, "War Memoir," *Solitudes*, p. 53. Also see "Hollywood," *Solitudes*, pp. 24–26.

11. Kaufman, "Bagel Shop Jazz," *Solitudes*, pp. 14–15. For more on Kaufman's pluralism in this poem see Maria Damon, "Jazz-Jews, Jive, and Gender: Ethnic Anxiety and the Politics of Jazz Argot," *Jews and Other Differences: The New Jewish Cultural Studies*, Daniel and Jonathan Boyarin, eds. (Minneapolis: University of Minnesota Press, 1997), pp. 150–175; Damon, "Other Beats," *Hambone*, 13 (spring 1997), pp. 177–185.

12. See Maria Damon, "Triangulated Desires and Tactical Silences in the Beat Hipscape: Bob Kaufman and Others," *College Literature*, 27, 1 (winter 2000): 139–157 (quotation, 147).

13. Ginsberg's quotation is from "America," *Howl*, p. 34. Letter from Ginsberg, *City Lights Records*, December 20, 1956. I want to mention that Robert Duncan stirred a local commotion in 1944 when he published "The Homosexual in Society" in Dwight McDonald's *Politics*. Duncan confessed his sexual preference in the article and signed it. Also, see Grieg, "The Lively Arts in San Francisco," p. 142.

14. Comments about ruth weiss and her memories of gays in North Beach and in *The Brink* come from ruth weiss, interview (February 6, 2000). Poetry from ruth weiss, "Tale about Dori or Lioness with a Mane," no pagination. In correspondence Maria Damon says weiss's turn to "Alaska" may reference the children's geography joke, "If Mississippi wore her New Jersey, what did Delaware? Idaho, Alaska." Thus, the pursued does not simply change the subject, but weiss adds erotic mystery by feminizing and homosocializing place names.

15. For more about how the Beats paved the way for the coming out of gay culture, see John D'Emilio, "The Movement and the Subculture Converge: San Francisco during the Early 1960s," *Sexual Politics, Sexual Communities: The Making of a Homosexual Minority in the United States, 1940–1970* (Chicago: University of Chicago Press, 1983), pp. 177–195.

16. The following quotations from weiss, *Gallery of Women*, no pagination.

17. Kerouac, *On the Road*, p. 8.

18. weiss was immersed in African American culture. Most of the other Beat writers felt the vibrations of African American culture from farther away. Their sensibilities collide with black culture more than their biographies. Unless otherwise noted, biographical information and quotations are taken from weiss, "ruth weiss," *Contemporary Authors Autobiography Series*, pp. 325–353. The epigraph about bebop is from a conversation I had with weiss after she read at the M. H. De Young Museum, October 12, 1996.

19. For Herb Caen's remark see the *San Francisco Chronicle* (February 15, 1993). weiss also says she started the readings at the Cellar in "ruth weiss," *Contemporary Authors Autobiography Series*, p. 329. She told me the same in

a telephone interview (May 17, 1996). Sonny Nelson's comments came from a telephone interview (February 24, 2000). During the 1990s weiss read with the Larry Vukovich Trio at different Bay Area venues. They have recorded twice: ruth weiss, *Poetry and All that Jazz*, vols. 1 & 2 (San Francisco: Awarehouse, 1994).

20. See Ted Gioia, *West Coast Jazz: Modern Jazz in California 1945–1960* (New York: Oxford University Press, 1992), p. 327.

21. Gleason's album notes are from Kenneth Rexroth and Lawrence Ferlinghetti, *Poetry Readings in the Cellar with the Cellar Jazz Quintet* (Fantasy, 1958): 7002.

22. The quotations about "white skin" and Pleasant come from weiss, "ruth weiss," *Contemporary Authors Autobiography Series*, p. 340. Also, weiss told me that her artistic rapport with Pleasant had rarely if ever been matched (interview, October 17, 1996). weiss continues to facilitate poetry and jazz in the United States and abroad.

23. Quotation from weiss, telephone interview (October 17, 1996). weiss told me the Philip Lamantia/Auerhahn story in a telephone interview on February 6, 2000. With respect to Rexroth, Ferlinghetti, and women poets Ponsot and Levertov, see Barry Silesky, *Ferlinghetti: The Artist in His Time* (New York: Warner Books, 1990), pp. 32, 36, 86.

24. weiss, "Tale about Dori or Lioness with a Mane," no pagination.

25. ruth weiss, *The Brink,* originally 16mm, 41 minutes, black and white (Albion, Calif.: ruth weiss, 1961; videocassette, 1986). The narration is a collage of various poems such as *Blue and Green* (San Francisco: Adler Press, 1960); "Chopsticks" and "The Brink," *Single Out* (ms. mid to late 1950s, Mill Valley, Calif.: D'Aurora Press, 1978), no pagination.

26. weiss, telephone interview (August 30, 1999). The scenes in *Pull My Daisy,* though famous for being improvised, were at the same time carefully planned, orchestrated, and edited. See John Hanhardt, "A Movement toward the Real: *Pull My Daisy* and the American Independent Film: 1950–'65," *Beat Culture and the New America 1950–1965* (New York: Whitney Museum and Flammarion, 1995), pp. 215–233. Ornette Coleman's *Free Jazz* is free within a frame that consisted in the predetermination of instruments and players, the order of solos, and pre-set ensemble passages to introduce the soloists in their turn. See *Free Jazz* (Atlantic, 1961): 1364–2.

27. My reference to hermeneutics draws upon George E. Marcus's discussion of the hermeneutic problems of ethnography. If it is impossible to represent the familiar world as directly knowable, then how much more problematic is it when one attempts to represent the unfamiliar other? In poetry, fiction, cultural studies, and the sciences, it is a difficult thing to write one's way out of one's own cultural patterns—that is, to write about the world without really writing about one's self. As we have seen, weiss disrupts selves' attempts to impose stable illusions on the page as if it were the world. See Marcus, "Ethnography in the Modern World System," *Writing Culture: The Poetics and Politics of Writing Culture,* ed. James Clifford and George E. Marcus (Berkeley: University of California Press, 1986), pp. 165–193.

weiss shares some of the contemporaneous concerns of concrete poets and sound poets. And she is a forerunner of the language poetry that would emerge in the coming decades. Sound and concrete poetry had their beginnings in the late romanticism of Mallarmé, in the jazz-inspired *poemes negres* by Tristan Tzara and other Dadaists, and in Gertrude Stein's fascinating attempts to objectify the linguistic structure. After World War II, sound and concrete poets were busy in the divided Germanys. The Lettrists, whose diverse practitioners gave the movement an international flavor, also emerged after the war. At the risk of oversimplification, the concrete poets sought to objectify the word by placing it in visual circumstances that made its signifying qualities beside the point; i.e., "Tale about Dori." Sound poetry reduces and complicates words' signifying function by placing them in contexts that highlight their aural qualities. Finally, the more current language poets are engaged in a poetry that highlights the coercive force of linguistic structures. Similarly to weiss, these poets assiduously deny conventional narrative authority. See Jon Erickson, *The Fate of the Object: From Modern Object to Postmodern Sign in Performance, Art, and Poetry* (Ann Arbor: University of Michigan Press, 1995), pp. 137–182.

28. Much of my biographical information about Kaufman comes from Henderson's introduction, which is based on the National Public Radio documentary, "Bob Kaufman, Poet." Henderson and Vic Bedoian produced the two-hour program. KPFA-FM in Berkeley aired the show first in April 1991. Also, see Damon, *Dark End of the Street,* pp. 67, 32–76; Damon has researched Kaufman's biography and written critically about his work. She has

encountered "multiple and conflicting accounts of Kaufman's genealogy, his life story, and other putatively relevant aspects of his life work." She adds, "Beat scholarship will never stand on incontrovertibly firm ground, because legend, hyperbole, and a scorn for official forms of documentation have constituted such primary elements in the Beat Aura." Also see Damon, "Triangulated Desires and Tactical Silences," p. 143; "Victors of Catastrophe: Beat Occlusions," pp. 141–152. Also, for biographical information that discards all pretense of fact, see Mel Clay, *Jazz—Jail and God: Bob Kaufman, an Impressionistic Biography* (San Francisco: Androgyne Books, 1987), pp. ix–xii. Also see Steven Watson, *The Birth of the Beat Generation: Visionaries, Rebels, and Hipsters 1944–1960* (New York: Pantheon Books, 1995), pp. 225–227.

29. Norman Mailer, *The White Negro: Superficial Reflections on the Hipster* (San Francisco: City Lights Books). Kaufman refers to queerness in two other poems and more sympathetically; like Kaufman, they are identities in flight: "Grandfather was Queer, too," and in "Unhistorical Events," "Riff Raff Rolfe had to flee his home state because he was queer." For the former see *Solitudes*, p. 13 and for the latter, see Kaufman, *Cranial Guitar*, ed. Gerald Nicosia (Minneapolis: Coffee House Press, 1996), p. 53. Damon, *Dark End of the Street*, p. 67.

30. The information and quotations about Russell Fitzgerald and his diary come from Damon, "Triangulated Desire and Tactical Silences," 153–155. Gerald Nicosia learned of Kerouac's sleepover at Kaufman's apartment in an October 1977 interview with Kaufman who gave Nicosia a copy of Kerouac's poem. See Nicosia, *Memory Babe*, pp. 618, 737. Also, I am not arguing that Kaufman or Kerouac were clandestine homosexuals or bisexuals. In fact, Fitzgerald's diary is full of frustration at the unobtainability of Kaufman. Fitzgerald apparently had oral sex with Kaufman once after the poet had "managed to pass out." And afterward, Fitzgerald was flooded with a sense of sin and guilt (Damon, p. 154). I cite these examples because they help show the sense in which Kaufman was a black object within the Beat milieu; black jazz musicians, and more recently black rock 'n' roll, soul, and hip hop artists constantly face this issue and have come to resent white objectification from admirers and detractors, alike. For a discussion of this issue as it relates to hip hop, see Ewan Allison, "'It's a Black Thing': Hearing

How Whites Can't," *Cultural Studies,* 8, 3 (October, 1994): 438–456. These examples also help disclose the presence of gay sociality in the Bay Area art scene in ways that much Beat writing may try to occlude. As to the meaning of Kerouac's poem, I do not read it as necessarily a memento of a sexual encounter. I read it as a memento to Kerouac's squinting to see, that is, know and understand, Kaufman as a human being. For material on Kerouac's sexuality ("homophobic when sober, bisexual when drunk," said Gore Vidal), see *Queer Beats* conference (San Francisco: Harvey Milk Institute, fall 1996).

31. Kaufman, "West Coast Sounds—1956," *Solitudes,* p. 11.

32. See Kaufman, "Cincophrenicpoet," *Solitudes,* p. 49.

33. See Kaufman, "Would You Wear My Eyes," *Solitudes,* p. 40.

34. Kaufman, "Song of the Broken Giraffe," *Solitudes,* pp. 34–35. I have quoted the poem at length but still only in part.

35. Sex Pistols, "Pretty Vacant," *Never Mind the Bollocks Here's the Sex Pistols* (Burbank, Calif.: Warner Brothers, 1977): 3147–2. See Greil Marcus's subcultural take on the Sex Pistols—the negation of familiar identities—in *Lipstick Traces: A Secret History of the Twentieth Century* (Cambridge, Mass.: Harvard University Press, 1989).

36. Dizzy Gillespie, "Salt Peanuts" and "Opp Bop Sh' Bam," *Groovin' High* (Newark, N.J.: Savoy Record Company, 1946): MG-12020.

3 CELLULOID BEATNIKS

1. All film quotations taken from *The Subterraneans,* an Arthur Freedman production (Metro Goldwyn Mayer, June 1960). Because I quote extensively from Kerouac's novel *The Subterraneans* (1959), page numbers of quotations are cited in the text.

2. Whalen wrote to Ginsberg between 1954 and 1956. Department of Special Collections, Box 5, Folder 42 (Stanford, Calif.: Stanford University Libraries, undated). Kerouac's quotations about spontaneous prose are from the introduction to the Norwegian edition of *The Subterraneans,* which is published, in part, in Ann Charters, *The Portable Kerouac* (New York: Penguin, 1995), p. 481. "The Essentials of Spontaneous Prose" was first published in *Evergreen Review No. 2,* v. 5 (summer 1957): 72–73. It is also in *A Casebook on the Beat,* ed. Thomas Parkinson, pp. 65–67. For the facts about

how Kerouac's spontaneous prose and Rexroth himself influenced Ginsberg's "Howl" and other poets' work, see Ginsberg, "Improvised Poetics," *Allen Ginsberg: Composed on the Tongue,* ed. Donald Allen (Bolinas, Calif.: Grey Fox Press, 1980), p. 42. Also see Barry Miles, *Ginsberg: A Biography,* pp. 166–187. Burroughs's letter to Kerouac, February 12, 1955, Tangiers, is found in *William S. Burroughs: 1945–1959,* p. 265.

3. Gerald Nicosia agrees that the movie travestied the book. He adds that it made Leo Percepied into a "murderous brawler," which is a bit overstated. See *Memory Babe,* p. 619. The movie's Percepied character never actually strikes anyone. He does threaten violence when someone demeans Mardou, when he himself encounters hostility, and when he's drunk and jealous. Dennis McNally condemns the film's trite plot and Percepied's adoption of Hollywood's favorite "fists-and-whiskey" manner, and concludes that in the face of Kerouac's naked confession, "this trivializing film was almost too ugly to grasp." See *Desolate Angel: A Biography,* p. 278. I am sympathetic to these viewpoints, but for reasons stated in the text, I do not believe the film should be dismissed or condemned out of hand.

4. With respect to capitalism's containment of Beat culture, Lisa Phillips notes the humorous, trivializing examples I have cited. She says the Beats found themselves powerless to fend off the "co-option, packaging, and containment" of their style. Phillips's point is well taken. Yet as Chapter 1 indicates, Ferlinghetti and Ginsberg did not feel or act as if they were powerless. Moreover, I am writing from the perspective of how the Beats expanded the terms of capitalism and used its strategies in order to reach audiences and change the culture. See Phillips, "Beat Culture: America Revisioned," *Beat Culture and the New America 1950–1965,* ed. Lisa Phillips (New York: Whitney Museum of Art / Flammarion, 1995), pp. 23–24. Max Shulman wrote the television series *The Many Loves of Dobie Gillis* and the books and short stories upon which it was based (these do not feature the beatnik figure). At least one person on the internet BeatList (now defunct) said they came to the Beats through Krebs because he was "cool." A now-defunct internet fan page devoted to *The Many Loves of Dobie Gillis* called Krebs subtly subversive. "Can you name any other 1950s sitcom where Dizzy Gillespie and Thelonious Monk were praised on a regular basis?" the page asked. Moreover, Bob Dylan was influenced by the fictional Krebs. He told *Rolling Stone*

magazine he got his inspiration for "If Dogs Run Free" from the Maynard Krebs album "Like What?," which had a brief release, then was canceled along with the TV show in 1962. Bob Denver played Krebs in the television series. Kenneth Rexroth's quotation is in Steven Watson, *The Birth of the Beat Generation,* p. 258. Kaufman's poem "Hollywood" is in *Solitudes,* pp. 24–25. For an assessment of the film *The Beat Generation,* also by MGM, see David Sterritt, *Mad to be Saved: The Beats, the '50s, and Film* (Carbondale, Ill.: Southern Illinois University Press, 1998), pp. 146–152. Kerouac's article appears in Charters, *The Portable Jack Kerouac,* pp. 565–572; originally published in *Playboy* (June, 1959).

5. Mass media caricatures made the Beats ridiculous and laughable, which also implied that the Beat way was not the way to wisdom; such is the trajectory of Renaissance comedy. It makes a fool of waywardness in support of social norms. The Shakespeare quotation is taken from Leo Salinger's discussion of mimesis in *Shakespeare and the Traditions of Comedy* (London: Cambridge University Press, 1974), p. 2. Kerouac, "Essentials of Spontaneous Prose," *A Casebook on the Beat,* pp. 65–67.

6. For examples, see John Brooks, "Of Growth and Decay." *New York Times Book Review* (March 5, 1950): 6; Victor P. Hass, "Good Story Lost In Flood of Rhetoric," *Chicago Tribune,* "Magazine of Books Section" (March 5, 1950): 4; Carter Brooke Jones, "John [sic] Kerouac's First Novel Reveals Vigorous New Talent," *Washington Star* (March 5, 1950): C-3.

7. See Baldassare Castiglione, *The Courtier,* trans. George Bull (1528, New York: Penguin, 1967). In many ways Kerouac's Mardou is a lady according to the Castiglione ideal; indeed, modern western notions of the gentleman and the lady can be traced to the widely translated *Courtier.* The courtly woman affects delicate femininity. She plays the role of the beautiful, charming, witty, and liberally educated woman. She may paint and play music or write poetry. With all of these talents she realizes a male ideal, but knows her place and does not challenge it. Mardou challenges it.

8. Kerouac grew up speaking the French-Canadian vernacular. The Beat Generation itself, as Ginsberg put it in "Howl," was forever "yacketayacking" in streets, bars, and flats; indeed, the range, depth, intimacy, and quantity of its spontaneous speech was a hallmark of the Beats. Kerouac traveled widely and sought new experiences of people. The legends and lore of indigenous

Mexicans, African Americans, and various immigrant groups fascinated him. He was not especially effective in conveying speech patterns. He was no linguist, but he attended to different ways of speaking and tried to convey them. Wherever he was, he was forever taking notes on his small front-pocket notepads. Sometimes he used a tape recorder to help him recall and portray what people said and how they said it. This is especially evident in the novel *Visions of Cody* (1972).

9. The underlying assumption of my position on cultural theory is that political economy is influential but not determinative of cultural products themselves, nor audiences' interpretations of them. Both culture makers (artists; in this case, a film crew) and consumers (also culture makers) make representations and meanings out of the intersecting crucibles of dominant and subordinate interests that compete with each other. In the context of late capitalism, the Beats and their audiences creatively forced their subordinate interests into the complexion of U.S. power; they changed the expression on the culture's face. In seeing consumption as a creative act, I am following Paul Willis, *Common Culture* (Buckingham, U.K.: Open University Press, 1990), p. 145. Also see Dick Hebdige, *Subculture: the Meaning of Style* (London: Routledge, 1979). And before them, as I demonstrate in Chapter 4, I am following Kerouac, who expressed amazement at the creativity of audiences in his experimental novel *Visions of Cody* (ms. 1951, New York: Penguin, 1972).

10. On the Bread and Wine Mission, see Miles, *Ginsberg: A Biography*, p. 262, and Watson, *The Birth of the Beat Generation*, pp. 189–190. For the Delattre quotation, see the interview in Arthur and Kit Knight, "Pierre Delattre Remembers Neal Cassady," *The Beat Vision* (New York: Paragon Publishing House, 1987), p. 57. Also see Pierre Delattre, *Episodes* (Saint Paul, Minn.: Graywolf Press, 1993) and Lewis Ellingham and Kevin Killian, *Poet Be Like God*, pp. 144–145, 150, 163, 171. On art during the the Great Depression, see Francis V. O'Conner, "The 1930s: Notes on the Transition from Social to Individual Scale in the Art of the Depression Era," *American Art in the 20th Century: Painting and Sculpture*, eds. Christos M. Joachimides and Norman Rosenthal (Munich, Germany: Prestel-Verlag, 1993), pp. 61–68.

11. "The Beat Friar," *Time* (May 25, 1959). Other quotations on Everson are taken from Steven Watson's profile in *The Birth of the Beat Generation*, pp. 203–205. Also see Lee Bartlett, *William Everson: The Life and Times of Brother Antoninus* (New York: New Directions, 1988).

12. Arthur Knight, "Jammin' the Blues, or the Sight of Jazz, 1944," *Representing Jazz*, ed. Krin Gabbard (Durham: Duke University Press, 1995), pp. 11–53.

13. Ibid., p. 19.

14. On Sonny Criss, see Ira Gitler, *Swing to Bop: An Oral History of the Transition in Jazz in the 1940s* (New York: Oxford University Press, 1985), pp. 168–169. About Granz and the JATP, see Dizzy Gillespie, *To Be, or Not . . . to Bop: Memoirs* (Garden City, N.Y.: Doubleday & Company, 1979), pp. 405–410.

15. With respect to realistic and pluralistic representations of jazz in Hollywood films, I will add the film *Young Man with a Horn* (1951), which gives a good role to Art Hazard (Juano Hernandez), an African American mentor to the film's hero (based on Bix Beiderbecke and played by Kirk Douglass), who is in search of "a note nobody ever heard before." Hernandez's role is subsidiary to the central love plot, however. See Thomas Cripps, *Making Movies Black: The Hollywood Message Movie from World War II to the Civil Rights Era* (New York: Oxford University Press, 1993), pp. 258–259. Also, in the 1920s and 1930s filmmakers photographed jazz on its on terms and in context, but these were independent, narrowly distributed, often documentary efforts. Knight's article and Cripps's book deal with Hollywood representations of jazz. Sam Donahue's quotation in Knight's article confirms musicians' feelings that dance audiences often did not appreciate musicianship. Moreover, musicians felt commercial forces, particularly Hollywood, frequently occluded the instrumental features of jazz by featuring sexy women singers; Cripps, *Making Movies Black*, pp. 11, 19.

On the lindy hop, see Robert P. Crease, "Divine Frivolity: Hollywood Representations of the Lindy Hop, 1937–1942," *Representing Jazz*, pp. 207–228. For a discussion of *Cabin in the Sky*, see Adam Knee, "Doubling, Music, and Race in *Cabin in the Sky*," *Representing Jazz*, pp. 193–204.

16. Quotations below taken from footage in the television broadcast

"Stage Entrance," which appears in the jazz documentary by Gary Giddons, *Celebrating Bird, Masters of America Music Series* (Toby Byron / Multiprises, 1987).

17. Through his small and big bands, frequent recording, and entertaining stage antics, Dizzy Gillespie was at the vanguard of attempts to widen bebop's audience. See Scott DeVeaux, *The Birth of Bebop: A Social and Musical History* (Berkeley: University of California Press, 1998), pp. 364–436. Certainly, he must have been pleased with the opportunity to show, without distractions of props or other entertainers, his and Parker's chops to a primarily white national audience. And here they were not supporting but supported by white musicians.

18. It is also true that black innovators of modern jazz styles such as bebop and experimental jazz in the 1960s developed their disruptive forms out of group cohesiveness that refused to compromise with white expectations for black demeanor: the happy negro, the clown, the primitive. Moreover, LeRoi Jones (Amira Baraka) in *Blues People*, pp. 175–136, and Eric Lott in "Double V, Double-Time: Bebop's Politics of Style," pp. 243–255, have provided subculture readings that parallel much in nationalist readings of avant garde jazz, such as that in Frank Kofsky, *Black Nationalism and the Revolution in Music* (New York: Pathfinder Press, 1970). Kerouac, too, heard black consciousness in the new styles of jazz and characterized its spread through the United States as a kind of reverse colonialism. Kerouac writes that the post-Depression generation heard in the music of Lester Young, Charlie Parker, Dizzy Gillespie, Billie Holiday, and Miles Davis "music . . . here to stay . . . history has washed over us . . . imperialistic kingdoms are coming." See "The Beginning of Bop" in Charters, *The Portable Jack Kerouac*, pp. 555–559. These styles were open to anyone (black or white) who would hear, learn, and contribute to the styles' development. At the same time black musicians were wary of whites' appropriations and dilutions of black music for profit. In other words, mixing among blacks and whites even in open-minded circles was far from immune to the political and economic tensions shaping social and cultural interactions in the mainstream—tensions that came forward in 1954 with the Supreme Court's *Brown v. Board of Education* decision. Jazz, for those who took the music seriously, provided a model for dealing with racial tensions; it made skin color irrelevant because

it disclosed diverse peoples engaged in a common artistic purpose. With respect to women, jazz was chauvinistic. It was usually taken for granted that
women were to serve creative music, not make it. Vocalists were accepted
more readily than instrumental players, but they had to carefully negotiate
the tensions between their artistic goals and male expectations for women.
Mary Lou Williams, Marian McPartland, Melba Liston, and Sarah Vaughn
were a few notable instrumentalists and vocalists who performed in predominantly male ensembles. See Porter, *What Is This Thing Called Jazz?*
(2002).

19. Knight points out that with the exception of the movie short *Jammin'
the Blues,* Hollywood did not credit jazz players unless they were celebrities
(pp. 29–34). This alludes to the reality that film producers typically dismissed as an aesthetic principle: jazz musicians' and audiences' need for
symmetry between the sound and performance image. This neglect revealed
not only producers' willingness to cut corners for profits but underlined an
ignorance or outright contempt for jazz musicians and mass audiences
whom they presumed would not notice or would not care.

20. Kaufman, "Bagel Shop Jazz," *Solitudes,* pp. 14–15.

21. With respect to the studio's response to Granz on including Kessel in
the film, the quotation comes from Knight's citation of Charles Emge from
Down Beat. See *Jammin' the Blues,* p. 41.

22. As mentioned earlier in the text, the synchronization between sound
and image breaks down on one occasion; this is it. The sound matches the
visual image until the last notes of the tune except for the drummer, who
stops playing two beats before the drum track ends.

23. Maria Damon, "Victors of Catastrophe: Beat Occlusions," *Beat Cul-
ture and the New America: 1950–1965,* pp. 141–152. Lisa Phillips, "Beat Cul-
ture: America Revisioned," *Beat Culture and the New America: 1950–1965,*
pp. 23–68. Saul Paradise speaking to Dean Moriarty in *On the Road* (New
York: Penguin, 1957), p. 122. Laura Mulvey, "Visual Pleasure and Narrative
Cinema," *Film Theory and Criticism,* ed. Gerald Mast and Marshall Cohen
(New York: Oxford University Press, 1985), p. 804. Originally published in
Screen, 16, 3.

24. Cripps points out that by this time Poitier's roles were Hollywood's favorite, but many critics had come to question them as evasive. Poitier him-

self admitted he felt trapped in the "one-dimensional, middle class imagery I had embodied," pp. 290–291. Harry Belafonte was an alternative at this time, but for the most part Hollywood shunned his work. *Odds Against Tomorrow* (1958) was a provocative exception that penetrated U.S. race relations via allegory. Because of the prodding of Max Youngstein, the United Artist producer, the company agreed to assist Belafonte's own Harbel company in the making of the film. Cripps, *Making Movies Black,* pp. 266–268.

25. See Harper, *Framing the Margins,* pp. 3–29.

26. For a discussion on the relationship between structure and spontaneity in Happenings, see Michael Kirby's introduction to *Happenings* (New York: E. P. Dutton & Co., 1965), pp. 9–52. For a similar discussion of free jazz, see Ekkehard Jost's introduction to *Free Jazz* (New York: Da Capo Press, 1975), pp. 8–16.

27. Dunham traveled the world to study indigenous dance. Haitian dance seems to have fascinated her most. She taught these "primitive" styles to her students and integrated them into her troupe's performances. See *Anna's Sin* (1954) and *Mambo* (1954) for examples in which her troupe is employed to provide exotic entertainment quite irrelevant to the films' drama. See Cripps, *Making Movies Black,* p. 273. Also see Ruth Beckford, *Katherine Dunham: A Biography* (New York: Marcel Dekker, 1979). The film seems to take Julienne's point of view in another dance scene in which Leo joins Roxanne. After approximately thirty seconds of dancing together, she realizes what's happening, stops in apparent horror, and comments, "I hate you. I hate all men." Then she runs away. Leo chases her and persuades her into his arms.

28. Burroughs, *Naked Lunch,* p. 205. About Kerouac's shame in selling *The Subterraneans* to MGM, see Nicosia, *Memory Babe,* p. 619.

29. Horkheimer and Adorno find little revolutionary potential (so central to earlier Marxist theory) in late capitalist hegemony with its capacity to swallow up individuality into ideological conformity. For these critics, corporate co-option of pop culture annuls the vernacular vitality and revolutionary potential of jazz, rock 'n' roll, and narratives—turns them into titillating distractions. See Max Horkheimer and Theodor Adorno, *Dialectic of Enlightenment* (New York: Seabury, 1972). Baudrilliard believes the technologies of simulation (the global web of communications and image control

systems) are so pervasive as to have superseded reality into a hyperreality of simulation. The air-brushed glossy simulacrum is more affecting to the senses than the real, which is passé. See Jean Baudrilliard, *Selected Writings*, ed. Mark Poster (Stanford: Stanford University Press, 1988), pp. 74–172.

4 READY FOR BREAKFAST

1. Jack Kerouac, *Visions of Cody* (ms. 1951; New York: McGraw-Hill, 1972; edition cited, New York: Penguin Books, 1993). Kerouac's "Essentials of Spontaneous Prose" reveals his ideal permitted revision of "obvious rational mistakes, such as names or *calculated* insertions in act of not writing but *inserting*." *Evergreen Review* 2, v. 5 (summer 1957): 72–73. The *On the Road* scroll indicates as much. The first version of the novel was produced in the form of a scroll. Kerouac taped together hundreds of sheets of typing paper so that he would not lose momentum as he wrote. I saw the scroll on display at the exhibit *Beat Culture and the New America 1950–1965*, M. H. De Young Museum (San Francisco, October 1996). The scroll was encased in glass and only two pages were visible, but copious differences existed between these two pages and those of the published text. For example, the published text reads, "Marylou was a pretty blonde with immense ringlets of hair like a sea of golden tresses; she sat there on the edge of the couch with her hands hanging in her lap" (*On The Road*, p. 5). The scroll reads, "Luanne [her real name] was a sweet pretty little thing but awfully dumb and capable of doing horrible things which she proved a while later." This sentence occurs in the published text but later on the page. Also, the clause following the last pronoun "which" was dropped.

2. Lyotard's term indicates flouting or indifference to traditional standards—the collapse of high into low. It is also associated with postwar aesthetic experimentation and the mixing of aesthetics, genres, and disciplines. From "Answering the Question: What Is Postmodernism?" *The Postmodern Condition*, trans. Regis Durand (Minneapolis: University of Minnesota Press, 1984), pp. 71–82.

3. For examples of an antebellum popular culture that competed with and vitalized what are now canonical works from the period, see David Reynolds, *Beneath the American Renaissance: The Subversive Imagination in*

the Age of Emerson and Melville (New York: Alfred A. Knopf, 1988). For an account of how a nineteenth-century lumpen-proletariat expressed its resistance and activism via its stylistic identification with free and slave blacks, see W. T. Lhamon Jr., *Raising Cain: Blackface Performance from Jim Crow to Hip Hop* (Cambridge, Mass.: Harvard University Press, 1998).

4. In general, Kerouac did not permit refinements but neither did the preceding popular, reflexive, and interactive modern "epic theater" of Kurt Weill and Bertolt Brecht. *Threepenny Opera* (1928) and *Mahogany* (1927) do not disdain bawdy, even "unseemly" humor but view it as a resource for raising critical consciousness of the political economy. Although Kerouac shunned precooked political agendas, local speech, popular culture, lore, and the mundane shaped his life and prose. My point is that competitive interpenetration between high and low art has long been integral to U.S. culture and modernism. Attempts to theorize recent and substantial breaks in cultural history neglect the persistence of historical continuities and cycles. Rita Barnard, too, makes a persuasive contribution to historically situating a developed pre–World War II postmodernism characterized by a consumer economy, competition between high and low art, the loss of high art's auratic strength, and the dissolution of grounding truth structures. See Rita Barnard, *The Great Depression and the Culture of Abundance* (Cambridge: Cambridge University Press, 1995). Finally, as noted in Chapter 2, Philip Brian Harper remarks that theorists who base the postmodern designation on the presence of the fragmented, decentered subject, neglect to take into account the decentered experience of marginalized peoples in American territories since colonial times. Technology-driven capitalism disorients the psyche, but marginal status in society contributes the same and as much. See Philip Brian Harper, *Framing the Margins,* pp. 27–28. Unlike Barnard and Harper, again, I do not periodize and separate these features from modernism.

5. My use of the term simulacra derives from Gilles Deleuze's article "Plato and the Simulacrum," which roots use of the term in intellectual history. The distinction between the simulacrum and the copy is based on their relationship to the original, the ideal. Copies are "well-grounded claimants, authorized by resemblance" (47). Simulacra are "false claimants, built on dissimilitude, implying a perversion, an essential turning away" from the

original and legitimate claimant (47). Copies in unauthorized hands of individuals may also run errant into the pejorative sphere of simulacra, which pervert intended and established meanings (I develop this idea further in the text). See Deleuze, trans. Rosalind Kraus, "Plato and the Simulacrum," *October* 27 (winter 1983): 45–56. Jean Baudrillard argues that postwar capitalism has produced an era no longer based on production but on simulational codes and models that inform information processing, media, cyber-control systems, and social organization. The era of the hyperreal designates the moment when the simulation becomes realer than the real. It is the real airbrushed, the real standing in "hallucinatory resemblance" to itself (23a). Thus, the present era is an era in which the real stands in pejorative relation to its simulated model, the ideal. Therefore, the actual United States pales to Disneyland's simulation of it as America; the Vietnam War is not as nihilistically mysterious as *Apocalypse Now*. In *Visions of Cody* an ethic of simulation informs the novel's confrontation with authorized originals and copies and ideal simulacra. I will show how the novel's simulational strategies conspire to celebrate excluded vernacular culture in the Americas—set it up as a multifaceted, fluidly changing reality. See Baudrillard, *Simulations* (New York: Semiotext(e), 1983). Also see *In the Shadow of the Silent Majorities* (New York: Semiotext(e), 1983). Breton's epigraph comes from Walter Benjamin's article "The Work of Art in the Age of Mechanical Reproduction," *Illuminations,* ed. Hannah Arendt, trans. Harry Zohn (originally published in Frankfurt: Suhrkamp Verlag, 1955; edition cited, New York: Harcourt, Brace & World, 1968), p. 251. No source cited on Breton.

6. The mannerist developments that for the most part followed the Renaissance thrived on parody and pastiche of works and artists from the preceding era much as modernists-postmodernists have done in this century. It should be said, too, that the romanticism of the mannerists was by and large a relativistic and cynical one. However, if Machiavelli's *The Prince* is any indication, the mannerist tendency was strong as the Italian Renaissance peaked.

7. Benjamin, "The Work of Art in the Age of Mechanical Reproduction," p. 223.

8. Quotation taken from Bela Balazs, "The Face of Man," *Theory of the Film,* trans. Edith Bone (New York: Dennis Dobson Books Ltd., Dover Pub-

lications, 1952), pp. 60–62. Subsequent quotations from Kerouac, *Visions of Cody*, pp. 81, 10–11.

9. Kerouac, *Visions of Cody*, pp. 10–11.

10. Unless otherwise noted, all quotations for the "Joan Rawshanks" section of the chapter come from Kerouac, *Visions of Cody*, pp. 275–290.

11. Here I have drawn on Roland Barthes's comments on reading and pleasure—the Text as *jouissance*: "pleasure without separation. Order of the signifier, the Text participates in a social utopia of its own: prior to history, the Text achieves, if not transparency of social relations, at least the transparency of language relations. It is the space in which no one language has a hold over any other, in which all languages circulate freely." *Visions of Cody* peruses this open space. But more than this, Kerouac experiences the pleasure of the reader (the making of meaning) as he writes the social text of the film set before him. His insight is that audiences do likewise. See Barthes, "From Work to Text," *Textual Strategies: Perspectives in Post-Structuralist Criticism,* ed. Josue V. Harari (Ithaca: Cornell University Press, 1979), pp. 80–81.

12. Quotations from Kerouac, *Visions of Cody*, pp. 5, 49; reference to Cain, p. 364. Unless otherwise noted, the quotations for the Three Stooges section below are taken from Kerouac, *Visions of Cody*, pp. 300–306.

13. Jack Kerouac, *Jack Kerouac: Selected Letters 1940–1956,* ed. Ann Charters (New York: Penguin Books, 1996), p. 274.

14. Ephraim Katz, ed. *The Film Encyclopedia* (New York: Perigree Books, Putnam Publishing Group, 1979), p. 1099.

15. Kerouac, *Visions of Cody*, pp. 23, 24.

16. Gerald Nicosia, *Memory Babe* (New York: Grove Press, 1983; edition cited, Berkeley: University of California Press, 1994), pp. 124–125, 167.

17. Terry Martin, liner notes from *Intuition,* CDP 7243 (Hollywood, Calif.: Capitol Records, 1996). This disk includes Lennie Tristano's significant 1949 Capitol sessions and Warne Marsh's 1956 *Jazz of Two Cities* sessions.

18. Richard Cook and Brian Morton explicitly associate Tristano with Webern in *The Penguin Guide to Jazz on CD,* 3d ed. (New York: Penguin Books, 1996), p. 1279. Jost dismisses analysis of Tristano's experiments, call-

ing them European-based anomalies, though improvised. See *Free Jazz* (Vienna: A. G. Wien, 1975; cited edition, New York: Da Capo Press, 1994), p. 41.

19. As to Cook's and Morton's comment, see *The Penguin Guide*, p. 1279; as to the comments of Fishkin, Bauer, Konitz, Brown, and Kirchner, see Martin's liner notes for *Intuition*. See John S. Wilson's interview with Tristano, "Watered-Down Bop Destroying Jazz" (October 6, 1950); reprinted as a "Classic Interview," *Down Beat* 61, 10 (October 1994): 34.

20. I am referring to the emerging debate over the validity of cool versus hot jazz, west versus east, white versus black. Critics and aficionados argued whether or not the blues was essential to jazz. There were entrenched debates about the authenticity of jazz styles such as bebop, swing, and classic jazz. See Bernard Gendron, "'Moldy Figs' and Modernists: Jazz at War (1942–1946)," *Jazz among the Discourses*, pp. 31–56.

21. Martin, *Intuition,* liner notes.

22. The two quotations are from Kerouac, *Visions of Cody,* pp. 296, 351–352.

23. Kerouac, *Visions of Cody,* pp. 296, 392.

24. The comment about the tape recorder and the "Frisco: The Tape" section, itself, come from Kerouac, *Visions of Cody,* pp. 99, 119–247. Because of the high number of quotations from *Visions of Cody,* I will cite page numbers parenthetically in the text of the chapter.

25. "First thought best thought" was Kerouac's and other Beats' writerly rule. There's no evidence to suggest that Kerouac made any changes of content on the tapes.

26. Kerouac's preamble to *Visions of Cody* (no pagination).

27. Kerouac's letter was first published in the small magazine *Notes from the Underground* 1 (Berkeley, 1964). It can also be found in *Jack Kerouac: Selected Letters, 1940–1956,* pp. 241–245.

28. Kerouac, *Visions of Cody,* preamble.

29. Kerouac, *Jack Kerouac: Selected Letters 1940–1956,* pp. 326–327.

30. Gilles Deleuze and Felix Guattari, *A Thousand Plateaus* (Minneapolis: University of Minnesota Press, 1987).

31. Kerouac, *Jack Kerouac: Selected Letters,* p. 232.

32. James Clifford, "Introduction: Partial Truths," *Writing Culture: The Poetics and Politics of Ethnography*, ed. James Clifford and George E. Marcus (Berkeley: University of California Press, 1986), pp. 25–26.

33. Kerouac, *Visions of Cody*, preamble.

34. See W. T. Lhamon Jr. for the account of vernacular cultures',—particularly African American cultures'—emergence into the foreground of U.S. culture; *Deliberate Speed: The Origins of a Cultural Style in the American 1950s* (Washington, D.C.: Smithsonian Institution Press, 1990).

5 HOWL OF LOVE

1. Lhamon's lore cycle describes how "across . . . chasms of regional, racial, class, gender, and age differences quite various groups were crafting quite similar practices to accommodate the new social challenges and material conditions in their lives"—a new postwar style. See *Deliberate Speed*, pp. vi–xv. For a description of the freewheeling pluralism of desire, see Gilles Deleuze and Felix Guattari, *Anti-Oedipus* (Minneapolis: University of Minnesota Press, 1983), pp. 54, 116, 139. My spin on Lhamon's lore cycle is that Ginsberg's *Howl* shows how vernacular notions of spirituality/mysticism, madness and grass roots, left-wing political activity were part of the mix. Thus, I talk about styles in the plural in order to indicate the specificity of multiple overlapping and interacting styles.

2. "The line of flight is a deterritorialization." It is the taking up of territory hemmed in by rigid or supple lines—the lines of division and constriction. In Deleuze's and Claire Parnet's chapter "On the Superiority of Anglo-American Literature" they say that Anglo-American literature constantly shows the rupture of lines, that it "creates through a line of flight. Thomas Hardy, Melville, Stevenson, Virginia Woolf, Thomas Wolfe, Lawrence, Fitzgerald, Miller, Kerouac. In them everything is departure, becoming, passage, leap, daemon, relationship with the outside. They create a new Earth." Thus flight is not detached transcendence but involved and immanent transformation. See *Dialogues* (Paris: Flammarion, 1977; cited edition, London: The Athlone Press, 1987), pp. 36–37.

3. See Irving Howe and Lewis Coser, *The American Communist Party: A Critical Study (1919–1957)* (Boston: Beacon Press, 1957). Conflicts between

Socialists and Communists were particularly evident in the chapter "The Party Becomes Stalinized," pp. 144–174. Relations were most cooperative between the two parties during World War II—the so-called "popular front" years, pp. 319–386. Also, biographical notes in this paragraph are taken from Barry Miles, *Ginsberg: A Biography,* pp. 9–35. Much of Miles's information on Ginsberg's childhood comes from the autobiographical content in his poems, in particular, "Kaddish" but also "America."

4. The poem was published in Allen Ginsberg, *Kaddish and Other Poems* (San Francisco: City Lights, 1961).

5. Concerning Ginsberg's institutionalization, see Miles, *Ginsberg,* pp. 117–124.

6. Here I have drawn on Michel Foucault's study of madness, which ends at the point at which madness accuses civilization. *Madness and Civilization: A History of Insanity in the Age of Reason,* trans. Richard Howard (New York: Random House, 1965), pp. 279–289. Originally published as *Histoire de la folie* (Paris: Librairie Plon, 1961). Examples of Goya's critique of the fruits of the Enlightenment would include "Executions of the Third of May, 1808" (1814–1815); *Disasters of War* (1810–1820); "Saturn Devouring One of His Children" (1820–1823). George Grosz pilloried rational modernity in works such as "Fit for Active Service" (1918); "Street Scene" (date unknown).

7. The line is from Ginsberg, "America," *Howl* (San Francisco: City Lights, 1956), pp. 31–34. Subsequent quotations from "America" are taken from this source as are quotations from the poem "Howl," pp. 9–22.

8. The first slogan sums up the message of a 6 × 9 handbill announcing a 1932 rally at Woodside on Long Island for the release of the Scottsboro Boys as well as Tom Mooney. Mooney was a militant labor leader arrested in 1916—along with his wife Rena and a radical worker named Warren K. Billings—for a patriotic parade bombing on San Francisco's Market Street. He spent the next twenty-three years in prison before Governor Culbert L. Olson finally pardoned him. The International Labor Defense (ILD) issued the handbill. The second slogan appears on a $\frac{7}{8}''$ (22mm) black-and-white button. It was made by the Eagle Regalia Co. at 298 Broadway, New York. The ILD produced thousands of such items. The third slogan is my own paraphrase of the feelings felt by those U.S. citizens who volunteered to fight or in some other way act in behalf of the first democratic government of

Spain, which was in danger of being toppled by the old regimes of privilege as represented by Generalissimo Franco. The threat to democracy in Spain and Europe was all the more imminent because Hitler and Mussolini helped arm and finance Spain's rebels. The Communist Party in the United States did not distribute propagandistic objects like the ones mentioned because they were not in keeping with the party's contemporaneous strategy of maintaining the Popular Front, which shunned radical emblems in favor of integrating itself into the mainstream. Nor did the party wish to attract too many volunteers to fight in Spain because it needed most of its workers stateside. A Popular Front of Communists, Socialists, Anarchists, and Democrats lobbied the U.S. government to help the Loyalists and to drop its damaging embargo against Spain (implemented as a gesture of its "neutrality") but to no avail. Clearly, Ginsberg is exposing a strongly felt historical political position. See Robert A. Rosenstone, *Crusade of the Left: The Lincoln Battalion in the Spanish Civil War* (New York: Pegasus, 1969), pp. 50–84. Also see Alvah Bessie and Albert Prago, eds. *Our Fight: Writings by Veterans of the Abraham Lincoln Brigade Spain 1936–1939* (New York: Monthly Review Press, 1989).

9. Such identifications had occurred in the jazz community. Mezz Mezzrow was perhaps the most outspoken about his sense of solidarity with African Americans—his blackness. See Neil Leonard, *Jazz and the White Americans* (Chicago: University of Chicago Press, 1962).

10. For the latest demystification of the ALB, see Sam Tanenhaus, "Innocents Abroad," *Vanity Fair* 493 (September 2001): 286–302. Mary R. Habeck, Ronald Radosh, and Grigory Sevostianov, *Spain Betrayed: The Soviet Union in the Spanish Civil War* (Yale University Press, 2001).

11. The Communist Party mastered exploitation of the spectacle. The party viewed Sacco and Vanzetti, Mooney, and the Scottsboro Boys as propaganda opportunities. The party attracted attention to itself and gained members, but it also alienated most of the public from the party and exacerbated prejudice against minorities, workers, and the victims of injustice. See Howe, pp. 175–235. In the 1920s and early 1930s, during the Communist Party's so-called "Third Period," characterized by the frightening totalitarianization of the party under Stalinist ideology, the party argued that African Americans were a separate nation entitled to autonomy and

self-determination via nationhood and that territories in the South should be so designated. In other words, the party opposed integration. The party dropped this line in the mid-1930s, which began the Popular Front years. Moreover, during World War II, the Communist Party was ambivalent about African American protests of second-order citizenship in the United States, which tended to splinter the Popular Front. This position alienated African Americans. The party's thinking centered on defeating Germany, saving Stalin, then turning to problems at home. See Howe, pp. 178–198. See Ralph Ellison, *Invisible Man* (1947; New York: Vintage Books edition, 1989). See Habeck, Ronald Radosh, and Grigory Sevostianov, *Spain Betrayed.*

12. See Robin D. G. Kelley's excellent chapter, "African Americans in the Spanish Civil War," in *African Americans in the Spanish Civil War,* Danny Duncan Collum, ed., A Project of the Abraham Lincoln Brigade Archives, Brandeis University (New York: G. K. Hall, 1992), pp. 5–57. See John Patrick Diggins, *The Rise and Fall of the American Left* (New York: W. W. Norton, 1992), pp. 175–178. Also see Rosenstone, *Crusade of the Left.* Also see Alvah Bessie and Albert Prago, eds., *Our Fight: Writing by Veterans of the Abraham Lincoln Brigade Spain 1936–1939* (New York: Monthly Review Press, 1987), p. 18. The facts about the oil shipments can found here.

13. See Collum, ed., *African Americans in the Spanish Civil War,* pp. 63–98.

14. Rosenstone, *Crusade of the Left,* 68–69.

15. See Ginsberg, *Howl,* pp. 35–37.

16. "America" was written Jan. 17, 1956, so there is a good chance he was working for Greyhound then. For information on the navy jobs see Miles, *Ginsberg,* p. 205.

17. Edward Conze defines a sutra simply as "a text which claims to have been spoken by the Buddha." See *Buddhist Scriptures* (Baltimore: Penguin Books, 1959), p. 249. Also, for examples of sutras see Hisao Inagaki, *The Three Pure Land Sutras: A Study and Translation* (Kyoto: Nagata Bunshodo, 1994.) For translation and commentary on the "Diamond Sutra" and the "Heart Sutra," see Conze, *Buddhist Wisdom Books: Vajracchedika* (New York: Harper & Row, 1958). Quotations from Ginsberg's poem taken from "Sunflower Sutra," *Howl,* pp. 28–30. Miles says that Ginsberg wrote the poem in twenty minutes; *Ginsberg,* p. 200.

18. For Holmes's comment see William Plummer, *The Holy Goof: A Biography of Neal Cassady* (Englewood Cliffs, N.J.: Prentice-Hall, 1981), pp. 35–36. For a quotation on the beginnings of Cassady's street savvy, also see Chapter 4 and Plummer, p. 20. Also check Kerouac, who examines and celebrates the vernacular cunning of Cody Pomeray in *Visions of Cody*. Deleuze and Parnet write that "style belongs to people of whom you . . . say, 'They have no style.' This [their style] is not a signifying structure. It is an assemblage . . . of enunciation. Being like a foreigner in one's own language." *Dialogues*, p. 4. Yes, I agree to a point. It is a disorientation and therefore an opening, but it is still historical and therefore also significant.

19. I have drawn my description of Ginsberg's visionary experience from Miles, *Ginsberg*, pp. 99–104. Blake's poem "Ah! Sunflower" is among the poems in *Songs of Innocence and of Experience* (1794).

20. In his poem "Supermarket in California," Ginsberg indicates the U.S. amnesia of the "lost America of love" that Walt Whitman imagined. Ginsberg likens Whitman's America—its artifacts, the democracy of its multiple vernacular tradition—to a boat disappearing on the "black waters of Lethe." Ginsberg is a dam in the river. See *Howl*, pp. 23–24.

21. The quotation is from Ginsberg's intriguing poem "Transcription of Organ Music," *Howl*, pp. 25–27. Here the process of growth is the fulfillment of life's desire, and it is evident in the growth of plants and flowers (which have mastered the art of life) and selves expressed through the mediums of words, music, and art—love's tokens—and means to intimacy.

22. For an excellent treatment of the jazz discourse and black musicians' and intellectuals' interventions into it, see Eric Porter, *What Is This Thing Called Jazz? African American Musicians as Artists, Critics, and Activists* (Berkeley: University of California Press, 2002). Here it is clear that many black musicians felt hemmed in and trapped by the discursive matrix of jazz; as a result and as has been mentioned, not a few rejected the term out of hand. My point, however, is that the ecumenical and global perspective and practices of the music, its spirit of innovation, while at times muted, have nevertheless continued to push the music into frontiers of new associations and musical combinations.

23. Ginsberg's birthday was June 3, 1926. Coltrane was born September 23, 1926. Facts about the first Miles Davis Quintet come from Eric Nisenson,

Ascension: John Coltrane and his Quest (New York: St. Martin's Press, 1993; cited edition, New York: Da Capo Press, 1995), pp. 29–42. Also, see Cuthbert Ormond Simpkins, *Coltrane: A Biography* (New York: Herndon House Publishers, 1975), pp. 45–58; and Lewis Porter, *John Coltrane: His Life and Music* (Ann Arbor: University of Michigan Press, 2000).

24. See Gitler's notes on *Relaxin'* (Prestige, Original Jazz Classics, OJCCD-190-2, recorded October 26, 1956).

25. "Howl" underwent several revisions of word content and line sequence but never departed from the spontaneously composed (improvised) thought of the original draft. See Ginsberg, *Howl: Original Facsimile*. Similarly, *On the Road* underwent numerous revisions. See note 2 in Chapter 4.

26. About Coltrane's practicing routines, see Nisenson, *Ascension*, p. 52. Also see Simpkins, *Coltrane: A Biography*, pp. 58–73. The four albums were as follows: *Workin'* (Prestige, Original Jazz Classics OJC 296}; *Cookin'* (Prestige, Original Jazz Classics OJC 128); *Steamin'* (Prestige, Original Jazz Classics OJC 391); *Relaxin'* (Prestige, Original Jazz Classics OJC 190).

27. "Surrey with the Fringe on Top" is on *Steamin'* and "Four" is on *Workin'*. See note 24 above. *Blue Train* (Blue Note CDP 7460952). In all likelihood, the complex form of "Moment's Notice" can be linked to the influence of such tunes as Dizzy Gillespie's "Con Alma," which uses multiple chords to harmonize a single note and also through the harmonically sophisticated Thelonious Monk with whom Coltrane was playing at the time. See Porter, *John Coltrane*, pp. 114–131. My analysis of "Moment's Notice" is based on transcription: Carl Coan, *John Coltrane's Solos* (Milwaukee: Hal Leonard, 1995), pp. 28–32. Also, for Coltrane's comments on the Prestige sessions with Davis, see "John Coltrane, Un Faust Moderne," by Jean-Claude Dargenpierre, *Jazz Magazine* 78 (January 1962): 24. Extended quotations from the article are translated in Porter, *John Coltrane*, pp. 99–113. Terrific examples of Dexter Gordon's playing can be heard on any number of his recordings for Blue Note such as *Doin' Alright* (CDP 784007); *Dexter Calling* (CDP B21Y 46544); and *Go!* (CDP 746094). For Rollins, see his incomparable *Saxophone Colossus* (Prestige, Original Jazz Classics, OJC 291). John Coltrane, *Giant Steps* (Atlantic 781337-2).

28. During this period, unlike Davis, Coltrane rarely settled on a first take. He sometimes exasperated musicians because he always wanted to play

better on the next roll-tape. See Nisenson's discussion on Coltrane's recording preferences, *Ascension*, p. 37. There are two published takes of "Giant Steps" separated by a month, and they are vastly different. Each comprises a different rhythm section. The earlier version (alt. take, 1974) is in a slower tempo. Coltrane is the only soloist, and his playing is less dense over the changes. Clearly, the first version was not to Coltrane's standards. Pianist Tommy Flanagan's solo on the later original Atlantic release is spotty and doesn't connect the changes. In places the performance sounds more like comping than soloing. He probably didn't have as much time to work on the piece as Coltrane. On the other hand, his playing contrasts with Coltrane in a way that obviously pleased them enough to submit the record to press. It might have sounded exactly like they intended it to sound. See liner notes for *Giant Steps*. Ekkehard Jost's analysis of "Giant Steps" states that the tune modulates by "mediants, by chords a third away." According to Paul F. Berliner and Steven Strunk, however, it just as often modulates by augmented fifths. Strunk goes on to write that no other composition better indicates the general trend in jazz in the 1950s toward greater harmonic complexity and speed. See Jost, *Free Jazz* (Graz: Universal Edition, 1974; cited edition, New York: Da Capo Press, 1981), pp. 23–24; Paul Berliner, *Thinking in Jazz: The Infinite Art of Improvisation* (Chicago: University of Chicago Press, 1994), pp. 79–80; Steven Strunk, "Harmony," *The New Grove Dictionary of Jazz*, ed. Barry Dean Kerfield, vol. 2 (London: Macmillan, 1988), pp. 485–496. For discussion of *Giant Steps* as the "culmination of Coltrane's developing interest in third-related chord movement," see Porter, *John Coltrane*, pp. 145–158.

29. See Berliner, *Thinking in Jazz*, pp. 63–94. Here Berliner shows how musicians often reinterpret jazz compositions' melodies, harmonies, and rhythms. Moreover, such reinterpretations inform new solo work. The process may be quite conservative or quite liberal and innovative to the point where the original version of a particular piece becomes difficult to recognize—certainly, one of the hallmarks of bebop.

The collaborative and improvisational habits that the Beats derived from jazz helped push improvisation into other art mediums. For example, theater, dance, and happenings frequently consist of skeletal compositions for performers to improvise on. Happenings may be seen as a form of improvisational theater and may contain elements of dance, dramatic action and dialogue, poetry, music, painting, and other art. For a discussion of spontaneity and the structure of happenings see Michael Kirby, "Introduction," *Happenings* (New York: E. P. Dutton, 1965), pp. 9–52.

30. There are discrepancies among sources as to what the name of the tune is. In his discussion of modal jazz, Kernfield lists the tune as "Milestones." See entry for modal jazz, *The New Grove Dictionary of Jazz*, pp. 116–117. The CD lists the song as "Miles" on *Milestones* (Columbia 460827).

31. My analysis of "Milestones" draws on Kernfield's discussion of the piece. See the entry for modal jazz in *The New Grove Dictionary of Jazz*, pp. 116–117. For Coltrane, the western mode would become an open door to Asian and African modes, comprising different intervals and unfamiliar emotional qualities, which would soon seep into his music.

32. For Bill Evans's notes see *Kind of Blue* (Columbia 460603).

33. See Jost, *Free Jazz*, pp. 20–23.

34. Ibid., p. 27. The results of the quartet's spontaneous and open procedures can be heard in the differences between the same compositions from one day to the next when they played the Village Vanguard on November 1, 2, 3, and 5, 1961. Remarkable differences, dramatic and subtle, occur in timing, content, intensities, and instrumentation. Garrison, Tyner, Jones, and Coltrane were the core group, but other musicians participated including Reggie Workman, who often played a second bass with Garrison. Eric Dolphy (as and bass clarinet), Ahmed Abdul-Malik (oud), and Garvin Bushell (oboe, contrabassoon) also frequently contributed. See *Coltrane: The Complete 1961 Village Vanguard Recordings* (Impulse! IMPD4–232). Exceptions to the quartet's adherence to open form performance include the tightly arranged *Ballads* (Impulse! MCAD 5885, 1962) and *John Coltrane and Johnny Hartman* (Impulse! MCAD 5661, 1963).

35. Lhamon and Scott DeVeaux both note the ambivalence bebop musicians felt for commercial blues and older African American styles of entertainment, particularly entertainment that appealed to whites via Uncle Tom gestures. See Lhamon, *Deliberate Speed*, pp. 110–111; DeVeaux, *The Birth of Bebop: A Social and Musical History* (Berkeley: University of California Press, 1997), pp. 340, 415–417, 431–436. Principles underlying the blues, such as skewed notes and scales, strange beats, appreciation of individual

style, collective participation, and oral transmission of knowledge, however, cycled through bop. For accounts of early African American musics and their functions see Jeff Todd Titon, *Early Down Home Blues* (Urbana: University of Illinois Press, 1977); Christopher Small, *Music of the Common Tongue* (New York: River Run Press, 1987). For an account of the spread of Creole Society to Northern cities see Ira Berlin, *Many Thousands Gone: The First Two Centuries of Slavery in North America* (Cambridge, Mass.: Harvard University Press, 1998), pp. 47–63 (the quotation "after hours conviviality" comes from p. 60). For the source on the dancers at Catherine Market and the birth of the modern youth culture, see W. T. Lhamon Jr., *Raising Cain* (Cambridge, Mass.: Harvard University Press, 1998), pp. 1–55. Also, mixed conviviality among differences pushes Kerouac's prose in *Visions of Cody,* particularly the "Frisco: The Tape" section, the end of which includes a transcript of a radio broadcast of an African American religious meeting where the preacher and congregation enact a remarkable, united, oral ritual. They enact the kind of communal interchange the Beats and bop musicians sought to recover from modernity's fragments; *Visions of Cody,* pp. 119–247; also see Chapter 4.

36. For "Howl," this was particularly the case when Ginsberg wrote the poem (he wrote it for the voice) and when he read it. For a live reading of "Howl" and "Footnote to Howl," see Ginsberg's compact disc collection *Holy Soul Jelly Roll: Poems and Songs 1949–1993* (Los Angeles: Rhino Records, 1994).

37. Lewis Porter, "John Coltrane's *A Love Supreme:* Jazz Improvisation as Composition." *Journal of the American Musicological Society* 3 (fall 1985): 600–601.

38. For the Berkeley reading of "Howl" see the *Holy Soul Jelly Roll* collection. There are also vast differences in tone and content between recordings of readings of "America." The Berkeley reading (read the same night as "Howl") plays to the humor of the poem. The audience is constantly laughing. Ginsberg prefaced his reading by saying the poem was not finished and that there was a second half yet to write. But he never wrote a second half. Instead, for the City Lights edition he cut twenty lines. He read this edition for Fantasy Records on June 6, 1959. By comparison to the Berkeley reading the tone and style of delivery seems flat and perfunctory. See *Howl* (Fantasy

#7013). The recording is also included on disc three of the compact disc set, *The Beat Generation* (Santa Monica, Calif.: Rhino Records, 1992).

39. Lewis Porter has transcribed "Psalm" without measure lines. He also shows how Coltrane's melody adheres to the oral melodic patterns of African American preachers. Coltrane's grandfather was a preacher. For evidence Porter draws on Jeff Titon, "Tonal System in the Chanted Oral Sermons of the Reverend C. L. Franklin," conference paper, Society for Ethnomusicology, Wesleyan University, October 17, 1975; Porter, "John Coltrane's *A Love Supreme*," *Journal of the American Musicological Society.* All of this specifically supports the common knowledge that Coltrane was pulling vernacular, oral influences into his compositions. For an early and useful account of orality in African American culture and music, particularly with respect to modern jazz and Coltrane, see Ben Sidran, *Black Talk* (New York: Da Capo Press, 1971), pp. 116–160.

40. The biographical data on Coltrane's musical training at Ornstein and his induction into the navy can be found in Nisenson, *Ascension,* pp. 3–28; Simpkins, *Coltrane: A Biography,* pp. 19–44; and Porter, *John Coltrane,* pp. 25–40. Also, there is a photograph of Coltrane in 1945 looking hip in his sunshades in the navy band in the picture folio section of Simpkins's book. For an account of Coltrane's drug problems and the spiritual encounter that helped him leave them behind, see Nisenson, pp. 128–142.

41. Porter, *John Coltrane,* pp. 11–13. Originally August Bloom, "An Interview with John Coltrane," *Jazz Review* (January 1959): 25. Much of the ensuing biographical information comes from Porter's book, which represents the most thorough research to date on Coltrane's early life, as well as impressive musicology. Nevertheless, as Porter notes, there remain many conflicting accounts of events and statements of fact for ensuing research to sort out and clarify.

42. See Porter, *John Coltrane,* pp. 14–15. Two quotations have been joined by an ellipsis. The first half is from "John Coltrane: Une Interview," by Francois Postif, *Jazz Hot* (January 1962): 13; the second half from the liner notes to *Giant Steps* (Atlantic 1311, 1960).

43. Porter, *John Coltrane,* pp. 16–17.

44. See Porter, "John Coltrane's *A Love Supreme*" and note 39 in this chapter.

45. Porter, "John Coltrane's *A Love Supreme,*" p. 30.

46. Ibid. Both quotations are from pp. 39–40.

47. Ibid., pp. 41–53.

48. For documentation of these events in the Civil Rights movement, I have used Joanne Grant, ed., *Black Protest: History, Documents, and Analyses 1619 to the Present* (New York: Fawcett Publications, 1968), pp. 251–356. My reference to statistics on inequality during this period also comes from Grant's book, which drew on studies from the Research Center at the University of Michigan, pp. 476–479. Reference to the Coltrane Quartet's playing a benefit for the SNCC can be found in Frank Kofsky, *Black Nationalism and the Revolution in Music* (New York: Path Finder Press, 1970), pp. 221–222. The benefit never actually occurred because the chancellor at the University of California, Berkeley—Clark Kerr—forbade it. Kofsky was one of the organizers of the event, which apparently ended up becoming a gig at the Jazz Workshop, where Kofsky first met Coltrane. Also, the connection between the church bombing that killed four girls at a church in Birmingham and Coltrane's composition "Alabama" is well known, but reference to it can be found in Nisenson, pp. 142–143 and also in note 15 of Porter, "John Coltrane's *A Love Supreme,*" p. 613. Porter mentions that an opening recitative in the piece is based on words by Martin Luther King Jr.—presumably, words that responded to the bombings. "Alabama" is recorded on the *Coltrane Live at Birdland* (Impulse! MCAD 33109, 1963) album, but to my ears the most moving version was broadcast on live television and can be seen on the video *Coltrane's Legacy* (Jazz Video 69035). The statistic on sales of *A Love Supreme* comes from Brian Priestley, *Jazz: A History on Record* (New York: Bill Board Books, 1991), p. 128. Nisenson's comment can be found in *Ascension*, p. 152.

49. Radicalized artists include Tom Dent, Larry Neal, Amira Baraka and the Black Arts Repertory Theatre in Harlem and the Association for the Advancement of Creative Musicians in Chicago. It would include the generation of jazz musicians playing the "new thing," such as Pharaoh Sanders and Archie Shepp, both of whom played with Coltrane, and Albert Ayler. Coltrane unselfishly and tirelessly promoted the new musicians, many of whom were outspoken about the need for music to meet the specific needs

of black people in the United States. Frank Kofsky, certainly, was one of the alienated whites who felt a personal need for black consciousness. Other musicians such as Abbey Lincoln, Max Roach, and Charles Mingus were also sympathetic to the radical necessity. They were much more outspoken than Coltrane. Coltrane focused on the music. He thrived on the new sounds and devoted his symbolic prestige to the musicians he believed in. He believed the music could transform people and social relationships. I have read nothing to indicate that Coltrane had adopted black nationalist ideology, however. According to Nisenson, he had adopted a series of lifestyle changes like Ginsberg's: become a vegetarian, practiced yoga, experimented with LSD, chanted from the Tibetan Book of the Dead, and was engrossed in the holistic, more relativistic writings of Krishnamurti, Einstein, and the Kabbalah; Nisenson, *Ascension,* pp. 182–195. Coltrane's undogmatic thinking also comes through in the 1966 interview with Kofsky, *Black Nationalism,* pp. 221–243. For a fine account of the centrality of jazz in the Black Arts movement, see Lorenzo Thomas, "Ascension: Music and the Black Arts Movement," *Jazz Among the Discourses,* ed. Krin Gabbard (Durham: Duke University Press, 1995), pp. 256–274. For a further elaboration and expansion of Thomas's topics, see Porter, *What Is This Thing Called Jazz,* especially chapters 3–6.

50. See Porter's discussion of Coltrane's unified improvisation in the recording of *A Love Supreme* through the use of the pentatonic scale and motive, "John Coltrane's *A Love Supreme,*" 600–612. Also, see Jost's comments on Coltrane's use of motivic ties in the composition, Jost, *Free Jazz,* pp. 32–34. It's also important to know that during this period of his career Coltrane used these devices like an improvisational painter uses color. Each performance resulted in a different painting. Even the motives, derived from the established tonal colors, would change.

51. For an account of the invective of nihilism hurled at Coltrane, see Jost, *Free Jazz,* p. 31.

52. See Judith Butler, *Gender Trouble: Feminism and the Subversion of Identity* (New York: Routledge, 1990). Anne Waldman, "Forward," *Women of the Beat Generation,* ed. Brenda Knight (Berkeley: Conari Press, 1996), pp. ix–xii. See Sally Placksin, *American Women in Jazz: 1900 to the Present*

250

NOTES TO PAGES 194-200

(New York: Seaview Books, 1982). There are unfortunate omissions of instrumentalists in Placksin's book such as Alice McLeod (Coltrane) and Marian McPartland.

53. The line is from Ginsberg, "Song," *Howl*, pp. 39–41.

54. For an account of how Gillespie used stage persona to promote himself and popularize bebop, see DeVeaux, *The Birth of Bebop*, pp. 431–436. In 1958 Coltrane related his personal code to Ira Gitler: "Keep listening. Never become so self-important that you can't listen to other players. Do right. You can improve as a player by improving as a person." When Kofsky interviewed Coltrane in 1966, it was obvious the code was still with him. Kofsky, *Black Nationalism*, pp. 221–246. The only realm in which Coltrane exhibited behavior that might be construed as selfish was in the way he kept his practice time; see Nisenson, *Ascension*, p. 64.

CONCLUSION

1. John Coltrane, *Coltrane: The Complete 1961 Village Vanguard Recordings* (New York: MCA, 1997): Impulse-IMPD4–232. Miles Davis, *On the Corner* (New York: Columbia, 1972). Also see the proto-fusion album, Miles Davis, *Bitches Brew* (New York: Columbia, 1968).

2. Coltrane, *A Love Supreme,* liner notes (New York: Impulse, MCA Records, 1964).

3. Rhonda J. Nelson, "Albert Ayler Is Missing." Unpublished. Nelson sent me the mimeographs. Tampa, Florida, May 2003. "Jaco's bouncing bass" refers to Jaco Pastorius, deceased bass player for Weather Report; "rockets of samples," carried out by Henry Shsiao, who performs electronica in the band MOD. He puts together samples and strings them together to produce a beat. Technically, Nelson performed the poem with the band MOD, some of the band members of which also play in the Irritable Tribe of Poets. The players easily circulate from ensemble to ensemble.

4. Kerouac, "The Essentials of Spontaneous Prose," *The Portable Jack Kerouac,* ed. Ann Charters (ms. 1954, New York: Penguin, 1995), pp. 484–485.

5. Nelson, "Albert Ayler Is Missing."

CREDITS

Bob Kaufman, photo by Chester Kessler. Reprinted by permission of Robert Emory Johnson.

ruth weiss, Grant Avenue Street Fair, photo by C. R. Snyder. Reprinted by permission of ruth weiss.

Book cover, Bob Kaufman, *Solitudes Crowded with Loneliness*, 1959. Reprinted by permission of New Directions Press.

ruth weiss publicity photo by Paul Beattie. Reprinted by permission of ruth weiss.

Session at the Coffee Gallery, photo by Jerry Stoll. Reprinted by permission of Robert Emory Johnson.

Allen Ginsberg, San Francisco State, 1955. Photo by Walter Lehrman.

Venice Beach cafe, photo by Austin Anton. Reprinted by permission of Dana Anton.

ruth weiss at the Exploratorium. Reprinted by permission of ruth weiss.

INDEX

Waits, Tom, 198
Waters, Ethel, 97
Webern, Anton, 132
Webster, Ben, 188
weiss, ruth, 12, 35, 61, 152, 193, 198; interview, 23, 68–69, 222n22; and partner Paul Blake, 42; on jazz (bop), 42, 64; biographical details, 50–51, 64–66; undermining subjectivity and relation of selves to social world, 51–53, 69–70; *The Brink*, 52, 58, 62, 70–74, 80–81; use of queer sexuality, 52, 58–59, 73; poetic style and jazz, 62–64, 69–70; at the Cellar, 66–68
Weitsman, Mel, 66
West Side Story, 110
Whalen, Philip, 23, 25, 26, 61, 95; on Kerouac, 83
White Stripes, 198

Whitman, Walt, 12, 19, 79
Wichel, William, 58
Wieners, John, 57
Wilde, Oscar, 111
Wild Ones, 19
Williams, William Carlos, 29, 34, 66
Wilson, Earl, 99–102
Wilson, John S. 133
Wilson, Teddy, 97, 132
Wolfe, Tom, 10
Workman, Reggie, 177
Works Projects Administration, 95

Young, Lester, 9, 97, 105, 132, 138–139; epitome of American exceptionalism, 147–148; influence on Coltrane, 185, 188

Zoot suits, 41–42